IFIP Advances in Information and Communication Technology

564

Editor-in-Chief

Kai Rannenberg, Goethe University Frankfurt, Germany

Editorial Board Members

IFIP – The International Federation for Information Processing

IFIP was founded in 1960 under the auspices of UNESCO, following the first World Computer Congress held in Paris the previous year. A federation for societies working in information processing, IFIP's aim is two-fold: to support information processing in the countries of its members and to encourage technology transfer to developing nations. As its mission statement clearly states:

IFIP is the global non-profit federation of societies of ICT professionals that aims at achieving a worldwide professional and socially responsible development and application of information and communication technologies.

IFIP is a non-profit-making organization, run almost solely by 2500 volunteers. It operates through a number of technical committees and working groups, which organize events and publications. IFIP's events range from large international open conferences to working conferences and local seminars.

The flagship event is the IFIP World Computer Congress, at which both invited and contributed papers are presented. Contributed papers are rigorously refereed and the rejection rate is high.

As with the Congress, participation in the open conferences is open to all and papers may be invited or submitted. Again, submitted papers are stringently refereed.

The working conferences are structured differently. They are usually run by a working group and attendance is generally smaller and occasionally by invitation only. Their purpose is to create an atmosphere conducive to innovation and development. Refereeing is also rigorous and papers are subjected to extensive group discussion.

Publications arising from IFIP events vary. The papers presented at the IFIP World Computer Congress and at open conferences are published as conference proceedings, while the results of the working conferences are often published as collections of selected and edited papers.

IFIP distinguishes three types of institutional membership: Country Representative Members, Members at Large, and Associate Members. The type of organization that can apply for membership is a wide variety and includes national or international societies of individual computer scientists/ICT professionals, associations or federations of such societies, government institutions/government related organizations, national or international research institutes or consortia, universities, academies of sciences, companies, national or international associations or federations of companies.

More information about this series at http://www.springer.com/series/6102

Arthur Tatnall · Nicholas Mavengere (Eds.)

Sustainable ICT, Education and Learning

IFIP WG 3.4 International Conference, SUZA 2019
Zanzibar, Tanzania, April 25–27, 2019
Revised Selected Papers

 Springer

Editors
Arthur Tatnall
Victoria University
Melbourne, VIC, Australia

Nicholas Mavengere
Bournemouth University
Poole, UK

ISSN 1868-4238   ISSN 1868-422X (electronic)
IFIP Advances in Information and Communication Technology
ISBN 978-3-030-28763-4   ISBN 978-3-030-28764-1 (eBook)
https://doi.org/10.1007/978-3-030-28764-1

This Springer imprint is published by the registered company Springer Nature Switzerland AG
The registered company address is: Gewerbestrasse 11, 6330 Cham, Switzerland

Preface

The chapters of this book are drawn from papers presented at an International Federation for Information Processing (IFIP) working conference in April 2019, which aimed to address sustainability issues in ICT, education, and learning. The conference was held at the State University of Zanzibar (SUZA) and run by IFIP Working Group 3.4 (Professional and Vocational Education) in collaboration with other TC3 working groups. The conference sought to promote and encourage discussion on different facets of ICT education and learning initiatives: their promise, potential, and challenge for sustainable development, especially in the Global South.

All papers submitted for the conference were peer reviewed before being accepted for presentation in Zanzibar. Of these, a further selection was made after the conference for publication in this book, and those selected were again reviewed after the authors had the opportunity to make improvements following feedback discussions at the conference.

The Sustainable ICT Education and Learning conference aimed, guided by the WCCE 2017 conference declaration for development of ICT, education and learning in the developing countries context, to:

- Focus on new pedagogical opportunities offered by mobile learning applications and their adoption in the education field
- Consider infrastructure challenges, neither as a matter of funding nor as a technocratic approach, but with school administrators and parents being included in developing creative support and maintenance as part of a wider holistic approach to development
- Foster co-operation with countries with a high degree of ICT development in education in sharing their experience in IT skills and usage in the educational domain
- Foster best-practice approaches implemented when using digital technologies to enhance learning in multicultural environments in developing countries

Previous efforts in the context of sustainable development, ICT and education include a Symposium at SaITE 2016 Guimarães, Portugal, and WCCE 2017 Dublin workshop/symposium with input by Kenyan and South African presentations. This led to this conference in Zanzibar bringing together academics, postgraduate students, lecturers, researchers, NGOs, and practitioners such as teachers, experts in learning technology, planners, and consultants. The SUZA community atmosphere enabled the sharing of academic and research experience on conference themes such as:

- Peer and collaborative learning in informatics
- Pedagogical approaches to teaching specific informatics courses
- Case studies of workplace learning related to information systems
- Case studies of e-learning
- ICTs for development

- Mobile solutions in learning in the North and South
- Lifelong learning
- Applications for disabled students
- Traversal skills and computational thinking
- Teacher education in the Global South

The working conference gathered about 40 participants from different continents, and had a strong local representation from East Africa. It included 28 session paper presentations, a keynote and demonstrations from the State University of Zanzibar. The keynote by Mr. Aape Pohjavirta from Funzi, a mobile learning company based in Finland, stressed the importance of applying light-weight, relatively low-tech solutions for e-learning in the Global South. Mobile solutions are able to reach students even in poor and remote areas. Many of the papers also dealt with issues of e-learning and ICTs in developing country settings, allowing participants to exchange views on challenges of deficient infrastructure and funds. In addition to educational technologies, many papers introduced pedagogical solutions and innovations both in developed and developing countries. The first two conference days were held in the Seacliff Resort and Spa outside Zanzibar City, and on Saturday the State University invited participants to their premises where they were shown the laboratories for e-learning and video recording and the drone lab. Moreover, the hospitality students prepared and served delicious spice tea and a sumptuous lunch. Participants were taken for a walk in the historic Stone Town after the lunch.

One of the dimensions in discussing sustainability is how educational systems and learning of work life and entreneurship knowledge are represented in university curricula. The article by Taajamaa, Nkonoki, Järvi, and Hooli gives a Tanzanian example of entrepreneurial education innovation in four universities and how it can be aligned into a natural sciences curriculum. At the same time we have the challenge of institutional capacity building in the developing countries. Efforts to make changes, not just with funding but also in building knowledge and capabilities through international collaboration is discussed by El Nabahany, Mosbech, Mgeni, and Yunus. As a result, a digital learning center was launched at the State University of Zanzibar to promote the transformation of education and learning. Carvalho argues that flipped learning and mobile games increase student motivation based on a three-stage case study. Gabi and Mavengere describe the value of the transition from paper-based portfolios to e-portfolios in order to maintain and foster student learning. Andresen describes how certification of e-learning programs in vocational education has been introduced in Denmark. This provides a best practice opportunity for both developed and developing countries to adopt.

Unprivileged and in other ways disabled young adults with learning difficulties need special approaches. One of them is introduced by Mead, Williams, and Mead and is an application of computer-generated music files in teaching. In addition, Bottino, Chioccariello, Feina, and Travella describe the potential of an important emerging and provoking opportunity – using digital games in primary schools for developing long-lasting transversal skills such as logical reasoning, creativity, and computational thinking. Innovation, creativity, and computational thinking skills are addressed by Reffay and Viroonluecha, who look for future challenges in 21st century skills building. Tatnall looks at the educational and developmental efforts from the perspective of actor-network theory, one of the respected research lenses in information systems science and education. He also raises the topic of learning objects in the time of Internet of Things.

Japanese researchers Hagiya, Fukuda, Tanabe, and Saito have developed a system to automatically generate questions for university entrance examinations which can also be applied to e-learning systems. Another example of boosting programming learning is introduced by Kloos and his colleagues Alario-Hoyos, Munõz-Merino, Catalan Aguirre, and Gonzales Castro, namely, voice assistance in Java programming in the context of massive open online courses. Voice-based applications are growing in importance and lowering many learning challenges. Learning at workplaces and in organizations – workplace learning, lifelong learning, and other more adult-oriented approaches also need research. Kromidha introduces an interesting case study from Albania about implementing electronic registers in the public sector. This poses an institutional learning challenge.

Teacher education and use of ICT are discussed by El Nabahany and Juma, especially in a Zanzibari context. Virtual courses have been introduced as an opportunity for collaboration between developed and developing countries, and Mavengere and Ruohonen describe the results of an evaluation of using virtual Moodle-based approaches within a multi-university context. More experiences of using emerging applications, such as Kio-Kit digital contents toolbox in STEM education in a regional setting, come from Ahmada, Abdulla, Yunus, and Ismail. Pondiwa and Phiri review experiences of using social media records in learning institutions in Zimbabwe. Osorio and Nieves make an interesting comparison and present an idea-provoking discussion of vocational education arrangements between Northern and Southern Global countries. Educational technology, such as mobile learning, should have an impact outside of schools, too. Romeike offers a big and perhaps fuzzy picture of digital society development, called digitalization, and argues that the driving force behind this is computer science and ICT education.

Web 2.0 technology has provided many opportunities to developing countries as well. A Zanzibari example of using global social media platforms is presented by Yunus, El Nabahany, Abdulla, Ahmada, and Malliga. Holvikivi argues that the increasing visualization in Internet and mobile applications will dramatically change the ways of learning and languages of education, in particularly in the Global South. An interesting country example of using ICT in schools comes from Chile. Toro has investigated the change process, drivers, and burdens in the region of the Mapuche, Chile. Gioko and Waga present survey research from Kenya on how to develop digital literacy for a competency-based curriculum. They conclude that despite major IT device advances, there is still a relatively low implementation of digital literacy. One of the visionary memorandums with technological examples comes from Burgos, who addresses his concept of "transgenic learning," something that enables you to learn through new emerging technological means both inside and outside of the classroom over your whole life. One of these new opportunities is open educational resources (OER), which is discussed again from a Tanzanian-Zanzibari perspective by Ismail, Mgeni, Yunus, Abdulla, and Ahmada. Virtual reality (VR) is a new opportunity in the emerging world of educational technology. Rötkönen, Najmul Islam, and Sutinen have launched a teaching arrangement, through VR technology, between two schools in Bangladesh and Finland. Based on their work, their aim is to enlarge their network of VR-based teaching in the future. And finally Yakubu, Kah, and Dasuki raise an important topic for diffusion of educational technology and present experiences and results from Nigeria about the acceptance of learning management systems.

We hope you enjoy this book and find it informative.

July 2019

Mikko Ruohonen
Jaana Holvikivi
Nicholas Mavengere
Arthur Tatnall

Organization

International Program and Organizing Chairs

Mikko Ruohonen   University of Tampere, Tampere, Finland
Nicholas Mavengere   Bournemouth University, UK
Jaana Holvikivi   Metropolia University of Applied Sciences,
                          Helsinki, Finland

Editors

Arthur Tatnall   Victoria University, Melbourne, Australia
Nicholas Mavengere   Bournemouth University, UK

Program Committee

Idris Rai (Vice Chancellor), State University of Zanzibar
Ali Ussi (Deputy VC), State University of Zanzibar
Said Ali Yunus, State University of Zanzibar
Raya Ahmada
Ali Abdulla Abdulla
Umayra El Nabahany
Maryam Jaffar Ismail
Hassan Simba Hassan
Suleiman Mussa Yussu

The conference was financially sponsored by:

- FinCEAL+ Bridges Program of the Ministry of Education and Culture, Finland
- Finnish Information Processing Association FIBA, Finland
- Tampere University and TAU Foundation, Finland
- IFIP TC3

Reviewers

Javier Osorio Acosta   Cathy Lewi
Said Ali Said Yunus   Andrew Fluck
Elizaphan Maina   Eric Sanchez
Arthur Tatnall   Sue Cranmer
Lawrence Williams   Gioko Maina
Ana A. Carvalho   Josephine Gabi
Rosa Bottino   Nicholas Mávengere
Toshinori Saito   Mikko Ruohonen

Jaana Holvikivi

Joel S. Mtebe

Anneke Hacquebard

Timo Lainema

Tarja Tiainen

Timo Poranen

Mary Webb

Pekka Kamaja

Paul Nleya

Ari-Veikko Anttiroiko

Contents

Promoting Innovation by Adding Entrepreneurial Education to a Natural Sciences Curriculum-Case Tanzania

Ville Taajamaa[✉], Emma Nkonoki, Antero Järvi, and Lauri Hooli

University of Turku, 20014 Turku, Finland
{vimita, emma.nkonoki}@utu.fi

Abstract. This paper presents the results from train-the-trainer workshop held for Tanzanian university faculty from four different universities. The aim of the workshop was to build entrepreneurial education capacity and competencies of local faculty. Findings from the workshop were planned to be integrated into the existing curricula of the universities together with activating and student-centred teaching methods. Main approaches were Problem based Learning and Design thinking.

This was the first workshop in a multi-year project with main intention and focus set on innovative and entrepreneurial education from the perspective of knowledge, skills and mindset.

The results show that participants of the workshop understood both at a general and at a context level how to add entrepreneurial practices and mindset to the natural sciences based curriculum. This was also the main aim of the workshop. Concerning educational content challenges there was more distribution among answers. Participants had different challenges concerning the topic. Process wise the practical and activating approach to the training was well understood and received. One of the main challenges was the question how to implement new approaches to the existing curricula.

Keywords: Innovation · Entrepreneurial education · Design thinking · Problem based Learning · University curricula · East Africa

1 Introduction

This paper presents the results from train-the-trainer workshop held for East African faculty from four different universities from Tanzania. The aim of the workshop was to work on learn together how adding entrepreneurial competencies could be integrated into the existing curricula of the universities and what kind activating and student-centred teaching methods could be used.

The title of the workshop was; "Entrepreneurship, Innovation and Education". There were 12 participants, out of those 9 answered the survey, from junior faculty to professors with experience of department level management. All the participants were from natural sciences backgrounds mostly from either IT or Geography. Survey focused on knowledge base, quality of subject content, competencies and learnings

© IFIP International Federation for Information Processing 2019
Published by Springer Nature Switzerland AG 2019
A. Tatnall and N. Mavengere (Eds.): SUZA 2019, IFIP AICT 564, pp. 1–6, 2019.
https://doi.org/10.1007/978-3-030-28764-1_1

from the workshop before and after. Workshop lasted for three full days and a half day. There were two coaches, both of whom are authors in this paper.

Looking through scientific silos or lingua academica underlying epistemological approach in training meant adding both pragmatic and social-constructivist worldviews to a typically positivistic, neo-, or post positivistic worldviews [1]. In practice it meant integrating activating teaching methods coupled with business approaches such as Problem based Learning, and Design thinking at the level of activities, processes, mind-set and methods [2–8]. Method wise the workshop consisted team based challenges and tasks that included ideation, need finding, and prototyping in a team and project based environment with open challenge settings. The program also included some business concept exercises and basics [2–8].

2 Methodology

For the most part the results were derived from the anonymous feedback survey that was disseminated after the workshop. It had both quantitative and qualitative parts. The quantitative data using Likert-scale was analysed using statistical tools and average was calculated [1]. The qualitative data was analysed thematically using thematic analysis and also ethnographic observation [1]. The analysis happened through first reading the open data several times, then finding different themes that emerged from the text and then coding the qualitative data based on those themes. The approach was close to thematic analysis method and had some elements from Grounded Theory Method as well [1].

3 Results and Discussion

The results show that the main aim of the workshop that is how to add entrepreneurial practices and mindset to the natural sciences based curriculum was well understood both at general and at context level. Concerning the challenges of the content there was distribution of the answers. Participants had different challenges concerning the topic. Process wise the practical and activating approach to the training was well understood and received. One of the main challenge found was the question how to implement new approaches to the existing curricula.

3.1 Relevance to Work and Understanding

As seen Table 1, in terms of workshop topic relevance to participants work the average was 4.7 out of 5.0. Participants were however somewhat confused about the content as the average for content coherence was only 3.9. This is a clear point that needs to be taken into consideration when planning for the iteration of the next workshop.

Table 1. Relevance and coherence of the workshop topic. The participants understood well the importance of the topic and saw the linkage to their work. However, many of the participants felt that workshop content was something new to them. As discussed in the Discussion section one of the reasons can be that there was no pre-workshop material distributed to the participants who came from very different disciplines.

	1	2	3	4	5		Total	Average
I see no linkage with the topic to my work/studies	0	0	1	1	7	The topic was highly relevant to my work/studies	9	4.67
	0%	0%	11.11%	11.11%	77.78%			
Many topics remained unclear	0	0	1	4	4	I understood everything	9	4.33
	0%	0%	11.11%	44.45%	44.44%			
Workshop contents felt confusing	0	1	2	2	3	Workshop contents were coherent	8	3.88
	0%	12.5%	25%	25%	37.5%			
Total	0	1	4	7	14		26	4.31

3.2 Gaining of Practical Skills

As seen Table 2, on an average 4.2 out of 5.0 felt that their theoretical knowledge about the topic had increased substantially and average 4.4 felt that their practical skills had increased substantially. Especially the increased practical skills can be seen as one of the main aims of the workshop. In Table 3 the respondents share their view on their theoretical and practical knowledge and skills in terms of the topic. As can be seen here the average 2.94, which is relatively low.

Table 2. Gaining of knowledge and practical skills. Clear majority of the participants thought that their theoretical knowledge as well as their practical skills related to the topic were increased substantially. This was also one of the aims of workshop.

	1	2	3	4	5		Total	Average
I did **not** gain new **theoretical knowledge** about the topic	0	0	1	5	3	My **theoretical knowledge** about the topic has increased substantially	9	4.22
	0%	0%	11.11%	55.56%	33.33%			
I did **not** learn new **practical skills** about the topic	0	0	0	5	4	My **practical skills** have increased substantially	9	4.44
	0%	0%	0%	55.56%	44.44%			
Total	0	0	1	10	7		18	4.33

3.3 Most Important Learning and What Supported It

In Table 4 the respondents described the most important things that they learned during the workshop. Five persons answered that understanding the link between theory and

Table 3. Knowledge and practical background to the topic. In Table 1 it was shown that participants found some of the content confusing. As seen above in Table 2 this is supported by the fact that participants had little previous knowledge and practical skills of the topic.

	1	2	3	4	5		Total	Average
No previous theoretical knowledge	0	1	8	0	0	Good theoretical knowledge	9	2.89
	0%	11.11%	88.89%	0%	0%			
No previous practical skills	0	1	7	1	0	Good practical skills	9	3
	0%	11.11%	77.78%	11.11%	0%			
Total	0	2	15	1	0		18	2.94

practice was the most important one. Also understanding the importance of business was emphasized to some extent. In Table 5 this is taken into workshop material level in terms of how the material supported the learning. Here the fact that the respondents felt that they did not receive enough theoretical background is understandably as the workshop focused on experiential and Problem based Learning and practical processes and methods. Coaching team decided that learning theoretical background is something that the participants can learn by themselves.

Table 4. Results from the question 'most important learnings during the workshop' supports the observations and discussions with the participants. As teachers and practitioners their concern is how to embed and integrate lessons learned into their daily practice. This is also one of the key challenges for future research especially from the perspective of grassroots innovation.

Responses
How to deliver my contents artistically when teaching
Handling teaching and using different methods (design thinking) to allow students to gain skills in being creative and and innovative in their field(s) of study
Developing a working curriculum with practical inputs to help students get learning practical things
Pedagogical skills on how to design and teach different courses in entreprenueral model
Linking theory and practice in view of entrepreneurship and innovation education provision at higher learning education using existing curricula
About Isses to be considered for a successful business
HOW TO INTEGRATE BUSINESS SKILLS IN THE CURRICULUM
Our courses should be designed in a way that it incorporates entrepreneurship and innovation skills.
The most important thing I learned is how to integrate Entrepreneurial skills to our curriculum and the delivery of lectures with mix of both pictures, text and visual.

Table 5. How the workshop methods and material supported learning. According to results the participants would have needed more theoretical knowledge. The aim of the workshop was to focus on hands-on experiential experience about what it takes to use activating learning methods in the context of entrepreneurial education. From this perspective the result is logical. This topic was also discussed during and after the workshop and as a result a 'list of readings' was created and disseminated to the participants.

	1	2	3	4	5		Total	Average
The workshop methods did not support my learning	0	0	2	5	2	The workshop methods supported my learning	9	4
	0%	0%	22.22%	55.56%	22.22%			
The workshop materials did not support my learning	0	0	0	4	4	The workshop materials supported my learning	8	4.5
	0%	0%	0%	50%	50%			
There was not enough theoretical background in the workshop	0	1	2	4	1	The theoretical background was sufficiently presented during the workshop	8	3.63
	0%	12.5%	25%	50%	12.5%			

4 Conclusion

It is important to understand that entrepreneurial education is not about giving answers or even paths and tools for solving them. It is about creating an environment for disruption where the learner is able to go through experiential cycles of learning and through that understanding the uniqueness of each context and situation. This creates a mind-set that enables innovation through testing. As the results show especially the set goals of the faculty learning practical skills and understanding the linkage between theory and practice were achieved. Although the duration of the workshop was four days it was still seen as too short. The future practical interventions and research will focus on furthering and deepening the approach of building-to-think, and going through experiential learning cycles in an actual open challenge setting utilizing different activating methods from lean management and design thinking. Given the setting of this study one of the future emphasis could be on grassroots innovations. Grassroots innovations is one of the foundational contexts for East Africa and it has an important role to play in creating sustainable development and reduces inequality. Inequality is a very common challenge in developing countries and reducing it is actually one of the sustainable development goals 2030. One of the main hypothesis for one track of future studies is that that education and especially entrepreneurial education with the help of technology can function as a bridge builder between grassroots and systemic innovation. The general situation in East Africa now, sees a lot of top down approaches to innovations and less of the bottom up. The idea is that adding entrepreneurial education to the university's curricula will help students to empower themselves and empower others. Taking into account that everybody is creative and/or has the capacity to be creative, university graduates will be able to contribute into building an inclusive innovation ecosystem by emphasizing grassroots innovations.

References

1. Creswell, J.W.: Research Design - Qualitative, Quantitative, and Mixed Methods Approach, 3rd edn. Sage Publications Inc., Thousand Oaks (2009)
2. Savin-Baden, M.: Problem-Based Learning in Higher Education: Untold Stories. The Society for Research into Higher Education and Open University Press, Buckingham (2000). 126 and 124
3. Graaff, E., Kolmos, A.: Characteristics of problem-based learning. Int. J. Eng. Educ. **19**(5), 657–662 (2003)
4. Edström, K., Kolmos, A.: PBL and CDIO: complementary models for engineering education development. Eur. J. Eng. Educ. **39**, 539–555 (2014)
5. Lehmann, M., Christensen, P., Du, X., Thrane, M.: Problem-oriented and project-based learning (POPBL) as an innovative learning strategy for sustainable development in engineering education. Eur. J. Eng. Educ. **33**(3), 283–295 (2008)
6. Kimbell, L.: Beyond design thinking: design-as-practice and designs-in-practice. In: CRESC (2009)
7. Kimbell, L.: Rethinking design thinking: part I. Des. Cult. **3**(3), 285–306 (2011)
8. Kimbell, L.: Rethinking design thinking: part II. Des. Cult. **4**(2), 129–148 (2012)

Using Mobile Devices and Online Tools to Promote Students' Learning

Ana Amelia Carvalho$^{(\boxtimes)}$

University of Coimbra, 3000-115 Coimbra, Portugal
anaameliac@fpce.uc.pt

Abstract. Keeping students' attention in class and engaging them in learning is not an easy task. In this paper we report the approaches and strategies used in a university course 'Games and Learning'. An action research study was conducted involving three cycles. During the first one, a flipped learning approach was used to motivate students to read the papers before class. In the classroom, students had to use their mobile devices to answer quizzes, fill a form, and summarize the lesson. During the following cycles, students worked in groups, analyzing digital games. Along the second cycle students analyzed a video game and during the third cycle they analyzed a serious game. We realized that asking them to submit some tasks online before class, helped them to work more and achieve better results. From the first group work to the second one the majority of students improved their critical digital game analysis. The collected data supported the conclusion that students were engaged in learning.

Keywords: Mobile devices · Flipped learning · Students' engagement

1 Introduction

1.1 Challenges to Higher Education

Nowadays, one of the greatest challenges colleges and universities are facing is how to get students engaged in learning and how to provide an education of real value to their students. Some complaints about students are very common: students lack the required skills, they are short on motivation, and they have insufficient focus and attention.

Some faculty members try to motivate and engage students in learning, pushing them to active roles. However, some students often resist. Students' resistance to learning is a systemic problem, as Tolman and Kremling [1] analyzed in their book. Indeed, although the great majority of students prefer taking active roles [2–7], a few students resist to it [8].

1.2 Some Students' Characteristics

Some characteristics of our students, as reported by several authors [4, 9–11] are important to be considered when planning classes.

© IFIP International Federation for Information Processing 2019
Published by Springer Nature Switzerland AG 2019
A. Tatnall and N. Mavengere (Eds.): SUZA 2019, IFIP AICT 564, pp. 7–15, 2019.
https://doi.org/10.1007/978-3-030-28764-1_2

(i)   Students are used to being online, connected to friends using Facebook, Instagram, WhatsApp, etc. They are used to get feedback almost instantly. They are used to immediacy.

(ii) They bring and use their mobile devices all the time, facilitating the implementation of the idea of Bring Your Own Device (BYOD). Indeed, it is wise to use their mobile devices to get students engaged in learning.

(iii) Quite often they have a low capacity of attention. A traditional lecture class is difficult for them to follow. The alternative is to reduce the teacher's presentation time, replacing it with an active learning approach.

1.3   The Course 'Games and Learning'

In this paper, we describe and reflect on our experience in motivating and engaging higher students in learning. When planning classes and thinking about which approach to use, we considered the previous characteristics of students presented in Sect. 1.2.

The course 'Games and Learning' is for undergraduate students from the 2nd and 3rd year, of Education Sciences Program in the Faculty of Psychology and Education Sciences, at the University of Coimbra, in Portugal. One of our concerns is to keep students' attention and interest during the class but also to motivate them to be critical to digital games analysis.

The course is divided into three parts, all of them related to each other. The first part of the course focuses on theoretical background about games and particularly about digital games. Games definition, the games genres, and the pros and cons of playing digital games are discussed. The learning principles under digital games according to Gee [12] are presented. Finally, the last topic is about serious games.

The second part is about the critical analysis of a digital game, a mainstream game. It is a group work with no more than three elements. Students have to write a report about their game analysis and to give a presentation in class.

The third and last part of the course is about the critical analysis of a serious game. This second group work is more demanding. It also includes a study with game players, checking their satisfaction with the game.

The next section presents the teaching approaches used, supported by the use of apps and students' mobile devices.

2   Teaching Approaches and Online Tools Used

Throughout the last few years, we recognized that students have ever more difficulty in keeping attention during lectures. So we have embraced active learning approaches. Moreover, we are using their mobile devices to connect them to the web for searching, answering to quizzes or fill in questionnaires. We intend to motivate students to be critical about digital games: what is good and what is not, and how can they be improved.

2.1 Active Learning

Active learning is "anything that involves students in doing things and thinking about the things they are doing" [13] (p. 2). As Felder and Brent [6] pointed out, students should be "called upon to do other things than simply watching, listening and taking notes" (p. 2). But "you are not doing active learning when you lecture, ask questions that the same few students always answer, or conduct discussions that engage only a small fraction of the class" (ibidem). They must read, write, discuss, or be engaged in solving tasks. Students must engage in higher-order thinking tasks such as analysis, synthesis, and evaluation. The activity usually takes from 15 sec to 3 min [6], for example, to share a point of view or discuss a result. If more time is needed, Felder and Brent advise to break the problem into several steps and treat each step as a separate activity. Students "work individually or in small groups to come up with a response; give them some time to do it; stop them, and call on one or more individuals or groups to share their responses" (p. 2) [6]. There are several activities to be considered, for example, Quizzes online, Brainstorming, forms, Think-Pair-Share, Peer Instruction, One-Minute-Paper, MindMapping, Full Body Response (FBR), Exit ticket, and so on. Active learning engages students in the learning process [7].

Flipped Learning

The main idea of flipped learning, initially called flipped classroom [14], is to increase interaction and personalized contact time between students and teachers [15]. Students do activities traditionally considered "homework" in class and activities traditionally considered as in-class work out of class. Before class, students watch videos and/or read previously given references. They have to get familiar with concepts. During class they work in small groups applying knowledge, analyzing things, evaluating or creating things. They can solve problems or projects in the class and after.

2.2 Bring Your Own Mobile Devices

Students bring their own mobile devices, which may facilitate activities in the classroom. They can be invited to search for information, answer multiple choice questions or concept tests. They can be challenged to do short activities as proposed in the active learning approach.

Usually, two rules are important to be respected in the classroom: students must turn off the sound of their mobile devices and they used the devices only when asked by the teacher.

Using students' mobile devices in the classroom, to answer a quiz online, for example, allows all students to see their own and the class results. Based on their answers, the teacher may move further or explain again a concept that was not very clear to students [4].

2.3 Online Tools

We used several online tools during the semester for different purposes as we will explain.

Online Quizzes

The app Kahoot is motivating for students. It has music, the question is projected and each student can see, per question, his/her result and then the five best respondents. However, it has a problem. As students are seated side by side and answering the same question, they can check the answers with their colleagues or copy their answers. Usually, they have only a few seconds to answer each question, to avoid the chance to compare answers or to help each other. This problem is solved with the app Quizizz.

With the app Quizizz it is possible to randomize the order of the questions and the order of the list of options. Therefore, each student answers different questions simultaneously. It has also music. The teacher and the students in the classroom can see a results bar along the quiz resolution.

In Table 1, we compare some features of Kahoot and Quizizz regarding quizzes. Besides the previously referred features, it is important to note that Kahoot has a limitation in the use of characters allowed per question and per answer.

Table 1. Quizzes comparison between the apps Kahoot and Quizizz

Features	Kahoot	Quizizz
Background music	Yes	Yes
Timer	Yes	Yes
Projection of questions	Yes	No
Feedback per question	Yes	Yes
Random questions	No	Yes
Limit of characters	Yes	No
Leaderboard	Yes	Yes
Homework	Yes	Yes

Another app that we use quite often is GoSoapBox. It does not have music, nor timer per question, but it is possible to create open questions. In what concerns feedback for the students, they can only see their results at the end of the quiz.

Google Forms

Google Forms were used for collecting data from questionnaires, students' opinion about a topic, and to summarize what they had learned at the end of class.

During group work development, students had to fill in a form related to the task assigned for that week.

3   Methodology

Based on the difficulties of students to get attention and focus in the class, and to get engaged in learning, we delineated two research questions: (i) How to keep students' attention and interest in class? and (ii) How to promote students' learning?

We used an action research methodology [16–19] to reflect and to improve the educational practices. Each cycle of action-research has three parts: planning, action, and reflection.

The aims of this study are: getting students' attention and interest in the class, promoting students learning, and developing critical digital games analysis.

As data collection techniques we used questionnaires and observation.

3.1   Data Collection Instruments

We developed two questionnaires. One to characterize students' game preferences and another to collect students' opinions about the course 'Games and Learning'. The first one was filled in at the beginning of the semester and the second one at the end of the semester. The questions were multiple choice or open-ended questions.

3.2   Participants Characterization

The majority of respondents (n = 30) were female (73%). Their ages ranged from 18 to 35 years. The mode is on their twenties, the majority of respondents is between 18–20 years, one student is 24 and another 35 years.

Half of the students enrolled in this elective course named 'Games and Learning' are from the 2nd year, 39% from the 3rd year and 11% are Erasmus Mobility Students.

They selected the course due to their interest in the thematic and the syllabus. Most of the students (83%) liked to play games and some (17%) indicated that it depended on the game. The great majority (90%) also liked to play digital games on their smartphones.

They liked to play the following traditional games: card games (like Sueca and Poker), Monopoly, Pictionary, and Clue. Asked about digital games that they liked to play, they indicated the following: The Sims, Call of Duty, Candy Crush, and Clash Royale.

4   Data Analysis

The data analysis is structured into three parts, each one corresponds to a cycle of action research. Each cycle analyses the effect of the approach used in students engagement and learning, and, according to its results, we changed some aspects in the following cycle.

Each cycle corresponds to a different part of the course named 'Games and Learning', which has been explained in Sect. 1.3.

4.1   1st Cycle – Theoretical Background

To motivate students to attend the classes and to do the readings, we used the Flipped Learning approach [15]. Every week, they had to read a paper before class. Students were also requested to bring a mobile device because they would need it during class. Mobile devices were used to do short tasks during the class, according to the active learning approach [6]. By using their mobile devices to fill in some forms, answer online quizzes or to write some information, enabled us to have access to their responses. And this way, we avoided the use of paper, thus contributing to sustainable practices.

At the beginning of each class, students answered a quiz online about the paper read during that week, receiving immediate feedback for each question. Two apps were used: Kahoot and Quizizz. We identified two advantages to this approach: students read the papers and arrived on time to the classroom.

With the quizzes results, the teacher had the opportunity to emphasize the most relevant concepts or ideas of the paper and answered some students' doubts. The teacher asked students about some aspects of the paper, and stimulated them to develop critical thinking.

To help them to keep attentive during the two-hour class, they were invited to summarize what they had learned that day, using a Google Form.

Based on the questionnaire results, students liked the approaches used (97%). They read the paper at home, answered quizzes, and were able to discuss the main ideas. Only a resistant student indicated that she preferred a traditional approach instead. Either way, all students reported that they felt engaged during classes.

Almost all students considered that summarizing what they learned during each session, motivated them to be focused on the class (97%). The quizzes solved at the beginning of each class motivated them to study and read the papers each week (97%). For the following cycle we decided to keep the summarizing activity.

4.2   2nd Cycle – Video Game Analysis

The second part of the course was dedicated to the analysis of a video game. This work was developed in small groups (of 3 elements) and implied a critical analysis of a video game according to specific items, namely: general video game characterization, game description, identification of the learning principles of Gee [12] in the video game, tangential learning, and a final commentary about the video game. For the latter, they were asked to reflect on the most and least successful aspects related to challenges, engagement, immersion, and flow [20], as well as its adequacy to the target audience. Throughout two classes, students received support from the teacher and colleagues.

Before the 1st session of group work, students had to fill a form indicating their team members and the chosen video game, which had to be approved by the teacher. The games selected were: Age of Empires II: The Conquerors; Asphalt 8: Airborne; Battle Warship: Naval Empire; Clash of Clans; Clash Royale; Counter Strike 1.6; Counter Strike: Global Offensive; Fortnite; GTA; Matchington Mansion; Pokémon Go; and Two Point Hospital.

During the third week, they presented their analysis and submitted a report. Some students were not very confident during their presentation. It seemed that they left the work to the last minute. The grades were not very high.

According to our experience, having a task to be completed before class as advantages both to the students and to the teacher. Students will have to solve the task before the class and the teacher may give students a written feedback. In the classroom the teacher has more time to clarify some group's doubts. We realized that with no previous task online, some students did not work properly. Based on these observations, a task online has been included previously to each session to the next group work.

4.3   3rd Cycle – Serious Game Analysis

The third part of the course was dedicated to a critical analysis of a serious game. This group work is more demanding as students had to collect data about gamers' satisfaction.

The serious game analysis focused on a general serious game characterization, game description, and the identification of a learning theory under game development. The following step was to describe player's reactions to the serious game. Particularly, if they had some difficulties in playing it and the degree of satisfaction obtained by playing the game. Finally, a commentary about the serious game analyzed: the best aspects and those not so successful, as well as some solutions to the problems (if identified). Finally, they had to comment about its adequacy to the target audience.

They had four tasks. Three of them had to be filled in a Google Form one day before the class. Task 1 was about the team elements, a definition of serious game and the game selected, which had to be accepted by the teacher. Task 2 was a game description, and they had to identify the best and the worst aspects of the game. With this analysis, they knew quite well the game and were prepared for planning Task 3: analyzing gamers' satisfaction. This task intended to help students to define: What do you intend to observe?, Where are you going to observe?, What kind of data collecting instrument are you going to use?, How can you measure the gamers' satisfaction? Some groups filled it very well but others had difficulties. It seemed that they could not understand what was being asked. Most of the groups submitted their instruments to collect data for teacher's approval.

Task 4 was accomplished after group presentation. They had to fill a Group Self-Assessment questionnaire about the game analysis. If the group considered that the team members worked differently, they could indicate the difference among them. Only two groups indicated differences in team members engagement during group work.

Students (97%) reported, in the Questionnaire of Opinion, that the digital games analyses promoted the development of critical thinking about game features. When asked what they liked most in the classes, they mentioned the digital games analyses, the quizzes, the teaching approaches used, the interactive classes, and the summary to be written online at the end of each class. Relatively to what they disliked during the course, the great majority said that they did not have anything to point. A few reported some noise in the class during group work, and the fact that some colleagues did not work as expected in the group tasks. Asked about suggestions to improve the course, the majority liked it as it was, but some mentioned that they would like to design a game.

When asked about their prevision of the final grade (in a 0 to 20 scale), 40% indicated the correct grade, 33% were one value below, 10% were one value above, and 17% overestimated their grade.

5 Conclusion

In the course 'Games and Learning', attention and interest was achieved by keeping students active in class, namely: answering an online quiz using their mobile device, discussing paper ideas, and writing in a Google form "What did you learn today?". This last idea came up during the first class, when some students were distracted or talking to their colleagues. To keep them quiet and following the activities in the class, this idea emerged. Summarizing the class at the end was the leitmotif to keep them attentive and taking notes.

Students learning was promoted differently in the three parts of the course. The first part of the semester relied on reading a paper before class, based on the flipped learning approach. In class they began by answering an online quiz about the paper using their mobile device. This motivated the students to read the paper, and they were on time in the classroom.

The second and third parts of the semester were devoted to digital game analysis: a mainstream game and a serious game, respectively. It was very important to define tasks to be filled online by each group work. It helped students to be more organized, working and discussing in advance to the class. The teacher gave students an online feedback about the task accomplished, and supported in the classroom the groups with more difficulties.

Students liked the approaches used in the course, and they developed critical digital games analysis. The course tasks and activities are very demanding for the teacher. There are lot of things to plan, to create and feedback to provide to students. However, their engagement, performance and satisfaction compensated the effort and time consuming.

The results achieved are consistent with other studies. For example, Fisher, Perényi and Birdthistle [21] concluded that "flipped learning pedagogy is inherently satisfying to students independent of their perceptions of performance". Ranieri, Raffaghelli and Bruni [22] pointed out that the use of quizzes "showed a high level of student satisfaction and an overall improvement of learning outcomes". However, there are differences in terms of effectiveness according to the nature of topics: more theoretical knowledge or the use of knowledge in a more practical context [22].

The ideas and results presented in the paper are also relevant for developing countries. In this paper we explained how we used students' mobile devices to get them engaged in learning. Moreover, we presented approaches that can be used by other teachers interested in improving their teaching, motivating students to read the material before class, and getting them engaged in the class activities.

Acknowledgements. The research presented in this paper is in part supported by LabTE FPCE-UC and CEIS20 at University of Coimbra.

References

1. Tolman, A., Kremling, J. (eds.): Why Students Resist Learning?. Stylus, Sterling (2017)
2. Ahmed, I., Roussev, V.: Peer instruction teaching methodology for cybersecurity education. IEEE Secur. Priv. **16**(4), 88–91 (2018)

3. Budhai, S., Skipwith, K.: Best Practices in Engaging Online Learners Through Active and Experiential Learning Strategies. Routledge, London (2016)
4. Carvalho, A., Machado, C.: Flipped classroom and quizzes to motivate learning: students' perspectives. In: Information Systems and Technologies, AISTI, pp. 752–757 (2017). https://doi.org/10.23919/CISTI.2017.7975851
5. Eison, J.: Using active learning instructional strategies to create excitement and enhance learning. University of Florida (2010)
6. Felder, R., Brent, R.: Active learning: an introduction. ASQ High. Educ. Brief **2**(4), 1–5 (2009)
7. Prince, M.: Does active learning work? A review of the research. J. Eng. Educ. **93**(3), 223–231 (2004)
8. Tolman, A., Sechler, A., Smart, S.: Defining and understanding student resistance. In: Tolman, A., Kremling, J. (eds.) Why Students Resist Learning?, pp. 1–20. Stylus, Sterling (2017)
9. Carr, N.: The Shallows – What the Internet Is Doing to Our Brains. Norton, New York (2011)
10. Couch, C., Mazur, E.: Peer instruction: ten years of experience and results. Am. Assoc. Phys. Teach. **69**(9), 970–977 (2001)
11. Veen, W., Vrakking, B.: Homo Zappiens: Growing Up in a Digital Age. Network Continuum Education, London (2007)
12. Gee, J.: What Video Games Have to Teach Us About Learning and Literacy. Palgrave MacMillan, New York (2003)
13. Bonwell, C., Eison, J.: Active learning: creating excitement in the classroom. ASHE- ERIC Higher Education Reports Nº 1. The George Washington University, School of Education and Human Development, Washington, D.C. (1991)
14. Bergmann, J., Sams, A.: Flip Your Classroom: Reach Every Student in Every Class Every Day. ISTE, Eugene (2012)
15. Bergmann, J., Sams, A.: Flipped Learning: Gateway to Student Engagement. ISTE, Alexandria (2014)
16. Cohen, L., Manion, L., Morrisson, K.: Research Methods in Education, 8th edn. Routledge, London (2018)
17. McNiff, J., Whitehead, J.: You and Your Action Research Project, 3rd edn. Routledge, London (2010)
18. Ferrance, E.: Action Research. LAB – Northeast and Islands Regional Educational Laboratory at Brown University, Providence (2000)
19. Akker, J.: Principles and methods of development research. In: Akker, J., Branch, R., Gustafson, K., Nieveen, N., Plomp, T. (eds.) Design Approaches and Tools in Education and Training, pp. 1–14. Kluwer Academic Publishers, Dordrecht (1999)
20. Czikszentmihalyi, M.: Flow: The Psychology of Optimal Experience. Harper Perennial, New York (2008)
21. Fisher, R., Perényi, Á., Birdthistle, N.: The positive relationship between flipped and blended learning and student engagement, performance and satisfaction. Active Learn. High. Educ. (2018). https://doi.org/10.1177/1469787418801702
22. Ranieri, M., Raffaghelli, J., Bruni, I.: Game-based student response system: revisiting its potentials and criticalities in large-size classes. Active Learn. High. Educ. (2018). https://doi.org/10.1177/1469787418812667

A Transformation into Digitally Supported Education: Case from the State University of Zanzibar

Umayra El Nabahany[1(✉)], Anne-Marie Mosbech[2(✉)],
Mwanajuma Mgeni[1(✉)], and Said Yunus[1(✉)]

[1] State University of Zanzibar, SUZA, Zanzibar, Tanzania
{umayra.al-nabhany,mwanajuma.mgeni,
said.yunus}@suza.ac.tz
[2] University of Copenhagen, UCPH, Copenhagen, Denmark
anne-marie@sund.ku.dk

Abstract. The case discussed in this paper shares lessons learned from the project on how to build sustainable institutional capacity in e-learning environment at the State University of Zanzibar. The project was carried out in partnership with the University of Copenhagen as part of the larger Building Stronger University, BSU program funded by the Danish International Development Agency, Danida.

Keywords: Institutional capacity building digitally supported education · Digital learning · E-learning

1 Introduction

The use of educational technologies in higher education has increased over the last decades. A considerably large number of universities have by now a Learning Management System (LMS) which as a minimum is used to effectively distribute course content to students. Many other types of digital programs, tools and resources are embedded in the higher education teaching too. While a lot of attention seems to be focusing on the technological development and initiatives from few front movers, less attention seems to be given to the broad institutional capacity needed to build a sustainable model for scaling up a skilled u Use of ICT in education at SUZA.

The following section describes the overall approach and specific activities jointly supported and facilitated by SUZA and the University of Copenhagen while the Sect. 3 describes lessons learned throughout the BSU[1] programs specific work packages.

---

[1] "The Building Stronger Universities program aims at increasing the capacity of African universities in selected Danida priority countries to undertake teaching, research and outreach with the overall objective to generate and apply new knowledge to solve priority development challenges."

A. Tatnall and N. Mavengere (Eds.): SUZA 2019, IFIP AICT 564, pp. 16–23, 2019.
https://doi.org/10.1007/978-3-030-28764-1_3

2 Use of ICT in Education at SUZA

E-learning at SUZA can be traced back to 2006 where a very simple e-learning tool for distributing lesson notes in text formats to students was implemented. Because of very limited use of ICT in education at SUZA, the first BSU partnership, in 2011, decided to improve student and teacher access to course materials by implementing the Learning Management System, MOODLE. Since the implementation of MOODLE in 2012 until 2018 a much broader variety of activities have taken place with the aim to support new online and blended learning approaches. Activities covered; (1) capacity development (including educational video production, OER integration and production), (2) mapping of students and lecturers' use of ICT and MOODLE and (3) development of guidelines and procedures. The following sections describe these different activities.

2.1 Activity 1: Skills Development

ICT Staff and Lecturers
The experience shows that, only few lecturers and IT staff have the opportunity or skills to transform traditional teaching and course material types into digitally supported education without any help or incitement from experienced colleges and management. This is why staff capacity building has been an essential part of the BSU project. Since the SUZA MOODLE has become the backbone for online and blended learning formats since 2014, a series of hands-on workshops have trained IT staff and lecturers' capacity on the use of the MOODLE platform. As it shows in Table 1 below, the training has expanded to all 7 faculties by year 2018.

Table 1. Number of SUZA lecturers and ICT staff trained in the use of MOODLE during the period 2014–2018 and gradually including more campus - as part of the BSU II and BSU III programs.

Year/Campus	SoE	SNSS	SCOPE	SKFL	SHMS	SoB	IoT	Total number of staff trained
2014 + 2015								25
2018							2	30
Total number of staff trained								55

SoE (School of Education), SNSS (School of Natural and Social Sciences), SCOPE (School of Continuing and Professional Education), SKFL (School of Kiswahili and Foreign Languages), SHMS (School of Health and Medical Sciences), SoB (School of Business), IoT (Institute of Tourism)

During workshops, lecturers and ICT staff have been trained on basic level on how to set up a course room, structure course content, create student engaging tasks such as quizzes, discussion forums and online collaboration to develop courses.

On a next level, workshops focused on production of simple educational videos and how to critically evaluate and incorporate externally produced Open Education Resources (OER) into the existing SUZA accredited courses.

Further, and with the aim to strengthen evidence-based knowledge at SUZA as well as the institution's positioning, a group of researchers were trained in formulating educational research projects, specifically with regard to didactic and pedagogical strategies for online and blended learning.

Finally, 5 staff from SUZA Center for Digital Learning, CDL, were trained in a slightly different way. Staff from CDL were trained through a combination of a hands-on workshops and on-the side job-training during a pilot production of educational field research videos in 2017. The purpose of the training was to enable SUZA to independently produce high quality materials for the accredited courses as well as for broader dissemination as OER.

The center has video recording and editing facilities and staff supporting lecturers in planning and producing course content for digital delivery. CDL staffs were trained in project planning, script writing, video recording, video editing, graphic production and animation. Simultaneously, selected SUZA researchers received basic media training and gained experience on how to open up and disseminate their research and research methods. High quality SUZA OER made CDL staff and researchers experience online dissemination of SUZA research to relevant national, regional and international stakeholders, e.g. broadcasted from SUZA Television and published as contributions to the MOOC: Sustainable Tourism promoting environmental public health, hosted on the global platform coursera.org. This kind of outreach to the broader public is motivating for further digital course content development too.

Below, Table 2 shows the different approaches to training activities aimed at supporting the need for capacity within MOODLE course design, content development as well as formulating relevant research questions for future studies.

Table 2. Total number of workshop days, participants, the number of courses created in MOODLE and number of students in MOODLE courses per semester

Workshop title/numbers	Date	Workshop days	Participants	Courses	Students
MOODLE course design	Dec. 2014– Aug. 2018	14	50	30	500+
OER integration	May, 2016, Aug. 2017	3	32	11	
Formulating research objectives	May, 2016	3	12		
Video production	Aug. 2017	5	26		
Video post-production	Aug., Sept. 2017	10	6		

2.2   Activity 2: Pilot and Evaluation Studies on SUZA's ICT Infrastructure, LMS and OER Materials

Since the beginning of the SUZA-BSU partnership, it has been a crucial matter to ensure students' access to digital resources and platforms that enable a satisfying use. This allows the students to get the greatest benefit from their lecturers and ICT staff efforts.

To find the best way for the students to benefit we explored student's usage of and access to SUZA's ICT infrastructure, and a pilot study was undertaken as a survey targeting 352 students out of a total of 2099 SUZA students at the time of the study. The results of this study are shown in Table 3 below. Here you can see that for example only 79.8% are computer literate, only 40.1% have access to computers and that 16.2% lack access to internet. This testifies a needed emphasis on providing computer training as well as providing access to computers and internet connection.

Table 3. Selected results from pilot study on ICT structure and usage

352 students	Yes	No
Computer literate (self-evaluation)	79.8%	20.2%
Access to computers in SUZA labs	40.1%	18.4%
Internet access in University campus	83.8%	16.2%
Awareness on online education e-resources	54.5%	
Number of students using MOODLE for the first 11 courses designed	81.7%	

As part of the earlier mentioned workshops, 11 courses were developed on the MOODLE platform. Another online survey was conducted to evaluate the usage of the platform and the blended learning format for these 11 courses. The study also assessed levels of student satisfaction with the Moodle.

The evaluation showed that out of 155 diploma and bachelor students participating in the first 11 courses, 10 integrated with the Moodle, (81.7%). The result also shows that most of the students (60%) use laptops to access the Moodle, 56% of the students use smartphones, 20.7% use Desktop computers and 7.4% of students' access the MOODLE from tablets.

2.3   Activity 3: Development of SUZA OER Guideline

As many other universities around the world and particularly in developing countries, SUZA suffers from limited teaching and learning materials, inadequate number of teachers and high prices on course materials like traditional printed books. To meet these challenges it can be valuable for the academic institutions to support the so called OER movement which has the potential to reduce instructional costs while providing the students as well as academic staff with high quality educational content [1]. And to strengthen, communicate and broaden the use of this kind of OER among lecturers at SUZA, an OER guideline was developed. The guideline covers integration of external produced OER as well as the production of SUZA's own OER, utilization and distribution of OER, including the use of Creative Commons licenses.

A survey among 431 students, as seen in Table 4, shows that around 60% have had positive experience from OER, around 28% are neutral while less than 20% disagree. In this way SUZA would potentially benefit a lot from the usage of OER.

Table 4. Students perception on use of OER as part of their course content

Perceptions	Respondents (Total 431)	Agree N (%)	Neutral N (%)	Disagree N (%)
MOOC contents provided by instructor were relevant to this course content	Students	225 (54)	128 (30.7)	64 (15.3)
You tube video provided by instructor of this course elaborate more about most of the sub-topic	Students	248 (59)	99 (23.6)	73 (17.4)
Online tutorial given by lecturer were very useful	Students	243 (58.7)	98 (23.7)	73 (17.6)
Web links provided by instructor give more learning opportunities	Students	253 (60.6)	118 (28.3)	46 (11.1)
External forum give me opportunity to get answer of my questions than class room forum	Students	197 (47.2)	135 (32.3)	86 (20.5)
The use of video was very interesting in this course	Students	268 (63.9)	100 (23.9)	51 (12.2)

Aside from using OER developed by other institutions SUZA is also producing its own OER as part of earlier activities within the Centre for Digital Learning, CDL. From the three different activities described above, a number of lessons learned can be grouped within five main areas – or questions.

3   Lessons Learned

3.1   What Human Resources Are Needed?

From workshop participants' feedback, early experiences showed that lecturers and IT staff did not use digital learning technologies without being given some initial training. This means that only by investing time and resources to support a systematic and continuous training, lecturers and supportive IT staff will join the transformation of digitally supported education.

According to the participants, trainings with a practical hand-on approach were found to be the most valuable compared to the more theoretical workshops and lecturers become most motivated when they can easily apply the hands-on training to their own course development.

During the workshops it was also advised that lecturers and IT staff should have easy access to assistance when managing day-to-day inquiries related to the LMS. Ideally each of SUZA's seven campuses should provide technical support staff as well as staff with IT-pedagogical qualifications. Center for ICT services should assign staff to perform regular updates and maintenance of the MOODLE.

To support and to attract attention to the didactic and pedagogical strategies for online and blended learning at SUZA, research should be conducted on specific praxis close teaching activities. Therefore, more SUZA PhD studies in educational technologies are needed to realize this need.

3.2   What Should the ICT-Infrastructure Look Like?

One of the basic needs to achieve increased and improved access for SUZA students to course materials is to find an efficient way to share and distribute course materials. With this regard, SUZA MOODLE has great potential and is in this way supporting conventional classroom teaching by easing access to a wide range of educational resources such as html-formatted documents, graphics, audio, video, multimedia. Further, it includes features promoting student activation, such as assignment submission, discussion forum, a blog, quiz-creation, grading, an online calendar, announcements and more.

One thing is to install the software but to motivate students as well as teachers' use in high numbers. It is crucial to provide easy access and a user-friendly interface. This is why the MOODLE interface has been redesigned into a version that meets more of the inexperienced teachers and students (20% of students are computer illiterate, ref. Table 3) needs as well as why the MOODLE was also installed in a mobile version (56% of students use smartphones, ref. Table 3). The mobile version can be accessed via smartphones or tablets.

As for the remaining 44% of the students with no access to smartphones or computers, it was decided that they should be provided with low cost tablets during BSU III so as to improve equity in accessing this service across students.

Further, to ease access for students it is recommended to build an integration between different IT systems and thereby provide a seamless digital journey for students. For example, an integration between MOODLE and the student registration system would in a user-friendly way lead the students to the online course room. As an additional benefit, easy access saves a lot of time spent on trouble shooting for both admin and academic staff.

Functional plagiarism and a library software are two more areas related to ICT-infrastructure and learning materials and are obviously gaining value if integrated and accessible from the SUZA MOODLE platform.

3.3   Should You Rely on OER or on Own Content Production – or Both?

A common fear among universities in low income countries has been that the availability of free OER from the world's top universities could lead to a development, where only top universities are producers of OER while the rest of the world's institutions are consumers of OER. Many projects in low income countries have consequently focused on the production of local OER [1]. Experience from the project shows that taking the best from the two worlds could be the best way to go on.

Attention should though be on ensuring teachers' critical approach to OER as well as to maintain production cost and lecturers' time used on content production is low.

This is where Centre for Digital Learning (CDL) has the potential to offer just-in-time support that can contribute to saving costs and save lecturers' time at the same time producing materials of high quality.

A guideline for integration, production, utilization and distribution of OER developed at SUZA provide the procedures on all matters regarding the OER within the university in consideration with other policies and guidelines operating within and outside the university.

3.4 What Support Is Needed from Management?

From the survey, increased use of ICT in education highly depends on a reliable internet connection and equipment for students to access online materials.

Further the use of ICT in education needs more awareness e.g. via a clear institutional vision on digitally supported education to enhance study efficacy and students' performance along with a guideline on minimum standards for the use of SUZA MOODLE.

As human resource is probably the most serious constraint, the university should consider reducing workloads for lecturers and instructors who are participating in developing online materials and blended learning course formats so that they can concentrate on these project activities.

Finally, more funds should be allocated on research studies on the use of digitally supported education. There is a need for research to be conducted to assess the contribution of blended and online courses at SUZA.

4 Conclusion

The BSU e-learning project approach, including parallel activities on staff capacity building, hard- and software implementation and institutional development about guides and policies, showcased in this paper, has demonstrated efficacy in driving the development of e-learning capacity at SUZA.

The south-north collaborative effort filling the gap of institutional capacity needed to build a sustainable model for scaling up a skilled use of educational technologies and inclusion of digital learning resources has until now showed successful and is greatly appreciated among staff responsible for a large number of courses. The overall achievement of the activities described have developed beyond expectations with four times as many courses on MOODLE and many more course instructors trained than anticipated.

The project has enhanced staff's capacity by training a total of 55 SUZA staff on designing, development and uploading online and blended course materials. Those members of staff have also been acquainted with the use of OER materials in teaching and learning process.

The utilization and integration of OER on existing accredited SUZA courses has been enhanced too.

Challenges also remain, e.g. for students to fully access online materials given, poor internet, and a lack of access to devices. Additionally, far from all SUZA lecturers have been trained in developing and transforming teaching into well-functioning digital supported teaching. In this respect a continued effort is needed to meet a satisfactory level for institutional capacity capable to implement new didactics and pedagogical principles to improve teaching and learning across SUZAs six faculties.

References

1. A New Way to Motivate Faculty Adoption of OER https://www.insidehighered.com/digital-learning/. Accessed 15 Mar 2019
2. Mgeni, M.S., Yunus, S. et al.: Explore Usage of ICT for Teaching and Learning at SUZA. Unpublished Manuscript (2016)
3. Giving Knowledge for Free: The Emergence of Open Educational Resources. Paris, France: OECD Publishing (2007). https://doi.org/10.1787/9789264032125-en. Accessed 15 May 2019

Making Use of Portfolios to Enhance Learning

Josephine Gabi[1]([⊠]) and Nicholas Mavengere[2]

[1] Manchester Metropolitan University, Manchester M15 6BH, UK
J.Gabi@mmu.ac.uk
[2] Tampere University, Kaventie 4, 33100 Tampere, Finland
nicholas.mavengere@tuni.fi

Abstract. Portfolios have been used in learning for a while. The value of the use of portfolios for learning has been well documented. For example, portfolios encourage students to reflect on their strengths, needs, errors, interests, challenges, and objectives, as well as, encourage interactive processes among students, teachers, and parents. Thus, it is value to strengthen the use of portfolio, for instance, by making use of appropriate pedagogical approaches and technological adoption. This research seeks to highlight the evolvement of use of portfolios from paper based to an electronic portfolio in the form of a word-processed document to students creating e-portfolios. To capture this process prior to the use of e-portfolios, students had been required to keep portfolios in the form of a word-processed document or paper based. The results show that the adoption of technology and improved pedagogical techniques enhanced students' educational performance and satisfaction. Therefore, this research advocates for the adoption of technologically-driven pedagogical philosophy to enhance the use of portfolios in learning and teaching.

Keywords: Paper-based-portfolios · Microsoft word-based portfolios ·
Electronic portfolios · Enhancing learning · Students' satisfaction

1 Introduction

Learning is increasingly demanding the skills set that meet the dynamic job demands. Thus, higher education institutions are being challenged to prepare students to effectively participate in the technologically advanced and fluid job market which demands the development of 'meta-competence' skills which will enable them to cope with what Barnett [4] characterises as 'supercomplexity'. This calls for transformative technology-mediated and imaginative pedagogies that create possibilities for experimental learning experiences. Technologies are being used in different dimensions to enhance learning and teaching as a paradigm shift from the view of students as consumers of knowledge to students as producers trajectory. In this research, we specifically focus on the utilisation of e-portfolios as a pedagogical, technological and outcomes-based tool. We argue that the potentialities of e-portfolios as learning, teaching and assessment instruments has not yet been sufficiently explored. Scully et al. [7] note that empirical evidence on the effectiveness of portfolios for learning and teaching remains sparse as research on the subject has 'either been purely theoretical in nature, or has focused on the technological platforms used to support learning portfolio construction'.

© IFIP International Federation for Information Processing 2019
Published by Springer Nature Switzerland AG 2019
A. Tatnall and N. Mavengere (Eds.): SUZA 2019, IFIP AICT 564, pp. 24–29, 2019.
https://doi.org/10.1007/978-3-030-28764-1_4

Portfolios have been widely used in educational contexts as both product and process of documenting learning [6]. Abrami and Barrett [1] noted the following possible advantages of portfolios;

- involve students in their learning (as a tool for reflection);
- allow students to increase their ability to self-evaluate;
- teach students to make choices;
- encourage students to better understand themselves and focus on their strengths;
- allow students to reflect on their procedures, strategies, and accomplishments so that they can improve and correct them and ultimately succeed;
- Promote feedback during the learning process, particularly during individual conferences;
- encourage students to reflect on their strengths, needs, errors, interests, challenges, and objectives;
- encourage interactive processes among students, teachers, and parents;
- shows student progress because it tracks performance over time;
- and they are used to assess competencies developed by students.

Electronic portfolios are used for different purposes, such as, process, showcase and assessment [1]. Electronic portfolios could be designed as process portfolios, that is, promoting how learning is conducted through structure and strategies. In essence, this way of using electronic portfolios makes them personal learning management tool as they enhance students' 'self-regulation, cognitive monitoring, and the development of a lifelong learning ethos as a habit of mind' [7]. Portfolios can help students in a number of ways including the following. According to Ali [2] it serves as:

- a reflective device of the students' skills and knowledge as they swiftly evolve over time.
- It helps articulate student accomplishment over the duration of study.
- It prepares the student for possible questions and answers during interviews.

Students reflecting on the bigger picture in terms of their wider personal, professional and academic experiences and how this impacts their development as reflective practitioners is central to learning in university setting. This research seeks to highlight the evolvement of use of portfolios from paper based to an electronic portfolio in the form of a word-processed document to students creating eportfolios. To capture this process prior to the students had been required to keep portfolios in the form of a word-processed document or paper based. Although this allowed for the development of ideas and evidence of reflection, students contributions and levels of engagement were somewhat limited by the medium. The following challenges were noted that lead to the adoption of e-portfolio.

- Students were limited to textual and graphical content in terms of the content they could add to their portfolios. External media could be linked to but felt removed from the portfolio itself.

- Students could not individualise their portfolios in design and layout.
- Students were not engaging significantly with the portfolio as reflective evidence or a platform through which to join parallels with other units or prior learning.
- A lack of content in the portfolios made it difficult to encourage deeper interactions and relationships to develop between Tutor's and Tutees whilst discussing portfolio content.

The adoption of technology to enhance portfolios could have the following aims;

- Increase quantity and depth of content in student portfolios by encouraging and enabling students to include a variety of media including textual, graphical and video content.
- Enable students to produce a more personalised portfolio with a bio section including an image representative of themselves, in addition to information on their interests and why they have chosen to study on the unit.
- Encourage students to draw connections to prior experiences and learning by using the portfolio on a regular basis as a reflective space.
- Develop relationships and interactivity between personal tutors and students/tutees. Tutors will give regular feedback by posting in the comments section on student's portfolios; this will also act as a platform to trigger more involved discussions during one to ones between Tutees and Tutors.

2 Methodology

Due to the requirements for students to have the ability to engage with multi-media content various e-portfolio platforms were considered. After evaluating the options available it was decided to use Weebly as the platform through which students would author their portfolios. Weebly was pursued for two reasons, firstly the tool uses a drag and drop mechanism easily allowing images, videos, audio and textual content to be added to student portfolios. Secondly, Weebly allowed students to add editors to their site which meant tutors could view student's portfolios without the content needing to be posted to the web. This solved any problems around plagiarism or any potential concerns student might have with their postings being in the public domain. In connection to this Weebly also allowed for students to export their portfolios as zip files which could then be uploaded as a submission within Moodle and date/time stamped for assessment purposes.

Initially staff created Weebly accounts and received some training on the use of the tool and then an introductory session was ran for all students to showcase the tool. Following on from this a series of video tutorials were created and embedded as a playlist on the Moodle unit area for students to work through to obtain all of the necessary skills to be able to use the tool. Throughout the unit time has been allocated for students to share skills whilst working on their Weebly site.

3 Results

The introduction of electronic portfolios aimed to:

- Increase quantity and depth of content in student portfolios by encouraging and enabling students to include a variety of media including textual, graphical and video content.
- Enable students to produce a more personalised portfolio with a bio section including an image representative of themselves, in addition to information on their interests and why they have chosen to study on the unit.
- Encourage students to draw connections to prior experiences and learning by using the portfolio on a regular basis as a reflective space.
- Develop relationships and interactivity between personal tutors and students/tutees. Tutors will give regular feedback by posting in the comments section on student's portfolios; this will also act as a platform to trigger more involved discussions during one to ones between Tutees and Tutors.

As a result of student creating e-portfolios a number of positive experiences were noted:

- Increase in student engagement: Tutors noted that students generally much preferred adding content to their blog and the ability to personalise the appearance of their portfolio and that the e-portfolio allow students to flexibly work on their assignment online. Students noted the following e-portfolios benefits; 'with the e-portfolio, I can be creative with what I do and its different to the usual essays and presentations.' 'The best thing about my assignment for this module is that I get to create something I have never created before a blog. This is something I have never done before so it is quite new to me. I am able to put all my experiences and my personal information into this blog and explain what I have been doing in my current placement.'
- Students as reflective practitioners: by using a portfolio on a regular basis, this allowed students to reflect on their wider knowledges and experiences. Students enjoyed having their own space online in which to reflect:
- 'I like the idea of web-based reflection as it allows me to go over exactly what I have learnt in seminars and in other units. It also leaves room for me to apply my knowledge in an active way'.
- 'The module itself is interesting as an individual I like to reflect on my professional development and always am looking in ways to become a better nursery practitioner etc.'
- Portfolio feedback: Tutors liked having the ability to use the portfolio as a mechanism through which to gauge student progress, offer regular formative/developmental feedback and forge stronger relationships with their Tutees. One Tutor commented:
- 'I like being able to make pages including one for feedback. Students can use these skills in the future'

- Overall student satisfaction improved from 70% (using word-based portfolios) to 94% (using e-portfolios). Students commented that they learned new methods of showcasing their work and building a portfolio of themselves
- Students develop a sense of both academic and social belonging: Students also appreciated the small class sizes (15 per tutor group) as these enabled them to get to know each other quickly and develop a sense of belonging. Most students commented that they felt confident participating in sessions without fear that they are being judged.

4 Discussion

This research emanated from years of observing students struggle to produce an end of year written assignment which sufficiently and appropriately reflects their personal, professional and academic development. This prompted a reconsideration of pedagogical philosophy in order to incorporate technologically-driven learning and teaching practice. The assessment method was changed from essay to e-portfolio which enabled the bridging of a gap between traditional literacy model and new multimodal digital literacies which was crucial for preparing students to cope with the realities of the technologically advanced world. Turning to web-based e-portfolios was also a paradigm shift from the view of students as passive consumers of knowledge to students as producers' trajectory.

Our learning and teaching strategies provided opportunities for peer collaboration which helped our students to purposefully engage with their portfolio thereby strengthening their capacity to monitor and self-regulate their own performance. Tutors provided formative feedback on work-in-progress throughout the academic year in order to enhance students' academic writing skills and chances of success. This process also offered tutors an in-depth knowledge of the student as a learner whilst opening up possibilities to proactively identify areas for improvement and individualise academic support. These predictive possibilities made it possible for tutors to anticipate and prevent possible problems before they occur or escalate. This was particularly important for our first-year students' transitioning from college to higher education. Shields [8] and Beard et al. [5] note that higher education is not merely a cognitive endeavour, but also an emotional learning journey for students. As observed by Barnett [3], it is a journey of becoming that is characterised by relentless and interminable processes of change and transformation individuals go through as they intra-act with others and materials within a given context. As such, students starting their educational journeys often plunge into a state of uncertainty where learning, according to Barnett [3] 'calls for courage on the part of the learner and a will to leap into a kind of void'. It was therefore, worth considering what it meant to be a student during this perceived period of uncertainty and the changes they are likely to go through in their educational journey. Perhaps more importantly are ways in which digital technology tools could be utilised to capture students' learning processes in order to improve their educational experience, success and progression. If using an external e-portfolio tool it is important to be aware of the following potential obstacles to consider when implementing the tool:

- Ensure students have sufficient technical skills within the tool before there is a requirement to post content. Although in the most part having a video tutorial series was sufficient some students did comment that they would have like some face to face technical support for the tool. Having an introductory task for students to create an 'about me' page worked well as a starter exercise in the portfolios.
- Adding Tutors as editors so they could view student portfolios and add comments offline only seemed to work sporadically in sending email invitations to staff giving them access to students Weebly sites. Students logging into their own Weebly accounts on the Tutors device and then adding their Tutor as an editor resolved this.

5   Conclusion

This research explained how different portfolios have been used in different academic years namely paper based to an electronic portfolio in the form of a word-processed document to students creating e-portfolio's. Students' satisfaction and academic performance improved with the adoption of technology. Therefore, we recommend that technology be adopted in using portfolios. However, we emphasize that appropriate pedagogical techniques be used to fully enjoy the benefits of technology adoption.

References

1. Abrami, P.C., Barrett, H.: Directions for research and development on electronic portfolios. Canadian J. Learn. Technol. **31**(3) (2005, online)
2. Ali, A.I.: Designing digital portfolios for technology support students. Issues Inf. Sci. Inf. Technol. **5** (2008, online)
3. Barnett, R.: Learning for an unknown future. High. Educ. Res. Dev. **23**(3), 248–260 (2004)
4. Barnett, R.: A Will to Learn: Being a Student in the Age of Uncertainty. Open University Press, Maidenhead (2007)
5. Beard, C., Clegg, S., Smith, K.: Acknowledging the affective in higher education. Br. Educ. Res. J. **33**(2), 235–252 (2007)
6. Lewis, L.: ePortfolio as pedagogy: threshold concepts for curriculum design. E-Learn. Digital Media **14**(1), 72–85 (2017)
7. Scully, D., O'Leary, M., Brown, M.: The learning portfolios in Higher Education: a game of snakes and ladders. National Institute for Digital Learning, Dublin (2018)
8. Shields, S.: 'My work is bleeding': exploring students' emotional responses to first-year assignment feedback. Teach. High. Educ. **20**(6), 614–624 (2015)

Sustainable E-Learning – A Case Study on the Pros and Cons of Certification

Bent B. Andresen(✉) ⓘ

Danish School of Education, Aarhus University,
Tuborgvej 164, 2400 Copenhagen, NV, Denmark
bba@edu.au.dk

Abstract. This paper deals with a case study on how to achieve sustainable e-learning through systematic certification. The case is a nationwide Danish project on the certification of 23 vocational e-learning courses conducted by 'The National Danish Knowledge Centre of e-learning' in 2018.

The research objective is to investigate the pros and cons of this e-learning certification. How and why does it promote sustainable e-learning and professional development among teachers in vocational education and training?

The research results provide evidence suggesting that the certification increases the sustainability of vocational e-learning. In particular, it promotes consistency between expected learning outcomes, preconditions as regards content, duration, flexibility, use of digital platform etc., and design in terms of organization and evaluation of learning activities.

The certification of e-learning also fosters professional development among the teachers involved. They appreciate the systematic nature of the certification process and the template applied as well as the provision of supportive and specific feedback from the certifier.

When the vocational teachers were assigned the role as e-learning designers, they stepped out of their comfort zone. In these cases, they greatly appreciated receiving supportive and challenging feedback. The combination of support and pressure helped them move forward towards new experiences and broader repertoires of sustainable e-learning methods.

In particular, the teachers benefitted from single-loop learning, which improved their planning actions, and double-loop learning, which improved their beliefs about sustainable e-learning. These results can be generalized and expanded to other projects. Consequently, the certification is important for the future development of sustainable e-learning.

Keywords: E-learning · Certification · Vocational teachers · Capacity building

1 Introduction

The paper deals with a project on e-learning certification at vocational colleges, which was carried out to promote the sustainability of e-learning. In this context, the term 'sustainable e-learning' is used as an umbrella term for various persistent quality aspects of e-learning. Focus is on the sustainability of e-learning instead of e-learning

© IFIP International Federation for Information Processing 2019
Published by Springer Nature Switzerland AG 2019
A. Tatnall and N. Mavengere (Eds.): SUZA 2019, IFIP AICT 564, pp. 30–38, 2019.
https://doi.org/10.1007/978-3-030-28764-1_5

for sustainability, i.e. education aimed at future development of the global environment, the climate etc.

Sustainability issues like the cost-effectiveness and usability of digital tools, platforms, and materials are outside the scope of the research. Rather, it deals with the sustainability of technology-enhanced vocational education that is flexible with respect to time and place. In this context, the notion of e-learning is used as an overarching term encompassing blended learning as well as purely distance learning.

1.1 Certification Process

In general, there are many visions regarding sustainable e-learning to be considered [1]. These visions include current vocational education and training (VET). Dealing with technological sustainability, the VET system takes into account ideas of increased flexibility and frequent use of digital technology.

Dealing with social and cultural sustainability, the system also takes into account constantly changing educational needs among participants in vocational youth and in-service education. Therefore, the certification project promotes precise descriptions of potential participants' various learning conditions and needs. The project also promotes explicit preconditions regarding content, duration, flexibility etc. Furthermore, it promotes consistent design, including organization and evaluation of learning activities.

The certified courses cover a spectrum from primarily face-to-face education to primarily online education. With an average of 59 h, the course duration varies from 4 to 185 h (see Fig. 1).

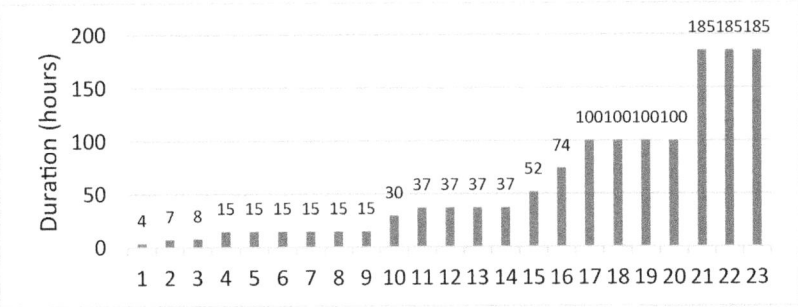

Fig. 1. Certified vocational e-learning courses

The certification project was launched in 2018 by 'The Danish Organization of Business Schools' (DEL) and the certification agency 'The Danish National Centre for e-learning'. In cooperation with the researcher (the author of this article), the certifier developed certification guidelines for qualifying e-learning at vocational colleges.

According to these guidelines, the certification process includes three main phases. First, the designer of vocational e-learning submits a draft concept to the certifier. The designer then receives supportive and specific feedback from the certifier to promote well-founded and sustainable e-learning. Then the designer uses this feedback to revise and refine the concept prior to bringing it into use.

The designers of vocational e-learning describe and submit their concept using a template provided by the certifier. The main themes in this template are based on an analysis of the main factors influencing the participants' learning outcomes [2]. The main themes are:

- Terms of the course
- Learning objectives of the course
- Participant's prior learning
- Organization of the course
- Activities and learning methods
- Assessment of the course

The vocational colleges are encouraged to use this template to increase the likelihood of successful learning outcomes for all participants. Most often, the learning objectives and course duration are determined by regional or national authorities. The developers of e-learning in the VET system are encouraged to explicate these objectives and make them understandable to potential participants. In addition, the developers have to explicate the organization of e-learning. For example, they have to clearly describe the relationship between face-to-face and online activities as well as the participants' individual and collaborative learning activities.

During the planning process, the developers are also encouraged to consider the participants' previous experiences, knowledge, and skills. For example, some participants in e-learning focusing on accounting principles and methods may already have a job as an accountant.

Moreover, the developers are encouraged to take into account general preconditions, such as the participants' oral, reading, and digital skills. About 25% of the population in Denmark aged 18–65 do not have functional reading skills and thus have trouble reading to learn something new.

By contrast, digital literacy is rarely a challenge. In Denmark, digital technology is used daily in connection with learning, and the 'bring your own device' principle has been fully implemented at all levels of the educational system for several years now. Among the participants, distraction from social networks and other non-curricular digital activities are, however, a challenge which many schools are currently struggling to overcome.

2   Research Objective

The overall research objective is to investigate the pros and cons of e-learning certification. Does the certification process support and promote sustainable development of e-learning in the VET system?

Moreover, the research objective is to investigate the perceived usefulness of this certification among the developers of vocational e-learning. Does it support and promote capacity building among these developers?

The program theory is shown in Fig. 2.

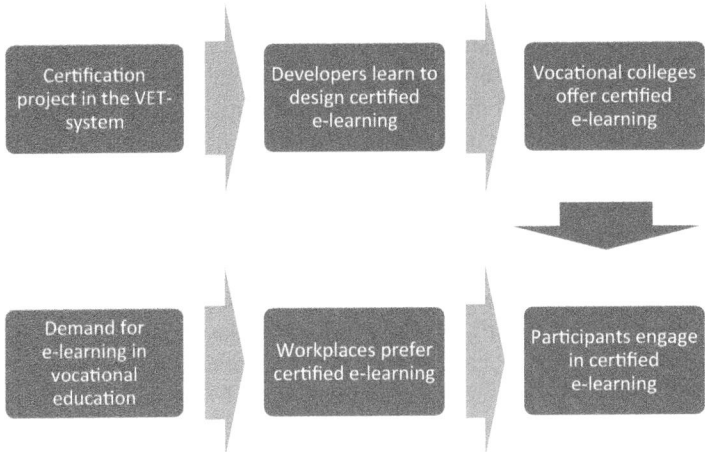

Fig. 2. Program theory

The upper row representing college level illustrates the potential influence of the certification project on the developers' professional development. Before that, their experiences in the area of e-learning varied. Some, but not all, had previous experience designing vocational e-learning. However, they all learned to design e-learning. In particular, they became better at creating certified e-learning, and in the end, they all succeeded, resulting in the 23 certified courses.

The bottom row in Fig. 2 represents the demand for vocational e-learning courses. This demand is expected to increase due to government initiatives encouraging timely and work-based vocational education. In the future, the demand is also expected to increase as workplaces become aware of and prefer certified courses.

2.1   Research Methods

The upper row representing college level illustrates the potential influence of the certification project on the developers' professional development. Before that, their experiences in the area of e-learning varied. Some, but not all, had previous experience designing vocational e-learning. However, they all learned to design e-learning. In particular, they became better at creating certified e-learning, and in the end, they all succeeded, resulting in the 23 certified courses.

The bottom row in Fig. 2 represents the demand for vocational e-learning courses. This demand is expected to increase due to government initiatives encouraging timely and work-based vocational education. In the future, the demand is also expected to increase as workplaces become aware of and prefer certified courses.

2.2   Research Methods

The case study is based on a mixed methods design. The methods used include semi-structured interviews with staff representatives in charge of e-learning initiatives as well as document analyses, i.e. analyses of descriptions and communication with the certifier regarding the 23 e-learning courses.

At the vocational colleges involved, the developers in charge of the development of the 23 e-learning courses had different positions and roles. Generally, they were supported by their team leader or immediate manager (distributed leadership).

In a few cases, the developers had been assigned the role as 'e-consultants' responsible for developing but not for running the course. In most cases, the certification was carried out by either individual teachers or small teams of teachers who would run the courses afterwards.

The teachers worked together in communities of practice. For example, three teachers each developed a certified course during regular meetings with a team leader and an 'e-consultant'. At another vocational college, a team of three teachers developed three certified courses while they were informally lead by one of the teachers who had substantial experience with vocational e-learning.

A third example concerns three colleges, which had each appointed a teacher. The three teachers then worked together on a certified e-learning course to be implemented by each of the three colleges afterwards.

In general, the teachers and e-consultants involved were intrinsically motivated due to personal interest in e-learning as well as inspiration from their colleagues, team leaders, and immediate managers. Their extrinsic motivation was related to expectations from team leaders and managers at the vocational colleges. For example, some developers participated in the certification project because they wanted to change roles from regular teacher to 'e-consultant' and some even considered further career development.

3 Research Findings

The research findings include new knowledge about the intended and unintended consequences of the certification process. In general, the perceived utility value of the systematic design of sustainable e-learning and the support and feedback from the certifier was high. The developers of e-learning involved at the vocational colleges appreciated the certification due to several reasons, which will be briefly described in the following.

First, the teachers involved express in the interviews that they consider the certification a relevant and valuable means of improving e-learning concepts.

Second, the certification fosters their professional development. They learn from the systematic development of sustainable e-learning and the associated dialog with the certifier. For example, they develop their knowledge about sustainability and other highly relevant e-learning issues.

Third, they generally consider the certification template useful. In the future, most developers will apply this template when designing e-learning courses. Some of the developers will use a similar template and some prefer to customize it a little bit.

Fourth, the certification is generally appreciated by the HR Departments in companies employing potential participants in vocational e-learning.

Fifth, these potential participants are assigned a more clearly defined role than before the certification project.

Sixth, the teachers learn to consider and describe more clearly than before what learning activities the participants are engaged in during the courses and what the specific learning objectives are. For example, a teacher involved in the certification project emphasizes that:

"They have ... elaborated more on the target group than in their own [previous] templates ... and they have included the learning objectives by going a little deeper into what they do".

Seventh, the developers learn to consider and describe the assessment of e-learning activities more clearly. The teachers describe the assessment methods applied in a particular course more systematically than they did before the certification project. For example, a teacher plans to conduct regular assessments during the e-learning course:

"The students will be assessed on each topic, whether they will get verbal feedback or online instruction. Sometimes the teachers give group feedback....They have clarified that for every single assignment. It's important to the students because they don't actually meet them".

Another teacher emphasizes the close relationship between learning objectives and the assessment methods applied:

"The assessment refers back to the learning objectives. After working intensely on them, we would look at them as we developed assignments for the topics and considered: 'What is it actually that we want to see that you are capable of once you have achieved the learning objectives?'"

Since the provision of feedback to participants in the e-learning courses is considered an integrated part of the assessment, the developers of e-learning are expected to describe their provision of feedback in detail. Teachers who at first neglected this were encouraged by the certifier to reconsider their provision of feedback and re-submit their description:

"You should go into more detail in your description of the feedback: What will the feedback consist of (e.g. type)? How will the feedback be provided (by whom and how?)?"

Eighth, the dialog with the certifier fosters capacity building among the developers of e-learning. In general, the developers appreciate the various comments they receive from the certifier on their draft concepts. In particular, the certifiers' submission of supportive and specific feedback promotes coherence between (1) learning goals, (2) organization of blended learning activities, and (3) formative and summative assessment of these activities.

Ninth, the certifier comments on the reasons given by the developers for the specific organization of the courses. In general, the developers submit two types of reasons, i.e. explicit and implicit reasons. Explicit reasons require that key decisions in the organization of e-learning are clearly described and justified.

Out of the 23 certified courses, ten contain explicit reasons that include the need to learn about information retrieval, create close links between theory and practice, support collaborative learning, and provide project guidance.

Implicit reasons for e-learning include consistency between the participants' prior knowledge and ability, their expected learning outcomes, and choices of organization and assessment methods. Implicit reasons also include given requirements for using digital technology, allowing greater flexibility through participation from home or a workplace.

In principle, implicit reasons can be difficult to communicate to colleagues who want to realize or further develop the courses. However, they may be rather obvious in practice. For example, the internship part of some vocational training programs can best be done by participating in dedicated facilities using suitable forklifts, kitchen facilities, accounting applications, etc.

In such cases, face-to-face learning activities at the vocational school are required. However, the developers have to justify the extent and nature of interaction in physical and digital learning environments.

Tenth, an unintended consequence was a significant lack of knowledge about e-learning methodology among a handful of the developers involved. These new e-learning developers all had experience with face-to-face teaching, and they were familiar with the approach called 'direct instruction' [3]. Moreover, they had extensive knowledge about the learning content but not about approaches combining face-to-face and online activities. Therefore, they experienced some challenges when asked to organize blended learning for specific groups of participants based on specific learning objectives.

To overcome these challenges, the certifier was in charge of some hours of in-service education focusing on proper description of learning objectives, well-founded organization of blended and collaborative learning, assessment methods, and the provision of formative feedback. In order to prevent such challenges in the future, entry-level educational knowledge among the developers of e-learning could be ensured.

In general, the teachers involved are experiencing balanced pressure and support, which helps them gain new experiences and broader repertoires of sustainable e-learning methods.

4 Discussion

There is research evidence suggesting that the learners' outcome of blended learning is generally greater than the outcome of merely face-to-face education or merely online learning, but the learning outcome highly depends on the participants' time on task and thus the developers' planning of such tasks [4]. Two other factors influencing the learning outcome are 'clear learning objectives' and 'teacher clarity' regarding information about planned learning activities [3]. Due to the previously mentioned lack of reading literacy among the participants in e-learning courses, a fourth sustainability factor is the vocational colleges' provision of digital video materials complementing text-based learning materials [5]. Depending on the learning objectives, at fifth major factor is learning in 'communities of practice' [6].

Teachers involved in the certification project are encouraged to carefully consider these factors when they design vocational e-learning. They participate as 'learners' engaging in focused and purposeful practice [7]. In general, they participate as a 'team' and learn from each other about sustainable e-learning approaches.

Since there is research evidence suggesting that teachers at vocational colleges seldom receive feedback on their teaching and organization of learning activities [8], the certification helps overcome this problem.

As discussed above, the teachers involved typically stepped out of their comfort zone when they were assigned the role as designers of vocational e-learning. In these cases, they greatly appreciated receiving formative and challenging feedback. In particular, they received supportive and specific feedback, including answers to questions, guidance, and supportive and specific comments on draft e-learning concepts.

Moreover, they engaged in single- and double-loop learning (see Fig. 3).

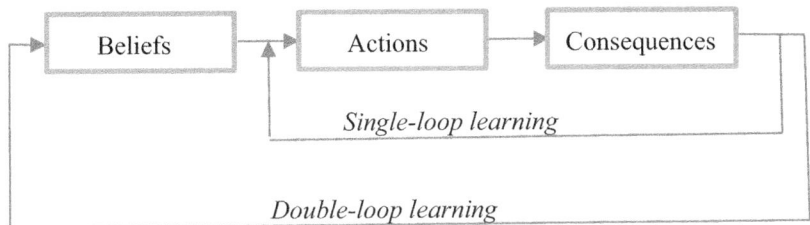

Fig. 3. Single- and double-loop learning [7].

According to the Theory of Action, three variables must be reconciled, i.e. beliefs, actions, and consequences. Single-loop learning refers to the relationship between actions (draft e-learning submitted to the certifier) and consequences (specific and supportive feedback from the certifier).

Double-loop learning refers to the developers' beliefs about sustainable e-learning. For example, the developers reflected on, questioned, and revised these beliefs causing changes in their theories of actions related to e-learning, thereby resulting in altered actions and improved design outcomes.

These results can be generalized to other projects. The findings in the case study probably also apply to other similar cases [9]. The certification is thus important for future development of sustainable e-learning.

5   Conclusion

This paper deals with the certification of vocational e-learning. It reports findings from a case study on systematic certification of 23 different e-learning courses, covering a spectrum from primarily face-to-face education to primarily online education. The average course duration is 59 h.

The overall research objective is to investigate the pros and cons of e-learning certification. In particular, the research objective is to investigate how the certification supports and promotes sustainable development of e-learning in the VET system.

Additionally, the research objective is to investigate how the certification supports and promotes capacity building among the developers of e-learning in this system.

The certification process was launched in 2018 by the certifier 'The Danish National Centre for e-learning'. In cooperation with the researcher, the certifier forwarded guidelines and a template for qualifying e-learning at vocational schools for certification. The template was based on research findings regarding factors with a high degree of influence on the learners' outcomes in vocational education.

The research findings include new knowledge about the intended and unintended consequences of the project. First, the research provides evidence suggesting a high relevance of the presented efforts ensuring the sustainability of vocational e-learning. In general, developers of vocational e-learning appreciate the systematic and associated dialog with the certifier.

Second, the research provides evidence suggesting that their dialog with colleagues and the certifier, including the associated feedback, fosters capacity building at the vocational school. This feedback regards, among other things, the coherence between learning goals, organization of blended learning activities, and formative and summative assessment of these activities.

The developers engaged in single-loop learning, which improved their planning actions, and double-loop learning, which improved their beliefs about sustainable e-learning. During some of these learning loops, the developers stepped out of their comfort zone.

Some teachers even stepped out of their zone of proximal development. In order to prevent such unintended consequences in the future, entry-level knowledge about learning objectives, formative evaluation, and e-learning methods among the developers of e-learning could be ensured.

Generally, the developers involved experienced balanced pressure and support. The research findings can be generalized to other projects regarding systematic provision of guidance and formative feedback from a certification agency. Consequently, the certification project is important for the future development of sustainable e-learning.

References

1. Christensen, C.M., Eyring, H.J.: The Innovative University. Changing the DNA of Higher Education from the Inside Out. Josey-Bass, San Francisco (2011)
2. Andresen, B.B.: Formative research on e-learning certification. In: Viby, J. (ed.) The National Danish Knowledge Centre of e-learning (2019). https://ec.europa.eu/epale/en/resource-centre/content/formative-research-e-learning-certification
3. Hattie, J.A.C.: Visible Learning. A Synthesis of Over 800 Meta-Analyses Relating to Achievement. Routledge, Abingdon (2009)
4. Means, B., et al.: Evaluation of Evidence-Based Practices in Online Learning. A Meta-Analysis and Review of Online Learning Studies. Washington, D.C.: U.S. Department of Education (2009). http://www2.ed.gov/rschstat/eval/tech/evidence-based-practices/finalreport.pdf
5. Hattie, J.A.C.: Visible Learning for Teachers. Maximizing Impact on Learning. Routledge, Oxford (2012)
6. Lave, J., Wenger, E.: Situated Learning – Legitimate Peripheral Participation. Cambridge University Press, New York (1991)
7. Fullan, M.: Nuance. Why Some Leaders Succeed and Others Fail. Corwin, London (2019)
8. OECD: TALIS 2013. Copenhagen: EVA (2013). https://www.eva.dk/projekter/2014/talis-2013/download-rapport/talis-2013-oecds-laerer-og-lederundersogelse/download
9. Flyvbjerg, B.: Five misunderstandings about case-study research. Qual. Inq. **12**(2), 219–245 (2006)

eHealth as the Trigger Initiative That May Foster Development in Health Care Delivery in Tanzania

Ernest Simon[1](✉) and Andrew Mushi[2](✉)

[1] Ministry of Health, Community Development, Gender, Elderly, and Children,
Mzumbe University, Morogoro, Tanzania
saiernest4@gmail.com
[2] Dar es Salaam Campus College, University of Mzumbe, Dar es Salaam,
Tanzania
amushi@mzumbe.ac.tz

Abstract. The Tanzania Ministry of Health, Community Development, Gender, Elderly, and Children developed eHealth Strategy aims to leverage the implementation of Information Communication Technology (ICT) in health service delivery [4]. The eHealth strategy in Tanzania was accord from the World Health Organisation after recognized the usage of ICT in supporting the delivery of health and health-related interventions [11]. The strategy promised various issues to be done by the Ministry in various capacities through its 16 Strategic Objectives (SO). Those promises were divided into four main categories of implementation which are eHealth Foundation with three SO, eHealth Solution with eleven SO, Change and Adoption with one SO, and lastly eHealth Governance with one SO. The implementation of eHealth initiatives has contributed tremendously to the changes and awareness of ICT in health services delivery in various capacities due to well-structured and adhering of the SO agreed on 2013. This has proven by changes of attitude for the health practitioners including doctors, nurses, administrators who are working to the health facilities in Tanzania. Clients who receive health care at health facilities are recognizing the importance of ICT in service delivery especially on reducing waiting time, and through the existing link between one department for example finance unit, medical record unit, and dispensing/pharmacy during the delivery of care to patients this link facilitate well-structured communication within the facility which smoothening the client/patients to practitioners interaction. Furthermore, it improved access of client information for the purpose of proper completion of a continuum of care to authorized practitioners within the facility.

Keywords: Health · Community Development · Gender · Elderly · Children · eHealth Strategy · Information Communication Technology

The implementation of eHealth initiative is accorded from various theories but the prominent one is the Unified Theory Acceptance and Use of Technology (UTAUT) which is a combination of various models which support the application of Information Communication Technology in service provision. Therefore this model borrowed constructs from each of the following models such as; Theory of reasoned action, the

A. Tatnall and N. Mavengere (Eds.): SUZA 2019, IFIP AICT 564, pp. 39–44, 2019.
https://doi.org/10.1007/978-3-030-28764-1_6

Technology acceptance model, the Motivational model. UTAUT is the key theory that supports the acceptance of ICT in service delivery. Venkatesh [1] identifies four key issues underpin the UTAUT which are performance expectancy, effort expectancy, social influence and facilitating conditions this issues have proven to have the close relation which influences the behavior of user to accept and use the ICT during delivering of services furthermore, issue like age, experience, and voluntariness have not left aside because it is believed to be moderators of technology acceptance and usage.

Therefore, for the successful usage of ICT, the human element should be taken into consideration and the user has to participate fully in organizing Information System in the organization to bring ownership and collective responsibility. It has been argued by Macleod [3] that, for successful implementation of any innovation including the use of ICT in service delivery user in the organization must be fully engaged in both hardware/software design with IT staff within the organization.

The implementation of ICT in health care delivery in Tanzania facilitated the Ministry to ensure that facilities are able to manage and identify the achievement of eHealth strategy implementation as follows; improved information sharing through Health Information Systems Integration to various partners, improved specialized health care services to patient in remote area using teleconsultation, facilitate early detection, rapid reporting and response via mobile platform, Strengthened Electronic Health Management Information System, improved resource management both human and financial and service delivery at health facilities, tracking of health commodities from Medical Stores Department to the facilities, Establishment of one source of facility register, improved network infrastructures to various Health facilities [5, 6].

The Health Sector Strategic Plan 2015–2020 (HSSP IV) emphasised on the engagement of population in the modality of interactive communication through e-health in order to establish the strong partnership between the government and community. This interactive communication is paramount important for the improvement of service delivery and is practically facilitated by the acceptability and usability of eHealth during the process of service delivery. The Ministry believed that the development and implementation of e-health strategy fostered usability of ICT hence improve service delivery in the country and contribute to the country development in terms of improving social services and will impact to the community at large [5, 6]. Due to the anticipated result, the Ministry set the target that by 2020, all public hospitals in the country make use of ICT applications for administrative and medical processes [5, 6].

Stakeholders in other sectors not limited to health services delivery can learn the effect of implementing eHealth initiatives in service delivery existing Tanzania particularly how service delivery was improved as a result of implementing eHealth which triggered client's satisfaction at the various level of care. ICT in Tanzania, like in other developing countries is an initiative that needs to be taken as a positive intervention to the social services (education, health, security, community development etc.) which involves clients or provider that are scattered and need to be coordinated for the purpose of delivered social services on time with little resources especially human resources.

The governance of health care delivery is done through various level of delivery from the national level to the community level. The Health Policy of 2007 and e-health strategy has little described how this intervention may lead to the improving governance in health sector instead its emphases on integrating mushrooming of health information technology system in order to have one system which is interoperability within a sector [4]. Therefore, implementation of e-health strategy of 2013–18 is part of ongoing health sector reform in Tanzania which brings about a positive intervention to leverage governance in the healthcare industry which can be adopted and applied in delivery of service to the public.

The Ministry of Health, Community Development, Gender, Elderly, and Children established feedback mechanisms at health facilities whereby clients/patient after receiving healthcare service can provide opinions/claims through dialling a short code given by Tanzania Communication and Regulatory Authority (TCRA) *152*05*03#. The feedback in terms of opinions/claims which was sent by the clients/patients is transmitted and analyzed through the web-based portal of www.maoni.moh.go.tz. This initiative of electronic feedback mechanism from the clients after receiving services is free of charge at the time of providing and has facilitated positive changes to the service provider hence improve service delivery. Immediately feedback mechanism from service user is paramount important as it indicates how the customer perceives the service provision. Stakeholders from different service provision authorities have to realize that direct electronic feedback mechanism from users can help to improve services when there is an integration of the system within the facility or at the point of delivery of the services.

The National guideline for integrated Health Facility Electronic Management Systems (iHFeMS) in Tanzania has indicated that all intervention regarding the usability of ICT is supposed to follow the e-health strategy [7]. It has been reported on Ministry's budget speech of 2018/19 that various public hospital from district hospitals to national level have managed to initiate a mechanism to collect revenue through e-electronics and some facilities have started to integrate patient records in an electronic system which helps to store and records of the patients information in a proper and accessible mechanism [10]. Furthermore, the introduction of Health Information Management System by the Ministry of health has facilitated the usability of District Health Information System 2 (DHIS2), Human Resources for Health Information System (HRHIS), Training Information Health System (TIHS), Emergence Information Diseases Severance Reporting (eIDSR). The Ministry is as the overseer of all eHealth initiatives implemented in a different level of care within the country.

Through the introduction of eHealth, Hospital Management Teams have managed to generate funds which are used on other interventions within the Hospital level and hence improve the quality of health provision. Doctors, nurses, administrators and other providers for health services are benefited in terms of receiving incentives due to the generated revenue which gave the morale to continue performing their duties. Therefore, this is the lesson to be learned to other stakeholders that it is paramount important to retain fund at the point of a collection as it is easier for the service provider to make rational decision on its allocation than been directed by higher authority also, it is a motivation for those who played a major role during its collection to be part of decision maker on how to utilize funds generated.

The current increased need for ICT in health has facilitated the Ministry of health to invest more on data quality management systems which facilitated an evidence-based decision as a compliment of the e-health strategy implementation. It was due to this fact the development partners have supported and facilitated the development of Tanzania Digital Health Investment Roadmap which is specifically for the investing on data systems and data use in order to strengthen the ability to make an evidence-based decision [8]. Therefore, it is important to adopt this investment roadmap as it outlines potential areas for investment and if well shared to the partners it may facilitate the institution to achieve the intended objective of providing quality service to the community.

Tanzania National Bureau of Statistics reported on 2018 that projected to be 89.2 Million in 2035 of which more than 60% are still estimated to reside in rural areas where are underprivileged with specialized medical care due to a low number of specialist in medical service provision or lack of equipment to provide high tech services. It have been reported by Ministry of Health that the shortage of healthcare provider is 52% whereas the available 48% also most of them are found in urban areas, according to Sikika [9] on their research report on "Tracking Study of Medical Doctors" identified that about 39.6% of tracked medical graduated are doing work that is not related to clinical practices. Therefore due to this scarcity of health practitioner to the rural areas telemedicine will provide alternative means for rural communities to access specialized healthcare services without traveling to the higher level facilities to seek for medical specialist or technology. Therefore, the scarcity of human resource is not the challenge only for health services provision but also the remarkable challenge has been reported in other sectors like education whereby the availability of teachers and instructors in rural area have still significant contribution to the performance of lower-level training facilities so the telemedicine initiative can be customized and contributed as part of solution to the community in need for quality provision of education services.

Furthermore, telemedicine as among initiative introduced by the country, the purpose of this initiative is to help the community to receive quality health regardless of the challenge existing of a shortage of human resources to the rural community. Therefore, this imitative of telemedicine in the country facilitated to foster the provision of telehealth services such as teleradiology, tele-oncology/telepathology, telecardiology to the areas where it was difficult to be offered especially to the rural areas which this service was not available. It is expected that telemedicine after its full implementation in the country it will ensure the wide scope of service delivery and hence the following impact will be realized to the community; to strengthening the provision of diagnostic, availability of specialized healthcare in under-served communities through the usage telemedicine due to the shortage of health practitioner at a lower level as it facilitates to have the ability to make consultations to the higher level facility connected to the network and hence improve delivery of services across the country. This initiative can be also implemented to social services sectors like education and the like as it capacitates lower level delivery unit to have a wide scope of delivery of services due to the fact that higher level is used as a backup where realized that needs arise.

The usage of the guideline and eHealth Strategy brought positive changes at facility level where curative services are delivered hence health facilities at the different level from Dispensary level to tertiary care facilities applies ICT in the delivery of health service in more than one department for Diagnosis purposes, drugs dispensing, revenue collection and billing system. The aim is that all activities within health facility should be integrated into the system which will make easier management performance of core and non-core function at the health service delivery at the health facility [2].

Implementation of eHealth and its performance are influenced by both internal and external factors of the organization this is infrastructures surrounding ICT implementation at the facility level such as connectivity of the internet, availability, and access of the device, privacy issues, and lack of sustainable power supply. This have been indicated by the study done in two region of Morogoro and Iringa by Busagala et al. [1] on the eHealth adoption in Tanzania which underlying the challenges facing both health workers and clients such as inadequate ICT skills, high cost of ICT in relation to economic status of community members, less developed infrastructure including lack of imaging equipment, small proportion of Internet users and lack of information about suitable ICT solutions. Therefore, for proper implementation of ICT in service delivery managers, Doctors, Nurses, and other key stakeholders should deal with those setbacks in order to influence smooth adoption and acceptability of ICT in developing countries like Tanzania.

It is recommended that the implementation of eHealth in developing countries in the health sector can be perceived as a trigger initiative that may foster development in healthcare delivery. The initiative uses information communication technology for its implementation, therefore, other sectors as an opportunity to learn the best practice of eHealth implementation in the health sector and customize it in order to fulfill the demand of improving service delivery to the intended user of the service which most of them are living in the unprivileged or rural areas.

References

1. Busagala, L.S.P., Kawono, G.C.: Underlying challenges of e-health adoption in Tanzania. Int. J. Inf. Commun. Technol. Res. **3**(1), 34–41 (2013)
2. Eysenbach, G.: Editorial: poverty, human development, and the role of e-health. J. Med. Internet Res. **4**, 34 (2007)
3. McLeod, L., MacDonnell, S.G., Doolin, B.: User participation in contemporary IS development: an IS management perspective. Australas. J. Inf. Syst. **15**(1), 113–136 (2007)
4. MOH: Tanzania National eHealth Strategy 2013–2018. URT (2013)
5. MOH: The Midterm Review Report of Health Sector Strategic Plan III 2015. URT (2015)
6. MOH: Health Sector Strategic Plan July 2015–June 2020 (HSSP IV): Reaching all Households with Quality Health Care. URT (2015)
7. MOH: Guideline and Standard for Integrated Health Facility Electronic Management Systems; Computerization of Health Facility Operation: Clinical, Administrative and Financial (2016)
8. MOH: Journey to better data for better health in Tanzania based on Tanzania Digital Health Investment Road Map. URT (2017)
9. Sikika: Where are the Doctors?-Tracking study of Medical Doctors. Unpublished Document (2013). Accessed 2 Dec 2018

10. URT: The Minister of Health budget Speech of the sector to the parliament for the financial year 2018/19 (2018)
11. WHO: International Telecommunication Union; National eHealth strategy toolkit (2012)
12. Venkatesh, V., Morris, M.G., Davis, G.B., Davis, F.D.: User acceptance of information technology: toward a unified view. MIS Q. **27**(3), 425–478 (2003)

A Pilot Teaching Project, "Keeping Safe", Exploring the Use of "Scratch 3" Computer Coding Files and Computer-Generated Music Files Created in "Sibelius", to Support Young Adults with Language Learning Difficulties and Disabilities at Lambeth College, in South London

Lloyd Mead[1], Lawrence Williams[2(✉)], and Beth Mead[3]

[1] Lambeth College (Further Education), London, UK
LMead@lambethcollege.ac.uk
[2] Brunel University London, London, UK
lawrencewilliams2060@gmail.com
[3] London, UK

Abstract. This case study outlines a continuing curriculum project, from 2009 to the present, now exploring "Scratch 3" to support the sequencing skills of young adults with learning difficulties (LLDD), at Lambeth College, south London. Student support files, in "Scratch 3" block coding, and in "Sibelius" music software, were created by a secondary school pupil, aged 12, and developed for use by the students at the Further Education College, as part of an on-going educational collaboration. While it has proved to be the most problematic and frustrating teaching and learning project of the learning series to date, nonetheless it has had very positive student outcomes.

Keywords: Curriculum innovation · "Scratch 3" · "Sibelius" · Further Education · LLDD students

1 Background

Young adults with learning difficulties and disabilities, aged 18 to 24 years, at Lambeth Further Education College in south London have a long tradition of exploring the use of ICT and Computing technologies to support their learning. This tradition has extended into cross-agency work (with Health and Education professionals); links with local secondary schools; commissions from the UK National Health Service; and to other agencies such as MirandaNet and ITTE, currently being amalgamated as the "Teaching, Pedagogy and Education Association", TPEA, 2019. In the past, Lambeth College students used Microsoft Office tools to support their learning [Note 1]; then "Scratch 1.4" block coding program [1]; and then "Scratch 2" [Note 2], and are now starting to explore the newest program version, "Scratch 3", together with music files

© IFIP International Federation for Information Processing 2019
Published by Springer Nature Switzerland AG 2019
A. Tatnall and N. Mavengere (Eds.): SUZA 2019, IFIP AICT 564, pp. 45–54, 2019.
https://doi.org/10.1007/978-3-030-28764-1_7

developed using the "Sibelius" music software program. The aim is for the College students to improve their sequencing and general skills (as part of their "Life Skills" course) through simple coding activities, and to keep themselves safe within the community. The most recent project, "Healthy Eating", using "Scratch 2", is currently posted on the MirandaNet World Ecitizens web site. To support the College students in this work, they were sent "Scratch 2" shell files created by a primary school pupil. Other cross-agency coding resources (Education and Health Care) can be found on the website [Note 3], and this project was later presented at the MirandaNet/ITTE Conference at the University of Winchester, in July 2018 (Fig. 1 below).

 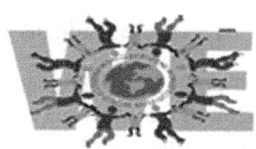 

Developing creative computer coding resources on the World Ecitizens web site

Lawrence Williams, MirandaNet Council
Lloyd Mead, Lambeth College Tutor
Beth Mead, West Wimbledon Primary School pupil
Paul Sebuliba, OT at Your HealthCare

Fig. 1. ITTE/MirandaNet International Conference 2018

The new project outlined in this paper is based, like previous projects, on Piaget's constructivist [2], and Papert's constructionist models [3], with students planning, problem-solving, constructing, developing, and then coding their original animated phone Apps, with their own Scratch Sprites and Backgrounds, with the addition of music, and voice-over sound files. It centres on activities created to support another ongoing College theme, "Keeping Safe". Some Lambeth LLDD students have difficulty in making the journey to College unaided, and so focussing on travel safety, and looking after their money, keys, and their mobile phones, is an important part of their "Life Skills" learning programme. Learning to sequence is also an important skill for all LLDD students.

2   Aims of the Project

The project aims to develop several aspects of the College students' learning development:

1. To help the students, by using "Scratch 3", to **organise** their thoughts, by **planning** an activity on paper, and carrying it through in a **sequenced** and methodical way.
2. To improve their **communication skills** by developing and sharing a topic of relevance to their own personal safety within the group, and with support staff.
3. To allow them **space to reflect on** and **review** what is important to them in relation to own their personal safety.
4. To develop **elementary coding skills** as part of a creative activity.

3   A Setback

When we first heard, in 2014, that "Scratch 3", written now in HTML5, would eventually run on androids, we were very excited. In September 2018, we therefore began to develop another teaching and learning project ready to start in January 2019, which would allow the Lambeth students to create "Keeping Safe" phone Apps, which they would learn to create using the new "Scratch 3". They could then, we fondly thought, run the files on their own phones when they were out and about in the community. This would have been a beautiful marriage between their College "Life Skills" studies, and practical safety support for them within the community. However, when "Scratch 3" arrived in early January 2019, it was sadly confirmed that the HTML5 Reader had been completely abandoned by MIT at only 40% completion, and offered rather vaguely to the coding community to develop. No-one seems to know how well the HTML5 Reader is progressing, if at all. So, while "Scratch 3" files can now actually be made on a phone or tablet, when used on-line, and can be saved onto a phone or tablet, as sb3 files, they cannot actually be run off-line without an HTML5 Reader, because it does not yet exist. So, we had reluctantly to revise our planned project.

"Scratch 3" has so far been poorly received by some users, [See: https://scratch.mit.edu/discuss/topic/326977/] with our own additional complaints about the limited sound file system, the unnecessarily complex new Paint option, and the revised (rather garish) screen appearance, which seems to direct the program towards much younger users while being, paradoxically, more complex to use. It is also unstable across a network.

At this juncture, we confess also that we are at a complete loss to understand why "Scratch 3" was developed in HTML5 (to run on android) but that the means to accomplish this in the real world (i.e. with a HTML5 Reader) was abandoned! A revised version of "Scratch 2", rewritten in HTML5 with a Reader, would have made much more sense to us. We hope that this omission will eventually be put right by MIT, and enable us to complete our earlier planned project, perhaps in 2020? On the plus side, "Scratch 3" does have helpful Tutorials embedded into it, and this is proving to be beneficial for the College students. Voice and movement activated elements of "Scratch 3" may be of later interest, when they are fully realised.

The presentation of these new resources, officially launched at the London BETT 2019 Exhibition, however, showed rather worryingly that these elements, too, are only partially successful, at present. And sb3 files, when emailed as attachments can, inexplicably, only be opened and edited in about 50% of cases. Much work still needs to be done, therefore, to make "Scratch 3" a reliable, rather than a disappointingly revamped program. MIT say they are working hard on all of these issues, but teachers will need to have more confidence if they are to adopt it.

The original learning objectives of our project (developing sequencing skills through computer programming, and keeping the students safe) were, of course, unaffected by most of these problems. And we felt that if we started to explore the music possibilities of "Scratch 3", and developed new links with the "Sibelius" music software, we could begin moving forward again, in a more musical direction. So, while the original aim was for the Lambeth support files to be used by the Lambeth students within their projects, they became, instead, exemplar material. From seeing their files displayed on the Interactive Whiteboard at the College, the students responded by making their own Apps unaided, a pleasing progression in terms of their independent learning.

4   Method

The College students were asked to discuss which aspects of their own personal safety they would like to develop as a phone App, using "Scratch 3". They decided, on an individual basis, to cover looking after their money, mobile phones, keys, and help with transportation to College. Building on their "Scratch 2" experience, the students were introduced to the "Scratch 3" coding program, and explored various aspects of how it could be used to sequence such personal information as photos, maps, and bus timetables, just as previous Lambeth College teaching groups had earlier done, using PowerPoint.

Parallel to this, the secondary school pupil set about creating two different sorts of support files for the College students: in "Scratch 3" the focus was on modelling possible App structures, to make the sequencing of the various elements (photos, text, maps, etc.,) more straightforward. This method had proved to be extremely successful in the earlier "Healthy Eating" project, and so suggestions were sent by email to the College. Exemplar music files were also created using "Sibelius", and dispatched accordingly. Additionally, to support one of the College students in using the Paint option to create her own Sprite, rather than just importing one from the Scratch library, the secondary pupil (aged 12) made a 4-min instructional video on a smart phone, which was then field tested by her younger brother (aged 8), and having proved successful, was taken into the College classroom. Placed on the college desk, it proved a successful tuition method.

5 Musical Aspects of the Project

Music sound files for the project were created by the young school pupil in six different ways: three within Scratch itself, and three using "Sibelius" files.

To create phone Apps that sounded more professional, and "cool", she set about creating a range of music jingles or fanfares, which would introduce or accompany the images within the App. The idea was to replicate the ubiquitous musical phone prompts, the bane of cinemas and theatres everywhere! The files created and sent from outside the College, acted as a catalyst for the Lambeth students to explore their own musical ideas.

This musical activity can be accomplished in a number of different ways:

(1) Scratch Music Files
Fanfares and other music can obviously be imported directly into projects from the Scratch Sounds library, but they can also be individually created very easily within Scratch itself, by using the Sound blocks. Single-note sound files can be programmed together algorithmically from the Sounds directory, and made into short, repeatable musical patterns as shown below (Fig. 2). Here the Trombone plays the sound an octave below the Trumpet, and by using Loops, it is repeated in order to make the short fanfare.

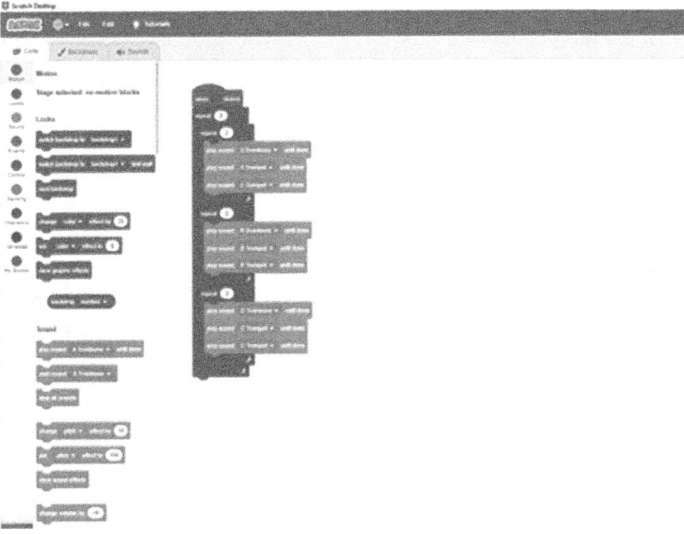

Fig. 2. Sound loops: simple App fanfare by a student (aged 12)

(2) Adjusting and Developing the Scratch Music Files
There are several ways in which sound files can now be manipulated in Scratch 3, such as faster/slower, louder/softer, spiral, echo and reverse. The secondary student created examples, which were shown to the Lambeth students as exemplar material (Fig. 3).

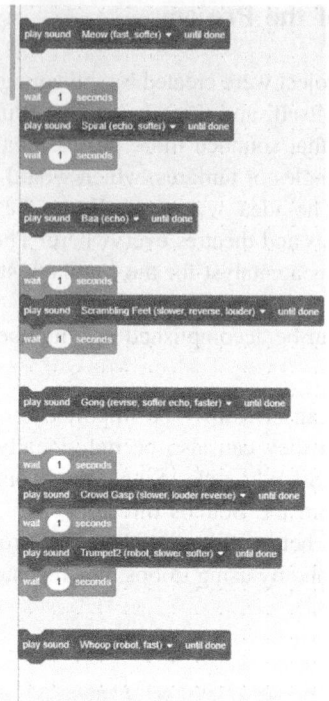

Fig. 3. "Reworked" sound files in "Scratch 3"

(3) Midi Music Keyboard Input
(i.e. Music played into the Record mode in "Scratch 3" from a piano or electronic Midi music keyboard.)

This is done by playing the music keyboard while it is placed adjacent to the "Scratch" computer. This works in just the same way as adding spoken sounds to speech bubbles. There is a short outline of how to do all of this on the "Literacy from Scratch" web site (using the earlier Scratch version 1.4 for writing bilingual Scratch stories, but the method is still relevant). See: https://www.literacyfromscratch.org.uk/teaching/music.htm.

Music played on an electronic keyboard can be added directly into Sibelius, through a Printer cable lead. This Midi input is converted by "Sibelius" into musical staff notation. Once the input has been played and saved, the playback can then be altered, changing the instrument's voice, for example.

(4) Music Input into "Sibelius": Option 1
Music created within "Sibelius" itself onto a musical stave (the manuscript page) in a variety of ways can also be played back live into Scratch, again through the red Record button. The music in "Sibelius" can be created in three ways, as follows:

Note by note (by hand, with mouse click and drag. Slow method.) (Fig. 4).

Fig. 4. A simple music file in G created "by hand and mouse" in "Sibelius", and showing the keypad

(5) Music Input into "Sibelius": Option 2

Music can be added to a manuscript by using the program's "virtual keyboard" (Faster method.) See Fig. 5. Here, the Virtual Keyboard is added to the screen on top of the manuscript page, and mouse clicks on the keyboard generate notes on the page.

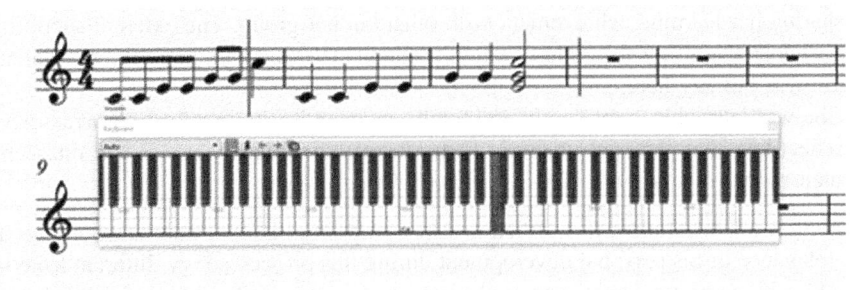

Fig. 5. The first bar of this fanfare in C was created using a mouse, and the second bar was created using the Sibelius "virtual keyboard".

(6) Music Input into "Sibelius": Option 3

Finally, music can be added onto a manuscript page by Midi music keyboard input, as mentioned above (Best method.) This is done by placing the Midi music keyboard next to the computer, and linking the two by use of a printer cable. Music played in real time on the Midi keyboard appears directly on the manuscript page, where it can be edited, developed and then played back into "Scratch 3", using the red Recording button, and in a variety of musical "voices" or instruments from within "Sibelius".

The musical developments in the project are on-going, but the major learning outcomes were completed by the end of the Spring Term.

1. Learning Outcomes (January to April 2019).

Student A: This young man has problems in engaging with other students, partly because of some behavioural difficulties, and he generally has a limited focus on learning tasks. He has some computer skills with Office programs, but also suffers anxiety issues, possibly related to his autism. Nonetheless, during the project he has developed much greater concentration on his learning tasks, probably because the work involved his own personal interests. He related his computer learning to his journey to College as an independent traveller on a 37 bus, and loved finding suitable images on the internet, and on the Lambeth Moodle, as well as taking appropriate photos out in the community, to add into his work. He was able, through a steady development process, to step outside his "Office comfort zone" to continue his project successfully.

As well as attending his Scratch classes more frequently than some other lessons, this personal development encouraged him to start problem-solving. Disliking writing, he started to use the recording device on his mobile phone as a means of recording his thoughts, so that he could include the text in his project. We were very pleased to see him using technology in this way to support his own learning.

Student B: Planning was the main focus of this student's learning. Starting with a hand-made drawing of herself (as an avatar/sprite), she was ably supported in developing this image as a sprite within her Scratch project by using a specially created instructional Paint video (made for her by a Year 7 school student, aged 12). She was inspired by this individually tailored support to create her own animated drawings of her avatar within her project. She was very excited by this success, and looked forward to sharing her learning achievement with others in her group. The external support for this student (by using the video) was a fundamental aspect of her success. Collaboration was the key here.

She was later able, confidently and totally independently, to adjust her avatar/sprite to reflect her own personal image in better detail. She hopes, also, to add music files created by her own keyboard skills to the finished project.

Student C: This student has difficulties in processing his own internal thinking, and the relevance of his personal development during this project is very different from that of others in the group. He is keen on drawing and story-telling, and he uses his drawing skill to externalise his thinking, which can sometimes be quite very dark and negative. Using "Scratch 3" has allowed him to **externalise** some of these sometimes violent emotions, and to create his animated characters, which allow him to discuss his thoughts with his teacher in a safe environment. He is able to draw his attention away from these dark thoughts into developing a creative, and cathartic, way of expressing himself, using computer animation and coding.

He later wanted to create further animation in "3D", that is with his sprite walking out towards the viewer. This activity allowed him to turn his focus away from death and killing, and towards the more positive direction of making his sprite come alive. This was an unexpected but very pleasing result.

The Group: Many of these students struggle with reading, writing, and mathematics work. Remarkably, however, all students involved in the project developed their sequencing skills and other important "Life Skills", by creating a series of correctly formulated algorithms for their "Keeping Safe" Apps. Attention span improved, as well as general behaviour. They were all very pleased with their progress towards final learning outcomes. We, too, were very pleased with some unexpected but rewarding outcomes.

6   Conclusions

We will have finished many of the learning outcomes of the project by the end of the Spring Term, April 2019. But it will not be possible for the students to use the Apps they have created at College on their phones until the HTML5 Reader is actually completed. Nonetheless, the students have once again focussed impressively on their coding work through their "Keeping Safe" project [5]; have developed their sequencing and personal skills effectively; and have worked successfully with the support of their young secondary school partner. They are also having fun developing the musical ideas sent to them by the school pupil, rather than importing them directly (pre-formed) from Scratch into their work. We are still developing this aspect of the project. As teachers, we are nonetheless very pleased by this learning progression.

What began as a planned celebration of "Scratch 3" rapidly became a project that had constantly to be remodelled in order to cope with its many newly-added deficiencies. (And we have not addressed the network instability of the program in this paper.) Nonetheless, we felt that knowing what does not work in the classroom is just as important to teachers, as knowing what actually does work.

So, there are two possibilities for the future development of this curriculum project. The first is to see if and when the HTML5 Scratch Reader is finally, if ever, completed, at which point we hope that we will be able to create usable "Keeping Safe" Apps for download onto the College students' phones, using a revised or more reliable version of "Scratch 3", as MIT has promised. The second option is to revert to reliable old "Scratch 2", (on-line and desktop) and then use rather complex conversion files to run the completed Apps onto the students' phones. Only time will tell. But we owe it to our most vulnerable students, to pursue the best potential uses of technology to support both their learning and their personal safety, however frustrating the task may at times turn out to be.

Notes:

1. Early cross-agency work undertaken by Lambeth College students, with secondary school pupil support, and UK National Health Service commissioning can be found in the MirandaNet archives at: https://www.mirandanet.org.uk/resources/
2. More recent work, this time developing students' computer coding and sequencing skills, using "Scratch 2" can be found at: http://www.worldecitizens.net/resource-materials-supporting-the-lambeth-college-projects/
3. For other simple background coding resources, including using Python for story-telling, see: http://www.worldecitizens.net/stories-for-children-2/ and https://sites.google.com/view/literacyfrompython/introduction-and-teachers-notes

4. For a brief report of the early, successful use of Sibelius 6 for classroom use, in the Times Educational Supplement, 1997, see: https://www.tes.com/news/sibelius-scores-girlsdo-it-yourselfmultimediait-interviewlawrence-williams

References

1. Williams, L.: Introduction to Computing. A Guide for Teachers. Routledge, Abingdon (2014)
2. Kalaš I., Mikolajová, K., Tomcsány, K.: Konštrukcionizmus. Od Piageta po školu v digitálnom. Keynote: DidInfo 2011, Slovakia (2011)
3. Papert, S., Harel, I.: Situating Constructionism. Ablex Publishing Corporation, Norwood (1991)
4. Doidge, N.: The Brain that Changes Itself. Penguin Books, London (2007)
5. Williams, L., Mead, L.: Using the "literacy from scratch" project to develop the computing and presentation skills of students with learning difficulties and disabilities. In: ITTE Conference, London (2016)

Digital Games in Primary Schools
for the Development of Key Transversal Skills

Rosa Bottino[(✉)], Augusto Chioccariello, Laura Freina,
and Mauro Tavella

Institute for Educational Technology of the Italian National Research Council,
Via De Marini, Genoa, Italy
bottino@itd.cnr.it

Abstract. Digital games are becoming more and more popular worldwide, arousing children's interest and fostering their motivation. Furthermore, tablets and smartphones are increasingly popular and widespread all around the globe, guaranteeing access to the web and to an ever-growing availability of games. This paper is based on the assumption that introducing digital game play into primary schools may support the development and consolidation of some transversal skills in a way that is perceived by students as interesting and motivating. When the games are carefully selected, the great effort spent by children in playing will provide them with the possibility to acquire and exercise, at an early age, basic skills which are important for their future. In particular, in this paper, different modalities in which digital games can be used in primary schools to foster basic transversal skills are presented. Logic and spatial reasoning skills as well as computational thinking are in particular considered. The reported experiments show that game based activities, when appropriately organized, can positively affect students' school performance as well as students' learning attitudes and behavior.

Keywords: Digital games · Reasoning skills · Visuospatial skills ·
Computational thinking · Primary school

1 Introduction

It is generally accepted that in education a fundamental role is played by transversal skills such as logical reasoning, visuospatial abilities, computational thinking, etc. Therefore, fostering the development of these basic skills at a primary school level can enhance the students' performance, affecting positively their future results. However, these skills develop slowly and need a prolonged supporting action stretching over several years [1, 2].

Digital games are becoming more and more popular worldwide, arousing children's interest and fostering their motivation. Tablets and smartphones are widespread all around the globe, guaranteeing access to the web and to an ever-growing availability of games, a lot of which are free.

This paper is based on the assumption that introducing digital game play into primary schools may support the development and consolidation of some transversal

© IFIP International Federation for Information Processing 2019
Published by Springer Nature Switzerland AG 2019
A. Tatnall and N. Mavengere (Eds.): SUZA 2019, IFIP AICT 564, pp. 55–65, 2019.
https://doi.org/10.1007/978-3-030-28764-1_8

skills in a way that is perceived by the students as interesting and motivating. When the games are carefully selected, the great effort spent by children in playing will provide them the possibility to acquire and exercise, at an early age, basic skills which are important for their future. Furthermore, if students' interest towards games is moved further and they are challenged to develop their own games rather than simply playing them, they can have the opportunity to develop computational thinking skills.

Many studies claim that computer games can positively affect learning and that their use can contribute to an effective educational innovation [3]. However, this assumption, taken as such, is too generic and there is the risk of falling into the old trap believing that the latest innovations are the best and should replace the previous learning approaches. The analysis of the efficacy for learning of the use of digital games is to be investigated in specific contexts and against clearly defined objectives and situations moving forward from the simple assumption that they are useful tools to engage and motivate students [4]. This paper reports studies in which the evaluation of the efficacy of games for learning is approached in a delimited context, while analyzing it in an articulated manner, making reference to the experience acquired in long-term studies and tackling the problem according to different perspectives which can complement each other.

In particular, different modalities in which digital games can be used in primary schools to foster basic transversal skills are presented. Logic and spatial reasoning skills as well as computational thinking are in particular considered. Specific reference is made to research projects performed at the Institute for Educational Technology of the Italian National Research Council. The experience gained in such studies supports the assumption that early and appropriately designed interventions focused on thinking skills carried out through game-based activities can positively affect students' school performance as well as students' learning attitudes and behavior [5, 6].

This paper presents a methodology useful to foster, in primary school students, some basic transversal skills in a language independent manner. Skills such as logical reasoning and visuospatial abilities are at the basis of learning Science, Technology, Engineering, and Mathematics (STEM) [7] and are considered crucial for a fruitful integration into the 21st Century digital world. The presented methodology and approach give several criteria for the selection of digital games, but do not rely on specific games. This guarantees that it can be adapted in time (as technology evolves and games change) and to different cultures and contexts.

Considering the specific context of developing countries and of Tanzania in particular, data from "We are Social – Hootsuite" [8] reports a great increase of the penetration of Internet in the last three years in Tanzania: in January 2019, 38% of the population was reported to be users of the Internet, while in 2017 and 2018 the percentage was 14% and 15%. Furthermore, 72% of the population has a mobile subscription, while the same percentage worldwide is lower (66% to 68% in the three years). This shows that the availability of connectivity and tools to use digital games covers already a large percentage of the population, and such a percentage is increasing very fast. However, games that were used in the projects presented in this paper could all be downloaded and installed on tablets or computers, to be used also without a web connection. Moreover, all the chosen games were free. For these reasons, the proposed methodology and approach can be of interest for a variety of different contexts and situations, also considering their flexibility and adaptation opportunities.

1.1 Playing and Making Games in Primary Education

Different modalities can be adopted to integrate digital games in primary school education:

- use games explicitly implemented for educational purposes;
- select and use games that are not built for education to foster the development of specific and clearly identified abilities;
- introduce children to the construction of digital games through programming.

Since the main aim of the project which is considered in this paper is verifying under which conditions the use of games that are meant for entertainment may have a positive impact on education, the focus is kept on the latter two modalities.

A wide spectrum of game types is currently available off-the-shelf, including role-plays, adventures, brainteasers or mind games, serious games, etc. These also feature a range of different strategies such as free exploration/navigation, question and answer routines, artefact making, etc. In our work, we have addressed the use of games to foster basic cognitive abilities (i.e. logical reasoning and visuospatial skills) that have a correlation with school performance in STEM subjects. In particular, we considered the use of digital mind games (i.e. games like puzzles or brainteasers that require the enactment of thinking and reasoning skills). Even if it was suggested that they can be used in schools to foster learning [9], they are not frequently studied from the point of view of learning outcomes [10]. Our research studies highlighted their pedagogical potential to support and foster problem solving, reasoning skills and visual spatial abilities, showing that their use under certain conditions may also have a positive impact on school performance in curricular subjects such as mathematics.

Game making can be a very valuable educational activity, able to trigger students' transversal skills, such as reasoning abilities, creative attitudes and computational thinking skills [11]. Kafai and Burke [12] argued that student-designed games can teach not only programming but also academic subjects and transversal basic skills such as collaboration and teamwork. However, they do not suggest a shift to game making from game playing but rather argue for a more comprehensive, inclusive idea of game use in education in which both making and playing should be considered. Specific environments to support game making activities are available and there is an increasing interest in their educational use.

2 The Project

In a previous experience, the cognitive skills involved in the use of a selected number of mind games were studied [13] and a methodology, based on the use of mind games, to assess logical reasoning skills in children in the last two years of primary school was defined and thoroughly tested with more than 500 students in Italy [14].

Starting from this experience, the research group organized a project with the main objective of using digital games to foster some basic transversal skill in Italian primary school children. For this purpose, specific digital games were selected and a methodology for their use in compulsory education was defined and tested.

Table 1. The phases of the project

Research questions	Focused skills	Participants	Results
How to use digital games in primary classes to foster the development of logical thinking abilities? Has their use an impact on students' math performance?	Logical thinking skills	Four classes (grades 4 to 7) 77 students from 9 to 13	A methodology (from skills analysis to games selection and their use in class) Analysis of the impact on students math performance (considering the results obtained in a national test)
Can games foster visuospatial abilities and have a positive impact on school results in mathematics?	Visuospatial Reasoning	Four classes (grade 4 and 5) 99 students from 9 to 11	Revised version of the methodology Better results in the math posttest for the experimental classes
Would a learning path focused on game making in support of computational thinking work in primary schools?	Computational Thinking	One grade 5 class 24 students from 10 to 11	A learning path for game making with a visual programming tool Teacher guidelines for the use of the learning path

The project was organized in three different phases (see Table 1). In the first phase, logical thinking abilities were fostered through the use of selected digital games. In this phase, a methodology for the use of digital games in formal education was defined.

In the second phase, visuo-spatial abilities were considered. These include the ability to imagine an object and how it changes due to specific transformations (i.e. rotation, translation, changes in size, etc.) and being able to move in space and recognize a scene from different points of view. Selected off the shelf digital games were used, along with a virtual reality game that was specifically developed for the purpose. A preliminary study was carried out to assess the impact of the immersion in a virtual world on performance in a visuospatial task, in order to better guide the choice of the games.

In the third phase, the activities moved to fostering computational thinking through game making activities in an online visual programming environment. In this paper, a preliminary case study is presented in which criteria for the introduction of coding in primary schools have been outlined.

3   Use of Digital Games to Foster Logical Reasoning Abilities

3.1   Introduction

In the first phase of the project we addressed the question on how to use digital games in primary classes to foster the development of logical thinking abilities.

The objective was to define a methodology addressing the analysis and selection of the games to be used as well as the organization and evaluation of the intervention involving primary school classes in close cooperation with the class teachers. Guidelines for game analysis and selection were developed as well as criteria to identify the specific skills to be fostered. This methodology can be adapted to different sets of abilities.

3.2   Game Selection

The chosen games were all freely available online, and were pre-selected according to the following criteria:

- they should entail some kind of logical reasoning (mind games);
- they were not linked to any specific arithmetic or language competence;
- the game play was not based on casual events, but rather strictly related to the player's moves;
- time, and therefore the speed of the player, did not influence results.

Some other characteristics of the games to be selected were also considered: the average duration of a play session, the availability of the game in different versions, languages, and levels of difficulty, the kind of immediate feedback provided by the game, its accessibility, as well as technical elements such as the needed technological support. Each selected mind game was then analysed with respect to the abilities needed to solve it. The following list reports the main abilities considered:

- knowing the rules of the game and being able to apply them in real game plays;
- making an inference based on the information available in a certain moment of the game and/or on constraints given by the game (one, two or more information/ constraints);
- evaluating if the available information at a certain time in the game was sufficient to decide whether a move or a configuration was correct;
- being able to combine previous reasoning to complete a schema in the game.

3.3   Methodology and Results

Guidelines for the organization of the training phase were then considered. This includes suggestions on the organization of the meetings and the needed tutoring support. Furthermore, guidelines on the duration of the whole intervention as well as each play session and their frequency were considered. Examples of supporting materials such as monitoring sheets, management of game feedbacks, final appreciation questionnaires for students, etc. are also provided.

The games were played in four different classes of the last years of an Italian primary school. Students played once a week with the selected games for a period of three months with the support of their class teacher and some researchers. All students showed a high interest in the game sessions. Qualitative data was collected both from direct observations and from final questionnaires and interviews with the students. Moreover, students' mathematics results from a national assessment test were analysed and the findings showed that experimental classes scored on average better than the other classes of the same school [5].

All students participated with great interest in the game activities and the impact of the experiment on the class climate was certainly positive.

The analysis of the collected data shows that strategies used by the students to solve the puzzles can improve significantly when the players receive a direct and personalized support when needed. The software characteristics that best support the addressed cognitive processes were analysed and specific recommendations have been added to the methodology. However, personalized support can be difficult to obtain when the number of teachers is limited with respect to the number of students. For this reason, the adaptation of existing games with the aim of making them more suited to actually support the development of the basic skills addressed, in particular with respect to the game feedbacks, was also considered. An open source version of the classic Master Mind game was modified to include both the possibility to trace the players moves and to give them personalized feedback based on the game play [15].

4   Use of Digital Games to Foster Visuo-Spatial Skills

4.1   Introduction

In the second phase of the project, the methodology developed in the first phase was applied to an intervention aimed at fostering visuospatial abilities in students of the last two years of primary school (aged 9–11) [16]. The methodology was thus tested and refined in order to guarantee that it could be applied to different sets of abilities.

Visuospatial abilities include several different skills and there is no unique definition in literature. Nevertheless, all authors agree in including two main elements: the ability to imagine a two or three dimensional object in space and understand how it changes when moved, rotated, reflected or stretched, and the ability to understand positions in space, to recognize the relative position of a set of objects, and to understand what it would look like from different points of view.

Several studies demonstrated that there is a close correlation between visuospatial abilities and achievements in STEM related subjects [7]. Other studies showed that these abilities can be improved with a specific training and such an improvement is transferred to different contexts and lasts in time [17]. Consequently, a game-based training of visuospatial abilities in primary students was organized and its impact on school results in mathematics was measured.

4.2   The Preliminary Study

As the addressed skills were analyzed, the strong embodied characteristics of visuospatial abilities emerged. A preliminary study was thus organized to assess the impact of immersion in a virtual world on the enactment of these abilities.

The digital game "In Your Eyes" was developed to be used for this preliminary study. The game is focused on Visual Perspective Taking: the ability to understand how a given scene would look like from the point of view of another person. The game takes place in a virtual living room, with a table in the middle and some objects on it. Four screens on the wall show the pictures of the table taken from the four sides. A virtual non player character moves to one side of the table, and then asks the player to select the picture showing the table as he sees it. The player can move in the room but has to go to a defined play position to answer.

The game is available in three different versions: a complete immersive version (which uses a Head Mounted Display), a semi-immersive version where the virtual world is seen through the computer screen, and a non-immersive one in which the player has only a fixed view of the room and cannot move.

"In Your Eyes" was tested with a limited number of students to measure the impact on performance of the different levels of immersion. Results show that the non-immersive version obtained the worst results, while the other two obtained very similar results, and differences were not statistically significant [18].

Due to these results, along with restrictions due to the limited availability of the Head Mounted Displays and some motion sickness experienced by some students it was decided not to use immersive games in the subsequent phase of the project. Thus, all the games chosen were either on tablets or standard computers.

4.3   Methodology and Results

Applying the previously defined methodology, the visuospatial abilities to be addressed were then detailed. The main abilities considered were: visual memory, visuo-motor coordination, the ability to imagine a bi- or three dimensional shape, the ability to understand what three dimensional object results from folding a two dimensional shape, finding strategies for filling an area or a volume, and orienting oneself in space.

Based on these abilities, a wide set of games was analysed and selected. At each meeting, one of the previously mentioned abilities was addressed, and several games were offered to the students, allowing them to choose freely according to their interests and abilities. A complete set of monitoring tools was defined, including observation sheets, questionnaires and interviews. A standardized math test was chosen to measure the students' mathematical achievements across different classes [19]. The test was given before the start of the training sessions and at the end of the project.

Data analysis showed that those classes that followed the game session performed statistically better at the standardized math post-test when compared to control classes that followed the traditional curriculum [16].

All the involved students were enthusiastic of the game activities and participated with great commitment, even though with large differences both with respect to the kinds of games they chose and the level of difficulty they could reach.

During the study, it was noticed that students are deeply involved in playing and participated with interest to all the different activities. Nevertheless, the involvement and interest measured were higher in those games that required a more active participation from the children. For instance, they particularly like Minecraft [20], a sandbox game that allows them to play with digital building blocks. Starting from this observation, it was decided to widen the proposed experiences to include not only game playing but also game creation and development. Actually, it is possible to play by the rules, following a given game as it was conceived by its creator, or with the rules, finding inspiration from known games to build a new, personalized one.

5 Boost Computational Thinking Through Game Making Activities

5.1 Introduction

In the third phase, a game making activity is introduced. The main objective was to foster the development of Computational Thinking (CT) abilities in students of the last year of primary school in a visual, block-based programming environment. Scratch [21], a visual programming environment where the instructions are assembled like LEGO building blocks, was chosen. Scratch is specifically designed for children from 8 up, it is free and available online, which allows students to continue their work outside school hours.

CT, as defined by Wing [22], is "the thought processes involved in formulating problems and their solutions so that the solutions are represented in a form that can effectively be carried out by an information-processing agent". It entails logical reasoning to solve problems and understand artefacts, procedures and systems. It includes a set of skills that are also at the basis of STEM subjects.

In order to define a methodology for the introduction of game making in primary schools, a single exploratory case study was organized, with students from the last years of an Italian primary school [23]. Among the main objectives of this phase was the definition of a learning path to be used in the following years directly by teachers.

5.2 Methodology and Results

The learning path was completely developed before the start of the school year, including a first part devoted to introducing students to the programming environment and to some basic concepts underlying the coding activity, followed by a role play in which students, organized into small groups, played the role of game developers.

In order to be ready to support students in the best possible way, a complete scaffolding was devised, to be used according to the class needs. This included a set of instructions that could be more or less detailed according to the needs, specific lessons with the class as a whole to solve together technical issues, some concrete activities to be used as a starting point to understand deeply a certain procedure, etc.

The learning path was then tested in a grade 5 class of an Italian primary school as a single explorative case study, involving all the students and their class teacher, for a period of about seven months. Some trainee teachers were also involved, mainly to carry out the observations. Teachers, trainee teachers, and researchers played the role of tutors to help the groups with their work. At the end of the project, each group managed to have a working prototype of their game, which was then presented to the families and the head of the school.

Students, in average, had no previous coding experience and few opportunities to code outside school hours; nevertheless, they all managed to play an active role in the creation of their own game. Results show that most students were very interested in the coding activities and gained an increasing amount of independence. Guidelines for teachers willing to organize a similar experience were then defined, with reference to the Italian context [23].

The case study, even though successful, evidenced some issues of concern that have to be closely considered when organizing similar interventions.

Since in the Italian primary schools there is no specialist information technology teacher, class teachers have to play an active role. However, teachers often had difficulty in managing learning paths involving programming activities.

Furthermore, the abilities that are at the basis of CT develop slowly. The case study showed that students would have needed a much longer time to really master the activities and their teachers were not yet adequately prepared to support their growth. For this reason, a longitudinal three-year long experiment has been planned, starting in the school year 2018–2019, involving the introduction of computational thinking skills by means of game-making and interactive story telling activities with pupils from the third to the fifth primary school grade.

6   Conclusions and Future Work

A project spanning over several years was organized to investigate the use of non-educational digital games to foster the development of some transversal abilities that are at the basis of the study of STEM related subjects. The project aimed at the definition of a methodology for the use of games in primary classes that can then be reused and adapted to different skills and contexts.

With respect to the use of off-the-shelf games, the methodology was defined and tested in the Italian context. It is sufficiently general to be adapted to different games and abilities. Some elements will need a deeper study. For example, results show that students improve better their play strategies when they receive personalized support. This could be achieved through an adaptation of the games to be used, enriching them with specific feedback functionalities.

In the third phase of the project, a game making approach was experimented, and gave good results. Nevertheless, a much longer time period, spanning over all the primary grades, would allow students to gain the needed experience and increase their coding abilities. At present, a long term study is being carried out including grades 3 to 5 of a primary school. Data is being collected with respect to every student showing their gradual improvement in coding and will be analyzed at the end of every school year.

References

1. King, P.M., Kitchener, K.S.: Developing Reflective Judgment: Understanding and Promoting Intellectual Growth and Critical Thinking in Adolescents and Adults. Jossey-Bass Higher and Adult Education Series and Jossey-Bass Social and Behavioral Science Series. Jossey-Bass, 350 Sansome Street, San Francisco, CA 94104-1310 (1994)
2. Edwards, S.: Digital play in the early years: a contextual response to the problem of integrating technologies and play-based pedagogies in the early childhood curriculum. Eur. Early Child. Educ. Res. J. **21**(2), 199–212 (2013)
3. De Freitas, S., Liarokapis, F.: Serious games: a new paradigm for education? In: Ma, M., Oikonomou, A., Jain, L. (eds.) Serious Games and Edutainment Applications, pp. 9–23. Springer, London (2011). https://doi.org/10.1007/978-1-4471-2161-9_2
4. Whitton, N.: Learning with Digital Games: A Practical Guide to Engaging Students in Higher Education. Routledge, Abingdon (2009)
5. Bottino, R.M., Ferlino, L., Ott, M., Tavella, M.: Developing strategic and reasoning abilities with computer games at primary school level. Comput. Educ. **49**(4), 1272–1286 (2007)
6. Bottino, R.M., Ott, M., Tavella, M.: Children's performance with digital mind games and evidence for learning behaviour. In: Lytras, M.D., Ruan, D., Tennysonm, R.D., Ordonez De Pablosm, P., García Peñalvom, F.J., Rusu, L. (eds.) Information Systems, E-learning, and Knowledge Management Research, WSKS 2011. CCIS, vol. 278, pp. 235–243. Springer, Heidelberg (2011). https://doi.org/10.1007/978-3-642-35879-1_28
7. Newcombe, N.S.: Picture this: increasing math and science learning by improving spatial thinking. Am. Educ. **34**(2), 29–35 (2010)
8. We are Social – Hootsuite. https://datareportal.com/reports. Accessed 05 Mar 2019
9. Vaegs, T., Dugosija, D., Hackenbracht, S., Hannemann, A.: Learning by gaming: facts and myths. Int. J. Technol. Enhanc. Learn. **2**(1–2), 21–40 (2010)
10. Facer, K., Ulicsak, M., Sandford, R.: Can computer games go to school? Emerg. Technol. Learn. BECTA **2**(5), 47–63 (2007)
11. Bottino, R., Chioccariello, A.: Computational thinking: videogames, educational robotics, and other powerful ideas to think with. In: KEYCIT: Key Competences in Informatics and ICT. Commentarii Informaticae didacticae (CID), vol. 7, pp. 301–309. University of Potsdam (2015)
12. Kafai, Y.B., Burke, Q.: Connected gaming: What making video games can teach us about learning and literacy. MIT Press, Cambridge (2016)
13. Bottino, R.M., Ott, M.: Mind games, reasoning skills, and the primary school curriculum: hints from a field experiment. Learn. Media Technol. **31**(4), 359–375 (2006)
14. Bottino, R.M., Ott, M., Tavella, M.: Serious gaming at school: Reflections on students' performance, engagement and motivation. Int. J. Game-Based Learn. (IJGBL) **4**(1), 21–36 (2014). https://doi.org/10.4018/IJGBL.2014010102
15. Bottino, R.M., Ott, M., Benigno, V.: Digital mind games: experience-based reflections on design and interface features supporting the development of reasoning skills. In: Proceedings of 3rd European Conference on Game Based Learning, pp. 53–61 (2009)
16. Freina, L., Bottino, R., Ferlino, L., Tavella, M.: Training of spatial abilities with digital games: impact on mathematics performance of primary school students. In: Proceedings of the Game and Learning Alliance International Conference (GALA), Lisbon, Portugal, 5–7 December 2017, pp. 25–40 (2017)
17. Uttal, D.H., et al.: The malleability of spatial skills: a meta-analysis of training studies. Psychol. Bull. **139**(2), 352 (2013)

18. Freina, L., Bottino, R., Tavella, M., Dagnino, F.: Immersion's impact on performance in a spatial reasoning task. In: Bottino, R., Jeuring, J., Veltkamp, R. (eds.) Games and Learning Alliance, GALA 2016. LNCS, vol. 10056, pp. 211–220. Springer, Cham (2016). https://doi.org/10.1007/978-3-319-50182-6_19

19. Cornoldi, C., Cornoldi, C., Lucangeli, D., Bellina, M.: AC-MT 6–11. Test di valutazione delle abilità di calcolo e soluzione dei problemi. Gruppo MT. Con CD-ROM. Edizioni Erickson (2012)

20. https://www.minecraft.net/. Accessed 14 Mar 2019

21. Resnick, M., et al.: Scratch: programming for all. Commun. ACM 52(11), 60–67 (2009)

22. Wing, J.: Research Notebook: Computational Thinking - What and Why? The Link. Carneige Mellon, Pitts-burgh (2011)

23. Freina, L., Bottino, R., Ferlino, L.: A learning path in support of computational thinking in the last years of primary school. In: Proceedings of the Game and Learning Alliance International Conference (GALA), Palermo, Italy, 5–7 December 2018 (2018)

Computational Thinking Nurturing Skills and Inspiring Pedagogy for Sustainable Education in the 21st Century

Christophe Reffay[1(✉)] and Phuwadol Viroonluecha[2]

[1] University Bourgogne-Franche-Comté, ELLIADD, FR-EDUC,
Besançon, France
Christophe.Reffay@ubfc.fr
[2] Top Sky Group, JobBKK, Bangkok, Thailand
vi.phuwadol_st@tni.ac.th

Abstract. Creativity, Innovation, Information search, problem-solving and data treatment are important not only in developed countries where people use many digital objects in their everyday life. Developing countries are necessary concerned by many aspects of the information society and digital era. Even if a large part of the population still does not access to the internet, because of a lack of reliable infrastructure, the information and knowledge societies are imposing their pace of innovation to the entire world. A more and more complex world is coming. Developing countries also feel the need to educate their people and give them the most of the 21st century skillset in order to face this complexity and the new challenges. For this reason, and because some of these competencies can be taught even without computers, Computational Thinking may nurture these skills even in developing countries.

In this presentation, we try to show how the integration of Computational Thinking with collaborative problem-based learning can cultivate learners how to learn and work on a real (authentic) problem together by bridging computer science main concepts and these skills to some efficient collaborative learning methods. Different recent viewpoints from developing countries are presented to show how they face this challenge in their nation.

Keywords: Computational thinking · 21st century skills ·
Collaborative problem-solving

1 Introduction

Our society is now built on a global scale. The development of each country has an impact on all others. Information processing allows us to regulate the transportation of people and goods from and to any part of the world, according to the special rules of each destination (political: visa, health: vaccination, financial: money change or withdrawal, cultural or religious: clothes and drinks, etc.) Many parts of everyday lives in many countries are already managed by using information processing (bank operation, medicine acts, commercial operations, media production and broadcast, etc.) Our world has reached such a complexity that computers became necessary to help us in managing more and more shift at all levels (individual, family, institutions, country) in

© IFIP International Federation for Information Processing 2019
Published by Springer Nature Switzerland AG 2019
A. Tatnall and N. Mavengere (Eds.): SUZA 2019, IFIP AICT 564, pp. 66–77, 2019.
https://doi.org/10.1007/978-3-030-28764-1_9

many domains: Army, Industry, Shopping. Education is often reluctant to change but the complex transformation of the society requires modification of the curricula to give more and more competencies to the citizen of the 21st century.

For [1], Computational Thinking (CT) is a skillset for everyone: not only for computer scientists and programmers. Many of CT concepts are related to Computer Science: correctness, termination, efficiency, determinism, parallelism [2]. The "Great Principle framework" draws Computer Science by the 7 categories: Computation, Communication, Coordination, Recollection, Automation, Evaluation and Design [3]. An interesting vision of the evolution of computer and education is given in [4] where ICT and Computer Science have evolving roles in the education system. In [5], the 4 roots of Computer science are algorithms, machines, languages and information.

As a current example in a developing country to illustrate the situation in teaching and learning digital competencies, a recent study [6] from a school of education in Cuba reports that: "[…] the current development of computer skills is insufficient, it was detected in the limited domain of work algorithms, as a result of the students who enrol in computer courses at the Young Club have little knowledge of the contents of the subject. They are afraid of the challenges and technological advances, so they tend to refuse to change, to develop and do not feel the need to enter the computer world because they do not consider the benefits they can achieve to develop even more professionally this way" [6].

We argue in this presentation that Computational Thinking (CT), and not only programming activity, can contribute to strengthen some of the important competencies of the 21st century skillsets and also that it may serve pedagogical design. Section 2 gives an overview of 5 frameworks on 21st century learning skillset. Section 3 emphasizes bridges between CT, selected competencies and learning design as presented in Table 2. Section 4 offers viewpoints from different developing countries over 3 continents and discussion and conclusion are briefly given in Sect. 5.

2   21st Century Skillsets: An Overview

More broadly, in the 21st century, many competencies are necessary to live in complex societies. In [7] authors decompose the 21st century learning skillset into three categories (to know, to value and to act) and 9 subcategories as presented in Fig. 1.

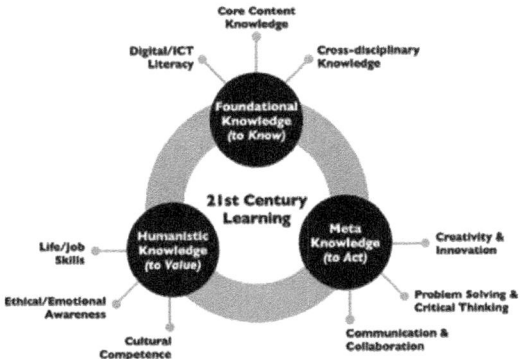

Fig. 1. Synthesis of 15 different 21st century learning frameworks [7]

The Partnership 21st Century Learning framework (P21) developed by Battelle for Kids [8] which are educators, education experts and business leaders who defined skill and knowledge that students require to succeed in their life. The framework is being used by many educators in several countries across the world. Key subjects, i.e. that are essential to student success include English, reading, or language arts, world languages; arts; mathematics, economics; science; geography; history; government; and civics. As presented in Fig. 2, the framework divides skills into three categories: (1) Learning and Innovation skills include creativity and innovation, critical thinking and problem solving, communication and collaboration. The next category is (2) Information, Media and Technology skills including information, media and ICT literacies. The last category is (3) Life and Career skills including flexibility and adaptability, initiative and self-direction, social and cross-cultural skills, productivity and accountability and leadership and responsibility.

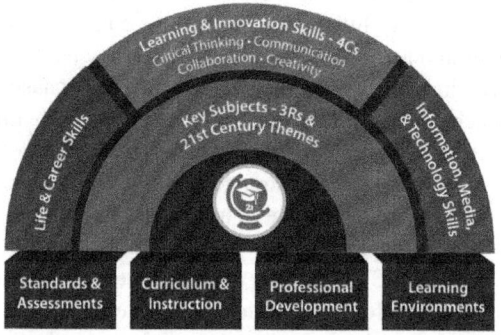

Fig. 2. The partnership 21st century learning framework (P21) schema [8]

Although the P21 Learning framework has gained popularity, a comparable Framework named EnGauge, presented on Fig. 3, was developed in 2003 by the Metiri group and the North Central Regional Educational Laboratory (NCREL) [9]. It proposed four categories of 21st century skills: Digital-Age Literacy (basic, scientific, economic, and technological literacies; visual and information literacies; multicultural literacy; and global awareness), Inventive Thinking (adaptability, managing complexity, and self-direction; curiosity, creativity, and risk-taking; higher-order thinking and sound reasoning), Effective Communication (teaming, collaboration, and interpersonal skills; personal, social, and civic responsibility; interactive communication) and High Productivity (prioritizing, planning, and managing for results; effective use of real-world tools; ability to produce relevant, high-quality products). The framework adds risk taking and effective productivity skills from P21.

Fig. 3. The EnGauge 21st century skills [9]

In 2005, the Organization for Economic Cooperation and Development (OECD) ministries emphasised: "Sustainable development and social cohesion depend critically on the competencies of all of our population – with competencies understood to cover knowledge, skills, attitudes and values." In the Programme for International Student Assessment (PISA), the OECD provided its conception of 21st century skills [10] combining three main categories of skills: Using tools interactively, Interacting in heterogeneous groups and Act autonomously. The highlights of this framework are managing and resolving conflicts skill in the second category. Leadership can be found in "The ability to form and conduct life plans and personal projects" in the third category. The OECD framework is more general than P21.

In 2007, the American Association of Colleges and Universities (AACU) [11] developed and presented their 21st century skills for college graduates who should obtain four categories of the essential learning outcomes. There are Knowledge of Human Cultures and the Physical and Natural World through study in the sciences and mathematics, social sciences, humanities, histories, languages, and the arts; Intellectual and Practical Skills, including inquiry and analysis, critical and creative thinking, written and oral communication, quantitative literacy, information literacy, teamwork and problem solving; Personal and Social Responsibility, including, civic knowledge and engagement - local and global, intercultural knowledge and competence, ethical reasoning and action, foundations and skills for lifelong learning; and Integrative Learning, including synthesis and advanced accomplishment across general and spe-cialized studies. This framework points out the necessity for graduates to have a curiosity about either arts or science and analytics skills such as inquiry and quanti-tative analysis.

Among the various skillsets referenced here above, we point out in Table 1 hereafter, the important skills shared on which CT may have an impact. And for each of these skills, we show the name of the global category it appears in each framework.

Table 1. Selection of skills from 5 frameworks

Skill	Kereluik's framework	P21	EnGauge	OECD	AACU
Creative thinking	Meta knowledge	Learning and thinking skills	Inventive thinking	–	Intellectual and practical skills
Critical thinking and problem-solving	Meta knowledge	Learning and thinking skills	Inventive thinking + high productivity	Interacting in heterogeneous groups	Intellectual and practical skills
ICT literacy	Foundational knowledge	ICT literacy	Digital-age literacy	Using tools interactively	Intellectual and practical skills
Collaboration	Meta knowledge	Learning and thinking skills	Effective communication	Interacting in heterogeneous groups	Intellectual and practical skills
Communication	Meta knowledge	Learning and thinking skills	Effective communication	Using tools interactively	Intellectual and practical skills
Leadership	Humanistic knowledge	Life skills	High productivity	Act autonomously	Intellectual and practical skills

3 Bridging Skills, Computational Thinking and Learning Methods

People tend to be a good collaborator when they share a common problem with others: the problem makes sense for pupils when it's authentic and realistic in their own environment. Problem-Based Learning (PBL) was initially used in medicine learning [12] but [13] showed that PBL method was widely used not only in medical education but in K-12, college level, and many fields of professional education.

Collaborative Learning (CL) involves groups of students working to solve a problem, complete a task or create a product [14]. CL is different from a traditional group learning in that CL is a well-organized method for learners to harmonize and to work along together with their own capabilities and expertise on tasks, not just dividing the assignment into pieces and assign to every single member. The Jigsaw Classroom [15] is one of the many approaches based on these concepts. In this method, a problem is given to many home groups in which, each team member is responsible for one part of the problem. Then, each member of all home groups will meet other pupils in specialized expert groups to solve their common specialized part of the problem. Then, home groups meet again to try to assemble the different partial solutions in order to solve the initial global problem.

CT could be involved in many ways of 21st-century skills' learning since it is required to think systematically. The algorithm is one of the main concepts encouraging learners to be able to solve the problem and improve their action step by step. For this reason, CT is an excellent introductory course for an experimental approach: hypothesis -> experiment -> validate or not.

Since the early stages, education must be efficacious on the method of information search. The Jigsaw could be a good way for example if expert groups have to find the missing part of the information. This method can also inspire students: naïve initial solutions may be discussed with experts to find or build a better one. In CT, this is called the optimization process.

Table 2. Bridges between selected skills, computational thinking and learning design

Selected skills	Computational thinking	Learning design
Problem-solving: complexity of a real-world authentic problem can be decomposed into smaller ones and solved by different specialized teams	"Computational thinking is a way humans solve problems; it is not trying to get humans to think like computers" [1] The decomposition can lead to specialized processes to treat the pieces of the whole problem (data or process)	**Problem-based learning** [12]. Jigsaw [16] is a collaborative learning method that implements this idea of decomposition and specialization
Information management: Managing data, information, knowledge and cultural heritage	Data (bit, Boolean, pixel, character, table, image …) representation, storage, access, and treatment are the basics. CT is the ability to "use big amounts of data to speed up computation; to see data as code or code as data" [1]. CT helps to define Boolean expressions like information search criteria. To reduce the information space by adding keywords or cutting branches. This is an evolving process (try and check until find and validate)	Learning is building knowledge upon previous data, experience, knowledge, information, using all accessible sources. **Inquiry learning** relies on information management. This can be applied individually or collaboratively. The collaborative version would promote peer-to-peer teaching and interactions
Critical thinking: reasoning and being able to take distance with arguments. Each position is supposed to be validated by an authority, personal experience or by empirical data	"CT is thinking in terms of prevention, protection, and recovery from worst-case scenarios through redundancy, damage containment, and error correction" [1]. Considering	The **debate** is one of the many learning activities that needs critical thinking. The socio-cognitive conflict [17] is more generally the suitable situation that needs critical thinking ability. The

(*continued*)

Table 2. (*continued*)

Selected skills	Computational thinking	Learning design
	the validity and optimality of a solution is also CT. Curiosity: to look inside the black box. From early stages, pupils have to discover, understand and experiment that technical objects that are emerging in our everyday lives, are not magical but follow algorithms, limited rules that organize their processes and behaviours. These considerations may help critical thinking	cognitive conflict also arises when the theory needs to be confronted with experimentation. **Project Based Learning** may often lead to such confrontation
Creativity, Innovation: Think globally and act locally. Don't reinvent the wheel but cite its inventors, so that you may invent tomorrow's world	In a programming learning context, [17] show how the Scratch network of publicly available projects give opportunities to the Scratchers to develop their creativity: "Creativity and learning are deeply social practices [...] "I can do different things when I have access to others" This enhances the need for collaboration and communication	Constructionism [18] is a well-known learning theory implemented in methods by "learning by making". Physical space and materials may be limited by physics laws where virtual ones may relax some constraints **Design thinking**: a method that may be used in the learning context
Collaboration and Communication: For authentic real size complex problems, collaboration became the major way to tackle them and communication is the necessary ingredient for collaboration	Sharing ideas and applying them to new contexts (by shifting various levels of abstraction), we can find solutions for parts of a problem. Computational thinking promotes multilevel abstraction and transfer of solutions. This can be achieved only by collaboration and communication. Information and Language are 2 of the 4 pillars of Computational thinking for [5]	**Learning** is a **social process.** "One learns alone, but never without the others": Learning needs an individual engagement and a community as context. Interaction, communication and collaboration are promoted by many learning methods. The **Jigsaw** may be one of them

In Table 2, we showed that CT, that can be studied from an early age, can be used to cultivate many facets of important skills and especially those presented in Table 1.

Furthermore, while enhancing learning by CT, learners can acquire leadership skill step by step which are: first level – planning, learners learn by thinking how to create a thing in steps, second level – solving a complex problem by splitting it into small pieces and the last level - parallel and distributed programming, how to properly assign tasks to processors or operators.

4   Application Examples

4.1   How Much Computational Thinking Is Considered by Educators in Latin America?

In February 2019, the conference entitled "*Pedagogía 2019: Encuentro internacional por la unidad de los educadores*" took place in Cuba. There were more than 2200 participants from 37 countries. The event official language was Spanish, but contributions were accepted also in English, Portuguese or French. The conference was split into 12 parallel sessions covering many aspects of Education at large. Each session produced its own proceedings. Among the 1550 articles in the proceedings, the vast majority was written in Spanish. We analysed the 17146 pages of the 12 conference proceedings, looking for occurrences of "*pensamiento computacional*" or "*pensamiento algorítmico*". Even if many countries consider computational thinking crucial to be taught in their schools, these expressions occur in only 5 articles among 1550 in 3 (among 12) chapters of these conference proceedings (Table 3).

Table 3. "Computational thinking" occurrences in "*Pedagogía 2019*"

Article	Title	#Occurrences
ESU	Current grand challenges of the pedagogical innovation in higher education [19]	1
TIC004	ICT strategy to strengthen problem-solving competence through computational thinking [20]	12
TIC140	Scratch in Education [21]	1
TIC141	Activities to develop skills using Scratch [22]	3
CED009	Didactic model for the development of algorithmic thinking in the systems engineering program [23]	6
Total	Pedagogía 2019 [24]	23

The first occurrence is in the conference of a University Rector in the chapter "Higher Education: challenges facing the 2030 Agenda" (ESU). This unique occurrence of CT is situated in the introduction in the following argument (translated):

"Information and knowledge societies generate new possibilities and challenges. They change the role of the teacher. The policy of technologies for a State becomes crucial. The use of technologies is the new school's alphabet. The distinction between knowing and learning helps us define the specificities of institutional spaces dedicated to education. Memory ceases to be a requirement after a long period in the realm of education. **Computational thinking** advances between fears, ignorance and uncertainties. Biology, genetic engineering and information technology become the disciplines of the future."

In the next 3 articles, belonging to the TIC chapter (ICT), we find contributions measuring the impact of the use of digital tools (EVA or Scratch) on problem-solving competencies for learners (in high school for the first and in primary school for the other two). Moreover, they emphasize positive shifts in more general learning attitude. In the conclusion of [21, 22], we can read:

"The Scratch is a development option for students and teachers can open doors to the healthy and intelligent enjoyment of technological means available to the school and the student. It is a tool to teach thinking logic, to learn and to show everyone that technology can be used not only as users but also as producers of content and games necessary for these ages. Scratch is a door to the development needs of the 21st century, of the world and to place Cuba in an international curricular standard, with the simplicity, modesty and intelligence that our development conditions demand" [21].

The last one, included in the CED chapter (Educational Science) presents a project design which aim is to define a didactic model in a school of engineers on systems.

4.2   Teaching CT in Thailand: An Example

The research in teaching CT through mobile technology and robotics by Phetsrikran et al. [25] is one example of a CT's application in Thailand. The study was conducted with grade 7 and 8 pupils in a provincial school in Thailand with 20 pupils. The research's purpose is to teach CT using technology such as robots and mobile technology. Pupils were divided into four groups with five team members. The brief introduction was given how to use the robot and command the robot with block coding via mobile device under less than five minutes. Then pupils had 2 h to solve as much tasks and puzzles as possible with at least assistance from an instructor. The result of the study is not only pupils improved CT skills but they gained better social interaction and enhanced collaborative skill.

In Thailand's public policy level, the new discipline in K-12 schools based on CT's concept namely "Computing Science" [26] was launched in May 2018. The objectives of this discipline are defined by levels of pupils in the school. The first level targets to pupils from grade 1 to 3, they learn solving simple problems using the troubleshooting steps, basic skills in using information and communication technology and protect their personal information. Next level, pupils from grade 4 to 6 learn to search for information effectively and evaluate reliability, deciding on information, using logical reasoning to solve problems, using information and communications technology in collaboration, understanding their rights and duties, and respecting the rights of others. Inputting primary data into the computer system; analysing, evaluating, presenting data and information with correct purposes; using computational thinking skills to solve real-life problems and write simple computer programs to solve problems, using information and communication technology knowingly and socially responsible are skills that pupils from grade 7 to 9 will be cultivated. The last level for pupils from grade 10 to 12 who will learn about applying of knowledge in computing science, digital media, information and communication technology to gather real-life data from various sources and knowledge from other sciences in order to create new contribution, understanding the change of technology that affects life, career, society, culture and safely use with ethics. Several learning concepts are applied in the classroom like peer-to-peer learning, creative-based learning, collaborative learning and real-life problem-based learning. Self and peer assessments are applied to evaluate pupils with summative assessment such as learning portfolio and subjective and objective tests.

4.3   Africa: 2 Examples

A first famous example that rid the world through social networks is the story of this Ghanaian teacher teaching word processor with (only) a chalkboard [27].

This story became famous especially when the Microsoft Corporation decided to help this teacher by a donation. However, as this teacher says: this was not possible because of the curriculum that imposes that students understand how to charge the system and configure the computer before any use of it. This example shows many interesting aspects. First, the passion and energy of this teacher to do his job. Second, the importance he puts in the ability to use a word processor. Third, the mismatch between this important need and (a) the material he can use and (b) the institutional constraints.

The second example on this continent is quite old. It is the story of a Swiss association "African puzzle" [28] that installed computer classrooms in Benin and proposed a truck for a mobile computer classroom. It deals with cooperation from a European country to help a developing country to access to the computer in order to develop ICT and related competencies. In this second example, we can see the importance of human exchange between association members (donators) and local teachers and technicians (receivers). Beyond technical problems due to lack of infrastructure, we can see such initiatives as impressive. They give unique opportunities to many pupils to experience moving a mouse and clicking on it to see the result on a real computer, not only on a video or a chalkboard.

There are also more positive examples of creativity using cultural handicraft abilities to produce (street) art from recycled material like for example: the African robots project [29] in Cape Town. Another impressive demonstration of engineering competencies in Africa (Kenya) is the first fly experience of the passenger drone project described in [30].

5   Discussion and Conclusion

The skills selected in Table 1 are important not only in developed countries where people use many digital objects in their everyday life. Developing countries are necessary concerned by many aspects of the information society and digital era because they are crossing frontiers and oceans: data and information on a natural phenomenon like a tsunami or earth quacks, meteorological forecast, migrations, transportations, global market, political shifts on the international scene. For this reason, and because it can be taught even without computers, CT may nurture these skills in order for the people to get more capacity to face new complex challenges. Especially in so-called developed countries, we are ingenious to build smart solutions for the next generation of smart houses, cities, aircraft and so on, but when we go back home by using one car per worker, we are still unable to collaborate and solve rush hours' traffic. Even if we face this problem every day as a citizen, we are still not able to solve it as a community.

In developing countries, we may consider this problem by using the experience of so-called "developed countries". For example, access to the internet is seen for educators in developing countries as a mine of information and knowledge. But we can also witness the time the children in developed countries are wasting in front of online dummy games! This should help us to design better curricula in schools in order to make learners more critical thinkers.

However, the problem to be solved, or the context of this problem, should be reachable by the learner. As a counterexample, this Ghanaian teacher on ICT that teaches Word processor by drawing the MS Word interface on a chalkboard [27]. Does it make sense if students never can use a computer to validate their learning? If they never confront theory to practice, an algorithm to a machine by an execution? In this presentation, we tried to show how the integration of computational thinking with collaborative problem-based learning can cultivate learners how to learn and work on a real (authentic) problem together. We also present some examples of Computational Concepts that can be connected to teaching methods and we suggest to use them to strengthen the skills selected among the various 21st century skillsets.

References

1. Wing, J.C.: Computational thinking. Commun. ACM **49**(3), 33–35 (2006)
2. Futschek, G.: Algorithmic thinking: the key for understanding computer science. In: Mittermeir, R.T. (ed.) ISSEP 2006. LNCS, vol. 4226, pp. 159–168. Springer, Heidelberg (2006). https://doi.org/10.1007/11915355_15
3. Denning, P.J.: Great principles of computing. Commun. ACM **46**(11), 15–20 (2003)
4. Dagienė, V.: Informatics education for new millennium learners. In: Kalaš, I., Mittermeir, R. T. (eds.) ISSEP 2011. LNCS, vol. 7013, pp. 9–20. Springer, Heidelberg (2011). https://doi. org/10.1007/978-3-642-24722-4_2
5. Dowek, G., Berry, G.: Une introduction à la science informatique pour les enseignants de la discipline en lycée. Paris: Centre régional de documentation pédagogique de l'académie de Paris (2011)
6. González Serra, G.I.: Multimedia para el desarrollo de habilidades informáticas. In: PEDAGOGÍA 2019, La Havana, Cuba, pp. 1522–1531 (2019)
7. Kereluik, K., Mishra, P., Fahnoe, C., Terry, L.: What knowledge is of most worth. J. Digit. Learn. Teach. Educ. **29**(4), 127–140 (2013)
8. Partnership for 21st Century Skills. https://www.battelleforkids.org/. Accessed 11 Mar 2019
9. Metiri Group: EnGauge 21st century skills: literacy in the digital age. North Central Regional Educational Laboratory, Metiri Group, Naperville (2003)
10. OECD: Definition and Selection of key Competencies. PISA: Definition and Selection of key Competencies, 27 May 2005. http://www.oecd.org/education/skills-beyond-school/definitionandselectionofcompetenciesdeseco.htm. Accessed 11 Mar 2019

11. College learning for the new global century: The National Leardership Council for Liberal Education and America's Promise, Washington, DC (2007)
12. Antepohl, W., Herzig, S.: Problem-based learning versus lecture-based learning in a course of basic pharmacology: a controlled, randomized study. Med. Educ. **33**(2), 106–113 (1999)
13. Barrows, H.S.: Problem-based learning in medicine and beyond: a brief overview. New Dir. Teach. Learn. **1996**(68), 3–12 (1996)
14. Macgregor, J.: Collaborative learning: shared inquiry as a process of reform. New Dir. Teach. Learn. **1990**(42), 19–30 (1990)
15. Aronson, E.: The Jigsaw Classroom. Beverly Hills, California (1978)
16. Asensio, J.I., et al.: Collaborative learning patterns: assisting the development of component-based CSCL applications. In: 12th Euromicro Conference on Parallel, Distributed and Network-Based Processing, Proceedings, pp. 218–224 (2004)
17. Brennan, K., Resnick, M.: New frameworks for studying and assessing the development of computational thinking. In: Proceedings of the 2012 Annual Meeting of the American Educational Research Association, Vancouver, Canada, vol. 1, p. 25 (2012)
18. Papert, S., Harel, I.: Situating constructionism. Constructionism **36**(2), 1–11 (1991)
19. Álvarez González, F.J.: Grandes desafios actuales de la innovacion pedagogica en la educacion superior. In: PEDAGOGÍA 2019, La Havana, Cuba, pp. 1–31 (2019)
20. Gutiérrez Rodríguez, C.A.: Estrategia TIC para fortalecer la competencia de solución de problemas mediante el pensamiento computacional. In: PEDAGOGÍA 2019, La Havana, Cuba, pp. 38–53 (2019)
21. González Marchante, I., Alfonso Rodríguez, H., Bess Constantén, Y.: El Scratch en la Educación. In: PEDAGOGÍA 2019, La Havana, Cuba, pp. 1435–1447 (2019)
22. Oceguera Martínez, S., Suárez Miranda, Z., Veloz Valdespino, Y.: Propuesta de actividades para desarrollar habilidades en el uso del Scratch. In: PEDAGOGÍA 2019, La Havana, Cuba, pp. 1448–1462 (2019)
23. Rúa Ascar, J.M., García González, J.: Modelo didáctico para el desarrollo del pensamiento algorítmico en los estudiantes del programa de ingeniería de sistemas. In: PEDAGOGÍA 2019, La Havana, Cuba, pp. 79–107 (2019)
24. Escalona Serrano, E.: International congress pedagogy 2019. In: Pedagogía Cuba 2019, February 2019. http://pedagogiacuba.com/en. Accessed 09 Mar 2019
25. Phetsrikran, T., Massagram, W., Harfield, A.: First steps in teaching computational thinking through mobile technology and robotics. Asian Int. J. Soc. Sci. **17**(3), 37–52 (2017)
26. Suebka, P.: Empower World Class Teaching and Learning Experience. The Institute for the Promotion of Teaching Science and Technology (IPST) (2017). http://eng.ipst.ac.th/. Accessed 13 Mar 2019
27. Asiedu, K.G.: The story behind a viral photo of a teacher in Ghana showing students Windows on a blackboard, Quartz Africa, 28 February 2018. https://qz.com/africa/1217879/a-ghana-teacher-shows-microsoft-windows-on-a-blackboard-is-a-viral-sensation/. Accessed 12 Jan 2019
28. Les 4 Baggio: 'African puzzle', African puzzle, 12 January 2015. http://africanpuzzle.blogspot.com/. Accessed 04 Mar 2019
29. Ralphborland.net. http://ralphborland.net/africanrobots/. Accessed 09 Mar 2019
30. Mbetsa, M.: Passenger drone. DroneDJ, July 2017

Researching Computers and Education Through Actor-Network Theory

Arthur Tatnall[✉] [iD]

Victoria University, Melbourne, Australia
Arthur.Tatnall@vu.edu.au

Abstract. The teaching of information technology and education needs to keep up to date to remain relevant. With technology changing rapidly this is no easy task. It is even more important that research into this area be sustainable and to keep up to date. The use of, or teaching about, computers in education involves both humans – teachers, students and parents, and non-humans – technology. Research into computers and education is socio-technical as it has to deal with both human and non-human actors, and so actor-network theory (ANT) can provide a useful research approach. This paper outlines actor-network theory and Innovation Translation (informed by ANT) and provides some examples of research using ANT as a lens for analysis.

Keywords: Information technology · Education · Research ·
Actor-network theory

1 Research in IT Education

For teaching about, or use of information technology in education to remain relevant and sustainable, research must keep up to date as new technologies appear, old one disappear or are substantially changed, new approaches to making use of IT in education emerge, and students' experience IT differently.

Research can be regarded as "*the systematic investigation and study of materials and sources to establish facts and reach new conclusions*" [1]. Research in education, however, is not just the province of academics in Faculties of Education (although they are the ones who formalise it in academic papers!). Teachers need to research new technology: how it works and how it could be used in their classrooms. Students need to research their school work, Parents need to research which school to send their children, and education authorities need to research new technologies and teaching approaches. This paper is thus about much more than just academic research into computer education.

2 Computers and Education

Education is about people: students, teachers and parents. Computers are about technology. Research into the use of information technology in education is concerned with the ways people use, and learn about computer-based systems to make education better.

© IFIP International Federation for Information Processing 2019
Published by Springer Nature Switzerland AG 2019
A. Tatnall and N. Mavengere (Eds.): SUZA 2019, IFIP AICT 564, pp. 78–88, 2019.
https://doi.org/10.1007/978-3-030-28764-1_10

It also has to deal with issues involving people and things: with both human and non-human entities [2]. Such research is thus truly socio-technical in nature. Researchers in this area need to deal with problems of how to handle complexities due to a multitude of interactions between people and computers [3]. It thus involves neither social nor technical determinism.

3 Actor-Network Theory

Social Determinism suggests that social interactions and constructs alone determine individual behaviour. On the other hand Technological Determinism assumes that a society's technology determines the development of its social structure and cultural values [4]. Clearly, as a study of the use of computers and education has elements that depend on people and others that depend on the technology, a simplistic view that it could be classed as either Social Determinism or Technological Determinism therefore cannot be valid.

Actor-Network Theory (ANT), or the 'sociology of translations' [5–7] is concerned with studying the mechanics of power that occurs through construction and maintenance of networks made up of both human and non-human actors. It was originally developed in the late 1980s by: Bruno Latour and Michael Callon (École Nationale Supérieure des Mines de Paris) and John Law (Lancaster University, UK).

In ANT an actor is seen as any human or non-human entity that is able to make its presence *individually* felt [8] by the other actors [9]. ANT deals with the social-technical divide by denying that purely technical or purely social relations are possible as nothing is purely social and nothing is purely technical [10].

Actor-network theory declares that the world is full of hybrid entities [11] containing both human and non-human elements. It was developed to analyse situations where separation of these elements is difficult [12]. You could ask, for example, which part of a software app is just an inanimate object and which is the result of human interactions. To differentiate a computer program's technical aspects from the influence exerted by the socio-cultural background of the software development team is quite difficult [13–15]. What part of a school class on geography that makes use of Google Maps is driven by the technology and which is due to the inclinations and approach of the teacher?

To address the need to treat both human and non-human actors fairly and in the same way, ANT is based upon three principles:

- Agnosticism – analytical impartiality towards all actors involved in the project, whether they are human or non-human.
- Generalised symmetry – explains conflicting viewpoints of different actors the same way for human and non-human actors.
- Free association – requires the abandonment of all a-priori distinctions between the technological and social [6, 16].

In summary, ANT requires all human and non-human actors to be acknowledged and their interactions to be treated in the same way. It is their interactions that matter.

4   Researching the Use of Computers and Education

Several examples of the use of actor-network theory in educational research in which I have been involved are now described. ANT is not a research methodology as such and can best be described as a lens through which to analyse data, usually collected through the use of case studies, action research, and other qualitative methods.

4.1   Factors Determining the Balance Between Online and Face-to-Face Teaching: An Analysis Using Actor-Network Theory

Papers published by Wong and Tatnall [17, 18], based on Wong's PhD research, involved an investigation of approaches to teaching a first-year accounting subject at Victoria University. Wong had recently introduced some online teaching using Blackboard (previously known as WebCT) into her classes and wanted to understand how its use compared with that of face-to-face teaching: which the students preferred, and which was most educationally effective.

In this case a simple investigation quickly showed that a large number of different entities had an effect on determining how much online and how much face-to-face teaching to include in this subject, and that not all were human as the technology itself has an important determining effect [19]. This suggested an investigation through the lens of actor-network theory.

The first step in an actor-network analysis is to identify the actors involved. In this case these were:

- **Human Actors:** Bachelor of Business Course Coordinator; BAO-1101 Subject Coordinator, Lecturers, Tutors and (Contract) Tutors; other lecturers; Faculty Dean; Head of the School of Accounting, Students
- **Non-Human:** University Administration, Policy and Infrastructure; IT Services; Computers; computer laboratories; other e-learning technologies (including remote access) and the Blackboard e-learning environment itself.

Each of these human and non-human actors potentially influenced the balance between an online and a face-to-face approach.

One of the issues brought out by the ANT investigation was the effect that force of personality and presence has in a teaching and learning environment and how this contrasts with the effect of the technology. Many students believed that as well as use of the technology, the personal interactions of face-to-face added value to their learning experience [20].

5   Technological Innovation and Education

Much of the research in the use of information technology in education relates to how or whether new technologies are adopted. This can be described as research into technological innovation in education. While invention can be seen as discovery or creation of new ideas, innovation involves putting these ideas into practice [21].

There are several approaches to researching technological innovation the most commonly used being: Diffusion of Innovations (Rogers [22]), TAM: Technology Acceptance Model (Davis et al. [23]) and UTAUT: Unified Theory of Acceptance and Use of Technology (Venkatesh et al. [24]). In this paper, however, I will make use of another approach: Innovation Translation from Actor-Network Theory.

When an organisation (or individual) is considering use of a technological innovation they do not always want to adopt it in its entirety but are interested in only some aspects and not others. Innovation Translation [6], informed by actor-network theory, provides a useful means for investigating adoption or non-adoption of new technology. In ANT terms this technology needs to be *translated* [6] into a form that is more appropriate for the potential adopter so that the innovation finally adopted is often not in its original form, but a *translation* into a form that is suitable for their use [25].

Callon [6] outlines four aspects or 'moments' in the process of translation:

1. *Problematisation* – key actors attempt to define the nature of the problem and the roles of other actors so that they are seen as having the answer.
2. *Interessement* – processes that attempt to interest and impose the identities and roles defined in the problematisation on the other actors.
3. *Enrolment* – if the interessement is successful through a process of coercion, seduction or consent [26] adoption of this innovation will follow.
4. *Mobilisation* occurs as the proposed solution gains wider acceptance with some working to promote the technology to others.

5.1 Adoption of Visual Basic in a University Curriculum

This section looks at an example of using Actor-Network Theory to understand the process of information systems curriculum innovation.

The discipline of Information Systems (IS) involves investigation of how businesses, and other organisational entities, can make the best use of ICT to further their business aims [9]. I will argue that changes in IS curriculum can best be thought of as innovations and considered using innovation theory.

This section provides an actor-network account of how Visual Basic (VB) entered the information systems curriculum at Bourke University of Technology in Melbourne in the 1990s [27]. Even though this innovation adoption and curriculum change took place twenty years ago, similar processes, interactions and associations to those here described are likely to be found in any current curriculum innovation.

This story begins in the early 1990s at a time when two Colleges of Advanced Education: Wills Institute of Technology and Bourke Institute of Technology were merging to form Bourke University of Technology[1] [27–29]. It will be considered in four parts.

First Attempts to Use Visual Basic

Not long after he began teaching at Wills Institute, Fred discovered Visual Basic for MS-DOS when undertaking an outside programming job. He liked the way that VB

---

[1] All human and institutional names in this article are pseudonyms to preserve a degree of anonymity.

allowed a programmer to produce a prototype solution very quickly, with less bother than in other languages.

At Wills Institute, Fred had just started teaching an introductory IS subject that required use of a screen prototyping tool. Unfortunately Wills had no prototyping tools that could be used in the MS-DOS student labs and so this topic could not really be handled practically. Fred wondered if some screen design aspects of VB could do the job. He did this by selecting some features of VB while ignoring others. He could only use VB in this way by *translating* [6] it from a 'programming language and visual programming environment' into a 'screen prototyping tool'. The following year after the student labs had been equipped with new Windows PCs Fred decided to give VB a try in an Operating Systems Programming subject. This involved another translation of VB to become a 'language to teach Windows operating systems programming'. None of this would have been possible if not for the formation of a VB actor-network consisting of Fred, the introductory IS subject, the operating systems programming subject, Visual Basic, the student labs and the students. VB had now become firmly *enrolled* at Wills.

Programming Languages Already in Place at Bourke Institute
At this time Bourke Institute of Technology used three programming languages in its teaching: Pick/BASIC, an assembly language system called Alice, and to a lesser extent COBOL (- not relevant to this discussion). This part of the story begins with seven actors: Bourke Institute of Technology, Pick/BASIC, Alice, COBOL, the IS curriculum and two humans: Stephen and James.

Starting our as a 'Working Man's College', Bourke's mission had always been to provide an *applied* tertiary education, and to achieve this it made every effort to ensure that its curriculum was based on 'real' (meaning industry standard) approaches, applications and technologies.

At the time Pick which is a specialised database-oriented operating system that makes use of a programming language called Pick/BASIC [30–32] was very much industry standard and 'real' for some applications. Stephen then began assembling a network to assist Pick's entry into the IS curriculum. Pick could not have entered the IS curriculum unaided and needed to expand its network by addition of a local ally who was in a position to assist. This was Stephen, who decided to introduce Pick/BASIC to his students and quickly produced a powerful *interessement* to convince his colleagues. He describes how his students quickly adapted to Pick/BASIC, and were able to gain a very rapid understanding of the business problems he wanted them to consider.

In the late-1980s James, another Bourke lecturer was developing an introductory subject in computer architecture and operating systems. He decided to build a software simulator: 'Alice' to teach assembly language, so that with this 'virtual machine' students would be better able to understand what went on inside a computer.

In terms of innovation translation, Stephen and James had thus each successfully *problematised* [6] a need for students to understand and use their respective approaches to programming.

Entry of Visual Basic and the Fate of the Existing Languages
After the merger of Wills Institute and Bourke Institute it was necessary that the new enlarged Bourke University of Technology to have the appearance of a *single*

university and so it was necessary to quickly merge the curricula for each degree at each campus. Negotiations about the new course continued over almost two-years until the final version was accredited.

While this was happening Visual Basic made its appearance in a new elective subject called *Graphic User Interface (GUI) and Event-Driven Programming*, giving it a toe-hold in the curriculum. When the new curriculum was finalised, it was agreed that the first and second programming subjects were to be taught using Pick/BASIC. The Alice virtual machine did not find a place in the new degree as knowledge of the inner workings of a computer had become largely irrelevant to IS students. This meant that the curriculum now contained Pick/BASIC and Visual Basic, but not Alice.

How VB Remained in the Curriculum

Debate on programming languages did not stop then however due to the entry of a new actor: Object-Oriented Programming. This might have destabilised or posed a threat to the existing networks [26]. If it had been unprepared to face this threat Visual Basic would probably have been displaced from at least one IS subject, but VB had always made use of objects in designing screens, and its whole programming approach was *object-based*. Also at about this time a new object-oriented version of VB became available. Visual Basic thus remained in the Bourke IS curriculum for some years.

5.2   Failure of the Victorian Education Ultranet

The Ultranet was a form of extranet released for use in Government Schools by the Victorian Education Department in 2010 as "*a student centred electronic learning environment that supports high quality learning and teaching, connects students, teachers and parents and enables efficient knowledge transfer.*" [33]. It was intended to support delivery of curriculum, online teaching and sharing of knowledge across all Victorian Government Schools. Although it seemed like a good idea at the time with lots of possibilities to do worthwhile things, by late 2012 it was not being used to any great extent in most schools and was abandoned by the Government in June 2013 [34]. This is the story of the life and death of the Ultranet viewed through an ANT lens.

An important Ultranet goal was to improve communication between schools, teachers and parents. The Ultranet was based on use of what it called *Spaces* (mini websites) using icons to identify each space and provide *Applications* for use in that space. Each Space was classified by its accessibility to different users (students, teachers, parents and the public) into one of the following categories:

- *Me Spaces* (private, and accessible only to the owner),
- *We Spaces* (shared with permission) and
- *See Spaces* (open, public access).

Any investigation of adoption of the Ultranet must consider its technical and its human components. It necessarily involves a socio-technical research approach and methods and so an investigation using ANT and Innovation Translation is appropriate. An innovation is of no value unless adopted, and it will only be adopted if adapted to fill a need – unless it is translated.

Problematisation

Research suggests that the intention, or problematisation, by the State Government for the Ultranet was to create a system to offer access to learning materials and to inform parents of their child's progress. Its problematisation was as "*a student-centred electronic learning environment that supports high quality learning and teaching, connects students, teachers and parents and enables efficient knowledge transfer*" [33]. This generally seemed like a good idea, but some teachers saw this as unnecessary as they were already using other learning management systems such as Blackboard or Moodle. Others saw connecting in this way with parents as a threat.

Interessement

The next step was to convince teachers and parents about the value of using the Ultranet. This got off to a bad start when the Ultranet was launched at a 'student-free day' of professional development for all teachers in August 2010. Unfortunately this day turned into a disaster when the Ultranet crashed at 9 am. When it was running later, many teachers experienced problems and reported it as running extremely slowly [35–37].

As an attempt to convince teachers of the Ultranet's value, each Education Department region appointed 'Ultranet Coaches' to visit local schools and promote Ultranet use, and each school was asked to appoint an Ultranet Champion known as a 'Lead User'. Many teachers, however, quickly became disenchanted with the Ultranet compared with other tools that were more easily adaptable. "*My experiences of the Ultranet so far have given me the impression that it is restricted and basic. While I can definitely see the value in what they are trying to achieve, it saddens me that so much funding and resources are being pumped into a clunky system in its infancy*" [38].

The State Government and Education Departments' attempts at interessement had clearly been unsuccessful.

Enrolment and Mobilisation

If all had been well, enrolment would have followed, but given the failure of interessement very few schools did became enrolled and an even smaller number became mobilised and attempted to convince others. The Ultranet was abandoned by the Government in June 2013.

5.3   The Internet of Things and How It May Relate to Education

The Internet of Things (IoT) involves connections of physical Things to the Internet and so is about inter-relationships between Things, or Non-Humans actors. The Non-Human actors, of course, cannot (yet) act alone and so we must also consider their interactions with Human Actors. In this socio-technical situation the use of Actor-Network Theory to frame the discussion is most appropriate [39, 40].

Use of the IoT brings up the concept of machine (or *Thing*) independence. Independence can be defined as: "*Free from outside control; not subject to another's authority*" and "*Capable of acting or thinking for oneself*" [41]. Another definition adds: "*Not subject to control by others*" [42]. Over the next few years the Things, with the assistance of advances in artificial intelligence, will begin to develop identities and virtual personalities. In the past non-human actors have only been there to serve and to interact with humans but with the IoT will this still the case? We can question where this leaves humans, will the things take over? Speaking of artificial intelligence in a BBC broadcast in 2014 [43] Stephen Hawking suggested that: *"The development of full artificial intelligence could spell the end of the human race"* and *"It would take off on its own, and re-design itself at an ever increasing rate. Humans, who are limited by slow biological evolution, couldn't compete, and would be superseded"* [43].

There are many possible uses of the IoT and these are likely to increase over the next few years. One important use is that of RFID in healthcare. Hospitals need to keep track of equipment such as trolleys, surgical equipment, wheelchairs, infusion pumps and defibrillators and RFID can assist with this [44]. Driverless smart trains, driverless trucks and driverless cars, making use of the IoT, are also in use today. With the IoT, control of appliances such as heaters, air conditioners, washing machines, dishwashers, refrigerators, ovens and home alarms can be done from a distance by the human owner with the aid of a smart phone.

Although not fully explored as yet education is not exempt from the impact of the IoT. This is a developing area and much more research needs to be done in its development. Some possibilities, though, are clear. In school management, RFID readers could be installed at the school gate, the library, and other places to identify the movements of students who carry an electronic tag. A noise sensor could be used to inform a neighbouring classroom that their noise has exceeded a certain level. IoT can potentially play a role in monitoring student emotional states and classroom environments, especially in relation to students with special needs [45]. Another possible use of the IoT in education is in science laboratories where it could be used as a tool for conducting experiments without the presence of the actual equipment [46].

As well as making *use* of the IoT in education though, an important consideration is curriculum development and what should be taught to students at all levels about the IoT [47].

It must be stressed that there is much more to be considered and researched in relation to the IoT and education. The possibilities are both very attractive and potentially rather frightening.

The Internet of Things and Other Possibilities

Not all IoT devices are serious in their application though and Amanda Davis [48] describes a video camera system that streams to your mobile phone to let you keep an eye on your cat while you are away. You can also talk to it through a two-way audio system and activate a moving laser pointer for your cat to chase to keep it amused until you come home.

In an article called: 'Do objects dream of an internet of things', Teodor Mitew [49] describes Brad the Toaster:

> *"Brad is a toaster connected to the internet, and to other toasters like him. He often exchanges information with his fellow toasters, with whom he tweets about the usage habits of their human hosts. He and his fellow toasters are not owned as other, simpler, toasters before them used to be. They are hosted by humans who have promised to use them. He loves being used, and is sensitive to learning that other toasters are used more often than him. When feeling underappreciated, Brad will draw attention to himself by playing pranks, throwing tantrums, and expressing his sadness loudly on Twitter. Eventually, Brad will become disillusioned and demand a move to another, more caring host. He will depart, leaving the smell of burned toast behind him"* [49: 4].

6 Conclusion

Research into computers in education is very important, but must be sustainable and kept up to date as new technologies and new approaches to teaching appear and changes in society result. This research must be socio-technical as it needs to investigate actions and interactions between teachers, students, parents, education authorities and the technology itself: to actions and interactions between humans and non-humans. In this paper I have argued that using the lens of actor-network theory and innovation translation can provide a useful research approach.

References

1. Collins English Dictionary. Definition of 'research', December 2018. https://www.collinsdictionary.com/us/dictionary/english/research
2. Tatnall, A.: Actor-network theory as a socio-technical approach to information systems research. In: Clarke, S., et al. (eds.) Socio-Technical and Human Cognition Elements of Information Systems, pp. 266–283. Information Science Publishing, Hershey (2003)
3. Tatnall, A.: Actor-network theory applied to information systems research. In: Khosrow-Pour, M. (ed.) Encyclopedia of Information Science and Technology, 2nd edn, pp. 20–24. Information Science Reference, Hershey (2009)
4. Wikipedia. Social and Technological Determinism, December 2018. https://en.wikipedia.org/wiki/Technological_determinism. https://en.wikipedia.org/wiki/Social_determinism
5. Latour, B.: The powers of association. In: Law, J. (ed.) Power, Action and Belief. A New Sociology of Knowledge? Sociological Review Monograph, vol. 32, pp. 264–280. Routledge & Kegan Paul, London (1986)
6. Callon, M.: Some elements of a sociology of translation: domestication of the scallops and the fishermen of St Brieuc Bay. In: Law, J. (ed.) Power, Action & Belief. A New Sociology of Knowledge?, pp. 196–229. Routledge & Kegan Paul, London (1986)
7. Law, J.: The heterogeneity of texts. In: Callon, M., Law, J., Rip, A. (eds.) Mapping the Dynamics of Science and Technology, pp. 67–83. Macmillan Press, UK (1986)
8. Law, J.: Technology and heterogeneous engineering: the case of portuguese expansion. In: Bijker, W.E., Hughes, T.P., Pinch, T.J. (eds.) The Social Construction of Technological Systems: New Directions in the Sociology and History of Technology, pp. 111–134. MIT Press, Cambridge (1987)
9. Tatnall, A.: Using actor-network theory to understand the process of information systems curriculum innovation. Educ. Inf. Technol. **15**(4 - Special Issue on Information Systems Curriculum), 239–254 (2010)
10. Law, J. (ed.): A Sociology of Monsters. Essays on Power, Technology and Domination. Routledge, London (1991)
11. Latour, B.: We Have Never Been Modern. Harvester University Press, Cambridge (1993)
12. Callon, M.: Society in the making: the study of technology as a tool for sociological analysis. In: Bijker, W.E., Hughes, T.P., Pinch, T.P. (eds.) The Social Construction of Technological Systems, pp. 85–103. The MIT Press, Cambridge (1987)
13. Tatnall, A., Gilding, A.: Actor-network theory and information systems research. In: 10th Australasian Conference on Information Systems (ACIS). Victoria University of Wellington, Wellington (1999)

14. Cusumano, M.A., Selby, R.W.: How Microsoft builds software. Commun. ACM **40**(6), 53–61 (1997)
15. Sahay, S.: Implementation of information technology: a space-time perspective. Organ. Stud. **18**(2), 229–260 (1997)
16. Singleton, V., Michael, M.: Actor-networks and ambivalence: general practitioners in the UK cervical screening programme. Soc. Stud. Sci. **23**(2), 227–264 (1993)
17. Wong, L., Tatnall, A.: Factors determining the balance between online and face-to-face teaching: an analysis using actor-network theory. Interdisc. J. Inf. Knowl. Manag. **5**, 167–176 (2010)
18. Wong, L., Tatnall, A.: The need to balance the blend: online versus face-to-face teaching in an introductory accounting subject. J. Issues Inf. Sci. Inf. Technol. (IISIT) **6**, 309–322 (2009)
19. Tummons, J.: Higher education in further education in England: an actor-network ethnography. Int. J. Actor-Netw. Theory Technol. Innov. **1**(3), 55–69 (2009)
20. Wong, L.: The e-learning experience - its impact on student engagement and learning outcomes. In: Business & Economics Society International Conference, Bahamas (2010)
21. Maguire, C., Kazlauskas, E.J., Weir, A.D.: Information Services for Innovative Organizations. Academic Press, Sandiego (1994)
22. Rogers, E.M.: Diffusion of Innovations, 5th edn. The Free Press, New York (2003)
23. Davis, F.: Perceived usefulness, perceived ease of use, and user acceptance of information technology. MIS Q. **13**(3), 318–340 (1989)
24. Venkatesh, V., Morris, M.G., Davis, G.B., Davis, F.D.: User acceptance of information technology: toward a unified view. MIS Q. **27**(3), 425–478 (2003)
25. Tatnall, A.: Information systems, technology adoption and innovation translation. Int. J. Actor-Netw. Theory Technol. Innov. **1**(1), 59–74 (2009)
26. Grint, K., Woolgar, S.: The Machine at Work – Technology, Work and Organisation. Polity Press, Cambridge (1997)
27. Tatnall, A.: Innovation and Change in the Information Systems Curriculum of an Australian University: A Socio-Technical Perspective. Central Queensland University, Rockhampton (2000)
28. Tatnall, A., Davey, W.: How visual basic entered the curriculum at an australian university: an account informed by innovation translation. In: Challenges to Informing Clients: A Transdisciplinary Approach (Informing Science 2001). Informing Science, Krakow (2001)
29. Tatnall, A.: Innovation Translation in a University Curriculum. Heidelberg Press, Melbourne (2007)
30. Johnson, W.: Pick, Universe, Unidata Resources (2009). Cited 2010 http://knol.google.com/k/pick-universe-unidata-resources#
31. Pick Systems: The Pick Systems Approach: Now more than ever (1998). Pick Systems: http://www.picksys.com/company/approach.html. Accessed 22 Sept 1998
32. Pick Systems: An Incomplete History of Pick/BASIC (1998). Pick Systems: http://www.picksys.com/articles/pw/119407.html. Accessed 22 Sept 1998
33. Department of Education and Early Childhood Development. Ultranet 2011, January 2012. http://www.education.vic.gov.au/about/directions/ultranet/default.htm
34. Tatnall, A., Davey, W.: Birth, life and death of the victorian education ultranet. Educ. Inf. Technol. **23**(4), 1585–1605 (2018)
35. Levy, M.: 'Massive fail': technical glitches upset Ultranet training day. In: The Age. The Age, Melbourne (2010)
36. Topsfield, J.: Rollout of ultranet postponed. In: The Age. Fairfax, Melbourne. p. 5 (2010)
37. Holden, S.: Ultranet crashes. Teacher (214), 5–8 (2010)
38. ReflectiveTeacher: Unlimited Potential … Unfortunate Ultranet, Melbourne (2012)

39. Tatnall, A., Davey, B.: The internet of things and beyond: rise of the non-human actors. Int. J. Actor-Netw. Theory Technol. Innov. **7**(4), 58–69 (2015)
40. Tatnall, A., Davey, B.: Towards machine independence: from mechanically programmed devices to the internet of things. In: Tatnall, A., Leslie, C. (eds.) HC 2016. IAICT, vol. 491, pp. 87–100. Springer, Cham (2016). https://doi.org/10.1007/978-3-319-49463-0_6
41. Soanes, C., Stevenson, A. (ed.): The Concise Oxford English Dictionary. 11th edn. Oxford University Press, Oxford (2004)
42. Merriam-Webster. Merriam-Webster Dictionary 2015, January 2016. http://www.merriam-webster.com/dictionary/independent
43. Cellan-Jones, R.: Stephen Hawking warns artificial intelligence could end mankind 2014, October 2015, 2 December 2014. http://www.bbc.com/news/technology-30290540
44. Unnithan, C.: Examining innovation translation of RFID technology in australian hospitals through a lens informed by actor-network theory. In: Information Systems. Victoria University, Melbourne (2014)
45. Kassab, M., DeFranco, J.F., Voas, J.: "Smarter" Education. IT Professional, pp. 20–24. IEEE Computer Society, September/October 2018
46. Muhammad, A.H., Nur Dalila, K.A., Zakiah, M.Y., Amar, F., Nooritawati, M.T.: Computer assisted e-laboratory using LabVIEW and internet-of-things platform as teaching aids in the industrial instrumentation course. Int. J. Online Eng. **14**(12), 26–42 (2018)
47. Voas, J., Laplante, P.: Curriculum Considerations for the Internet of Things. Computer, pp. 72–75. IEEE Computer Society, January 2017
48. Davis, A.: Boost Your Home's IQ With These Seven Gadgets 2015, January 2016. http://theinstitute.ieee.org/technology-focus/technology-topic/boosting-your-homes-iq-with-these-seven-gadgets
49. Mitew, T.: Do objects dream of an internet of things? Fibreculture J. **2014**(23), 1–25 (2014)

Automatically Generating Programming Questions Corresponding to Rubrics Using Assertions and Invariants

Masami Hagiya[1]([⊠]), Kosuke Fukuda[1], Yoshinori Tanabe[2]([⊠]), and Toshinori Saito[3]([⊠])

[1] Graduate School of Information Science and Technology, University of Tokyo, Tokyo, Japan
hagiya@is.s.u-tokyo.ac.jp
[2] School of Literature, Tsurumi University, Yokohama, Japan
tanabe-y@tsurumi-u.ac.jp
[3] Graduate School of Practitioners in Education, Seisa University, Yokohama, Japan
t-saito@gred.seisa.ac.jp

Abstract. The importance of programming in the context of primary and secondary education is increasing, reflecting incorporation of programming in the reformation of Japanese curriculum guidelines for schools, the release of which is planned in 2020. Earlier research developed proposed rubrics for assessment of student attainment levels in various fields of high-school informatics, including programming. The reformation requires that university entrance examinations should include informatics; it has thus become necessary to create a large number of questions exploring various levels of attainment. Here, we develop methods automatically generating questions in the field of programming; we use program correctness proofs and a theorem prover to this end. Questions corresponding to each level are automatically generated from a single program featuring a correctness proof by analyzing the source code and the proof with the aid of a theorem prover. These methods can help prepare questions for university entrance examinations, and can also be applied to E-learning systems when questions are used to allow evaluation of student attainment levels. We conducted a small experiment, and the results show that this is a promising approach.

Keywords: Programming education · Rubric · Examination · Correctness proof · Invariant · Assertion

1 Introduction

The teaching of computer science and information technology, or informatics in general, is increasingly common not only in higher educational institutions but also in primary and secondary schools. This world-wide trend is especially prominent in Japan. The Japanese government has decided to introduce computer programming in primary schools in the next standard curriculum guideline that will take effect in 2020 [1]. The subject "Informatics I" of the high school curriculum will also be modernized

© IFIP International Federation for Information Processing 2019
Published by Springer Nature Switzerland AG 2019
A. Tatnall and N. Mavengere (Eds.): SUZA 2019, IFIP AICT 564, pp. 89–98, 2019.
https://doi.org/10.1007/978-3-030-28764-1_11

to include programming as a mandatory field of study (this is presently optional) [2, 3]. Given this trend, it is becoming increasingly important to assess student understanding of, and skill in, informatics. In a research project funded by the government and led by Osaka University [4], attainment levels for each field of high school informatics, including programming, have been formulated as "rubrics", and methods for assessment of student performance using these rubrics are under development.

To assess student attainment levels, it is necessary to create appropriate questions for each level of all rubrics. Obviously, such questions must be posed during high school education to allow adjustment of teaching methods and materials with reference to student attainment levels. Such questions can also be used when evaluating admission to Japanese universities. The government is now investigating the possibility of introducing Informatics to the common entrance examination run by the Center for University Entrance Examinations.

1.1   Goal

Here, we develop methods that automatically generate questions in the field of programming to assess students' understanding of programs; we use correctness proofs and a theorem prover to this end. Questions corresponding to each level of rubrics mentioned above are automatically generated from a single program featuring a correctness proof by analyzing the source code and the proof with the aid of a theorem prover. Our assumed target is the common entrance examination of Japanese universities mentioned in the previous section. Therefore, it should be possible to generate a large number of questions. Also, because the score of the examination need to be automatically evaluated, the format of questions should be true or false, multiple choice, or the like.

To achieve our goal, we use the methods of software engineering, including software verification and testing, to automatically generate programming questions; this is a field of study within Informatics. Although these technologies were developed to verify or test programs written by humans, we use them to test humans. These two applications are not contradictory. Advanced software verification and testing algorithms are intended to replace humans who test and debug programs. We therefore apply these technologies to test whether humans (i.e., students) have the required knowledge and skill for testing and debugging programs.

Here, we assume that a program features a correctness proof. Questions are then automatically generated corresponding to each level of rubrics. It is therefore not necessary to create different questions for different levels of the rubrics.

A correctness proof is obtained by reference to the given program pre-condition and post-condition; appropriate invariants of while-statements and lemmas are also given and referenced to derive the post-condition from the pre-condition. Our hypothesis is that invariants used in the correctness proof of a program play an important role in understanding the program. We do not require even those who make questions of examinations to write correctness proofs. It is sufficient for them to provide appropriate loop invariants.

For question generation, we also use the theorem prover as a Satisfiability Modulo Theories (SMT) solver. When appropriate constraints are automatically generated from the program and the correctness proof, the SMT solver solves the constraints and produces inputs or variable assignments that are used to generate questions.

This method allows the preparation of questions not only for university admission examinations but also for E-learning systems where the questions must reflect differences in student abilities.

1.2   Rubrics

Matsunaga and Hagiya have formulated rubrics for the attainment levels of each field of high-school informatics [5] as part of the research project (mentioned above) led by Osaka University [4]. The suggested rubrics for programming are shown in Table 1.

At the lowest level 1-1, students can recognize the description of a given program, and can thus understand the structure of a program (such as declarations and if-statements) by reference to the grammar of the programming language. At the next level 1-2, at which the first major level is entered, students can trace the program after a given input. At this level, students are required to understand the meaning of each construct of a program and mechanically execute the program given a concrete input. At level 2-1, students can explain what a given program does. This requires that they understand the goal or specification of the program and how the program meets that specification. At level 2-2, in addition to correctly understanding programs, students can modify a given program to attain a different goal or specification, or repair an incorrect program to meet a given specification.

Table 1. Rubrics for programming

1-1	Being able to recognize the description of a given program
1-2	Being able to trace the execution of a given program
2-1	Being able to explain what a given program does
2-2	Being able to modify or debug a given program to solve a given problem
3	Being able to design an algorithm and write a program to solve a given problem
4	Being able to improve an algorithm or a program to solve a given problem more effectively
5	Being able to evaluate and improve a program during program construction

1.3   Approach

By reference to the rubrics explained above, we took the following approach to automatically generate questions corresponding to the three levels of the rubrics.

As Rubric 1-2 requires students to trace the execution of a given program, we use questions that ask students to explain what will happen when the program is executed after a given input. We have developed a method that generates an input, after which the program follows a given (appropriate) execution path.

Rubric 2-1 requires students to explain what a given program does. Such an explanation of functionality requires comprehension of the assertion that is always true at each step of the program. Therefore, we use questions that ask students to distinguish between states that satisfy the assertion and those that do not. We have developed a method that generates two kinds of states at any given point of the program.

For Rubric 2-1, we also use questions to see if students understand dynamic behavior of a program. Those questions give a pair of states at a point of the program and ask students if one state of the pair can precede the other in a certain execution path.

Third kind of question for Rubric 2-1 gives a list of conditions and asks students if each condition in the list is always true during execution of the program.

As Rubric 2-2 requires students to repair an incorrect program, we use questions that ask students to fill a blank in the code by choosing the correct expression from certain candidate expressions. Our method generates appropriate incorrect expressions.

We mainly focus on the above three levels of the rubrics because these levels are considered relatively important in high school education and for common entrance examination.

2   Related Work

A great deal of effort has been devoted to the development of methods that automatically generate questions for use in programming education; it is very difficult to exhaustively review the systems that implement such methods. However, most systems, including those of Radošević et al. [6] and Wakayama and Maeda [7], are based on question templates. Therefore, different templates must be prepared for different kinds of questions.

In contrast to such systems, we do not use question templates but, rather, programs with correctness proofs. Furthermore, a single program with a correctness proof can be used to generate different kinds of questions; thus, those for the different rubric levels in the present instance.

As related work, we could mention assessment systems which automatically test and grade submissions by students [8]. Since they evaluate programs written for a given goal, they mainly evaluate student ability of designing algorithms and writing programs, and correspond to Rubric 3 and higher levels.

3   Methods

This section presents the methods that we use and example questions generated by these methods.

We detail the methods for Rubric 2-1 and outline the others, because examining students understanding of a program is the most challenging among the three levels of the rubrics.

Although our methods are applicable to any programming language, we adopt a subset of Python as our target language because (1) Python is currently widely recognized as a common language for teaching programming to novices, (2) we actually teach Python in some classes of our schools, and (3) various tools for formal verification and symbolic execution of Python programs are available. In particular, we employ PyExZ3 [9], a tool for dynamic symbolic execution of Python programs, for generating questions for Rubric 2-1.

As mentioned in the introduction, we assume that a program features a correctness proof, which is obtained from the given program pre-condition and post-condition together with appropriate assertions embedded in the program. Invariants are typical assertions that are put in loop statements.

Although a theorem prover is required to obtain a correctness proof, generation of questions for the three levels of the rubrics in this paper is possible only with appropriate assertions embedded in the program, as far as those assertions are correct. Therefore, the methods can be used with limited knowledge about formal verification or theorem proving.

3.1 Rubric 1-2

Rubric 1-2 indicates the level at which students can correctly trace the execution of a given program. To generate questions, our tool finds an input to the program that satisfies the program pre-condition and produces a path when the program is executed with this input. An execution path is presented to the tool as a sequence of truth values indicating the conditions imposed on if-statements and while-statements along the path.

To find such an input, the tool generates the path condition under which execution of the code should follow the given path. The tool does this by examining the if-statements and while-statements along the path. This process is similar to the symbolic execution of Pex [10]. Although Pex automatically searches for paths to take, the tool views the path instructions as inputs and follows them, which allows question difficulty to be controlled.

The tool then finds a solution featuring conjunction of the generated path condition and the program pre-condition, using the SMT solver Z3 [11, 12].

3.2 Rubric 2-1

Rubric 2-1 indicates the level at which students can explain the behavior of a given program. We assume that the post-condition can be proven from the pre-condition with the help of invariants and lemmas. Consequently, each statement of the program satisfies a certain assertion, which is derived from the program post-condition and the loop invariants of while-statements in the program. If the program commences with an input satisfying the pre-condition, the assertion of each statement holds prior to execution. We thus reduce the ability to explain the behavior of a program to that of comprehending the assertion of each statement in the program.

To determine whether students comprehend an assertion in the program, we take the following approach. Those inputs that satisfy the program pre-condition always satisfy the program assertions whereas states that violate a program assertion can never develop from a correct input. If students can discriminate correct from incorrect states, they are considered to comprehend the assertions and hence exhibit some understanding as to why the program behaves correctly.

To generate inputs that satisfy the pre-condition, the tool automatically creates an execution path that leads to the specified point of the program. The tool then traces the path and generates the path condition via symbolic execution, obtaining an input.

Incorrect states are those falsifying conditions confirmed to be valid. Since all correct states satisfy the conditions, we generate incorrect states by modifying correct ones. We make as few modifications as possible, so that obtained states appear to be correct. The SMT solver is called to find the new value that falsifies the conditions.

As for dynamic behavior, we choose conditions that are always satisfied by a pair of states along an execution path of a program. Correct pairs are obtained from actual execution paths of the program. Incorrect pairs are obtained by modifying correct ones so that the conditions are falsified.

Finally, incorrect conditions are obtained by modifying correct ones. For a candidate condition obtained from a correct one, we search for an execution path of a program that actually falsifies the condition.

The questions generated by the method for the bubble sort program are shown below.

Question 1: Assume that the function in Fig. 1 is executed and reaches the point L1. Answer whether the designated combination of values is possible or not.

(1) `len(lst)=6, i=2, j=5, lst[1]=8, lst[3]=2`.
(2) `len(lst)=6, i=1, j=4, lst[2]=5, lst[5]=5`.

The answers are: (1) is IMPOSSIBLE and (2) is POSSIBLE.

```
def bubblesort(lst):
    for j in range(len(lst) - 1):
        for i in range(len(lst) - 1 - j):
            if lst[i] > lst[i + 1]:
                lst[i + 1], lst[i] = lst[i], lst[i + 1]
            # L1
        # L2
```

Fig. 1. Source for bubble sort function

Question 2: Answer whether both of the following two conditions can be satisfied or not.

The function in Fig. 1 reaches the point L1 and has the combination of values shown at [Before].

The function continues to run and reaches the point L1 again to have the combination of values shown at [After].

(1) [Before] len(lst) = 6, j = 3, lst[4] = 4; [After] j = 2, lst[4] = 8
(2) [Before] len(lst) = 6, j = 5, lst[2] = 4; [After] j = 1, lst[2] = 2

The answers are: (1) is IMPOSSIBLE and (2) is POSSIBLE.

Question 3: Assume the function reaches the point L2 and 2 <= j <= len[lst] - 1 holds. Answer whether each of the following is always correct or not.

(1) lst[j-2] <= lst[j-1]
(2) lst[j-1] <= lst[j]

The answers are: (1) is NOT ALWAYS CORRECT and (2) is ALWAYS CORRECT.

To generate Question 1, we specify an assertion that essentially means "for any index k of lst, if k < i + 1, then lst[k] <= lst[i + 1]". The tool inserts instrumentation code similar to the following at the point L1:

```
show([[i,j,lst]])                    # (A)
show(alter(other,[i,j,lst]))   # (B)
```

Function show is also generated by the tool and contains code similar to the following:

```
for k in range(len(lst)):
  if k < i+1 and lst[k] > lst[i+1]:      # impossible
    .... print(k, i, lst, ...) ....
  elif k < i+1 and lst[k] <= lst[i+1]: # possible
    .... print(k, i, lst, ...) ....
  elif k >= i+1 and lst[k] < lst[i+1]: # possible
    .... print(k, i, lst, ...) ....
  ....
```

While function alter generates a list of states each of which is obtained by replacing the value of either i, j or an element of lst with the value of other.

The tool then runs PyExZ3 with the instrumented bubble sort function. Its dynamic symbolic execution mechanism runs the code symbolically, meaning that it tries to run every possible branch of each conditional and gives a concrete value for each variable when it meets the print function. Thus, instrumented code (A) shows reachable states from the branches marked as "possible". Code (B) shows unreachable states, due to the assertion, from the branch marked as "impossible".

3.3 Rubric 2-2

Rubric 2-2 indicates the level at which students are able to correct a given program that does not behave as intended. To evaluate whether students have achieved this level, we use incomplete or buggy code.

Our tool, therefore, generates expressions which, when used to replace original expressions at specified lines in the code, fail to satisfy some of the intended properties and, thus, the post-condition, a loop invariant, and/or the well-found nature of the measures.

4 Small Experiment

We conducted a small experiment of the proposed methods.

Twelve undergraduate students in School of Literature of a university participated in the experiment. They have learned programming languages, including Python, for a half to three years, but they have not spent much time in practicing programming. All of them have learned basic control structures of python (for and while statements) in a course, but none has taken courses of algorithms or data structures. Some of them have difficulties in comprehending nested loops.

Two functions written in Python were used. Question A asks about a function which counts even numbers included in a given integer list. The function used in Question B receives a list of positive integers and a positive integer. It removes occurrences of the integer from the list, moves the remaining integers forward (to smaller indices), and pads the emptied positions with zeroes.

All the questions correspond to Rubric 2-1. Question A has two sub-questions A-1 and A-2, while Question B has three, B-1, B-2 and B-3. Each sub-question has four to eight cases that the examinee answers either true or false. Sub-questions A-i and B-i are in the form of Question i in Sect. 3.2.

The examinees were given 30 min to answer the questions. After they completed, the authors conducted an interview for each examinee to evaluate their understanding of the source code.

The results are shown on Table 2. An ID from 01 to 12 is given to each examinee. The number of different cases for each sub-question is shown in parentheses under the sub-question number; there are six cases for A-1, for example. The table shows the number of correct answers of each examinee for each sub-question. The columns of "A-eval" and "B-eval" show the authors' evaluation of examinees' understanding for each function through the interview. Label "Y" indicates an examinee who showed good understanding and "N" is given to those who poorly understand the code.

From the results, some statistics are calculated as follows.

For the two groups "Y" and "N", the Mann-Whitney U value of the sum of A-1 and A-2 is 2.5 and the p-value (for two-sided) is 0.043. The U value of the sum of B-1, B-2 and B-3 is 5.0 and the p-value is 0.045.

Spearman's rank correlation coefficients of a few combinations of the scores of sub-questions are shown in Table 3. Although a couple of combinations show correlation to some extent, we cannot draw definite conclusions from the results due to the numbers of questions and examinees.

The interview revealed several issues on the experiment.

The text of questions contains explanation of the function. A number of students answered the questions, not based on their reading of the source code, but relying on the explaining text. This type of explanation should not be removed entirely because it would give the examinee an excessive burden, but we may need to investigate appropriate expression in the text.

Some students felt difficulties in grasping the state expressions. For example, State (1) of Question 1 in Sect. 3.2 consists of five equalities including two indices of a list. Although all information is needed, this long enumeration may distract the examinee.

In this experiment, we did not precisely define the criteria with which the examinees are divided into two groups. The grouping was done based on the authors' impression and could be biased by various factors. Moreover, the number of examinees is small. We plan to conduct another experiment with improved questions, grouping methods and a larger number of examinees.

Table 2. Scores of examinees

ID	A-1 (6)	A-2 (4)	A-eval	B-1 (6)	B-2 (6)	B-3 (8)	B-eval
01	1	2	Y	2	3	5	Y
02	6	2	Y	4	3	4	Y
03	6	2	Y	6	5	1	Y
04	5	3	Y	4	4	0	N
05	5	2	Y	6	4	5	Y
06	6	2	Y	4	0	0	N
07	2	3	N	0	0	0	N
08	5	3	Y	6	6	8	Y
09	3	2	N	2	2	6	N
10	5	4	Y	5	5	7	Y
11	0	3	N	2	5	4	N
12	4	2	Y	3	5	5	N

Table 3. Correlation coefficients

Sub-questions	ρ	p-value
A-1 and A-2	0.25	0.43
B-1 and B-2	0.54	0.07
B-2 and B-3	0.50	0.09
B-1 and B-3	0.25	0.42

5   Concluding Remarks

As shown in previous sections, the tools that we have developed for Rubric 1-2, Rubric 2-1, and Rubric 2-2 can automatically generate questions to some extent. The tools can potentially aid the production of the large number of questions required for university entrance examinations. However, this requires human intervention at many stages. For example, additional constraints are necessary to avoid trivial questions because some incorrect states at a specified point can be immediately rejected by examining previous statements. Such constraints can be automatically generated by analyzing previous statements.

Since the tools can currently generate questions for only Rubrics 1-2, 2-1, and 2-2, it must be extended to generate questions for other rubrics. Rubric 1-1 seems relatively easy; we can insert grammatical errors to correct programs and ask students to detect them as we insert semantic errors for Rubric 2-2. For Rubric 3, methods developed for automatic assessment systems can be applied in the case of computer-based examination.

Finally, empirical evaluation of the quality of the questions generated, which extends the reported small experiment, is required. In fact, experimental testing of students using questions generated by our tool and evaluation of the effectiveness of our methods with a larger number of examinees are currently planned as part of the research project mentioned in Sect. 1 [4]. For such experiments, more questions must be generated from programs with correctness proofs.

Acknowledgment. This work was supported by Research on Evaluation Method in the Subject of Informatics for University Admission Examinations Based on Computational Approach supported by Ministry of Education, enPiT Pro Project supported by Ministry of Education, and JSPS KAKENHI Grant Number 16K00109.

References

1. MEXT, Curriculum guideline for high school, 2018 (in Japanese). http://www.mext.go.jp/a_menu/shotou/new-cs/1384661.htm
2. Hagiya, M.: Defining informatics across Bun-kei and Ri-kei. J. Inf. Process. **23**(4), 525–530 (2015). https://doi.org/10.2197/ipsjjip.23.525
3. Nakayama, Y., et al.: Current situation of teachers of informatics at high schools in Japan. Olympiads Inf. **12**, 177–185 (2018)
4. Research and Development of Assessment Methods in Selection of Applicants to Universities in the subject "Informatics" from Approach Based on Informatics (in Japanese). http://www.uarp.ist.osaka-u.ac.jp/index.html
5. Matsunaga, K., Hagiya, M.: Characterization of thinking, judging and expressing in the rubrics of common subject "Information". In: The 10th Congress of National High School Informatics Education Study Group (2017). (in Japanese)
6. Radošević, D., Orehovački, T., Stapić, Z.: Automatic on-line generation of student's exercises in teaching programming. In: Central European Conference on Information and Intelligent Systems, CECIIS 2010, pp. 7 (2010)
7. Wakatani, A., Maeda, T.: Evaluation of software education using auto-generated exercises. In: 2016 IEEE International Conference on Computational Science and Engineering, IEEE International Conference on Embedded and Ubiquitous Computing, and International Symposium on Distributed Computing and Applications to Business, Engineering and Science, pp. 732–735 (2016)
8. Douce, C., Livingstone, D., Orwell, J.: Automatic test-based assessment of programming: a review. J. Educ. Res. Comput. **5**(3), 4 (2005)
9. Ball, T., Daniel, J.: Deconstructing dynamic symbolic execution. In: Proceedings of the 2014 Marktober Summer School on Dependable Software Systems Engineering (2015)
10. Tillmann, N., de Halleux, J.: Pex–White Box Test Generation for .NET. In: Beckert, B., Hähnle, R. (eds.) TAP 2008. LNCS, vol. 4966, pp. 134–153. Springer, Heidelberg (2008). https://doi.org/10.1007/978-3-540-79124-9_10
11. de Moura, L., Bjørner, N.: Z3: an efficient SMT solver. In: Ramakrishnan, C.R., Rehof, J. (eds.) TACAS 2008. LNCS, vol. 4963, pp. 337–340. Springer, Heidelberg (2008). https://doi.org/10.1007/978-3-540-78800-3_24
12. The Z3 Theorem Prover. https://github.com/Z3Prover/z3

Principles for the Design of an Educational Voice Assistant for Learning Java

Carlos Delgado Kloos[(✉)], Carlos Alario-Hoyos,
Pedro J. Muñoz-Merino, Cristina Catalán Aguirre,
and Nuria González Castro

Universidad Carlos III de Madrid,
Av. Universidad, 30, 28911 Leganés, Madrid, Spain
{cdk, calario, pedmume}@it.uc3m.es,
crcatala@pa.uc3m.es, nurigonz@db.uc3m.es

Abstract. Conversational agents, be they text- or voice-powered, are acquiring a level of maturity that makes them useful for natural and smart interactions. In this paper, we explore some design principles for voice-commanded assistants for educational use, in particular, of one designed to train Java concepts as a complement to a MOOC (Massive Open Online Course) about programming.

Keywords: Conversational agents · Voice assistants · VUI · MOOCs · Java teaching · Design decisions

1 Voice Assistants for Education

We have seen improvements in the human-machine interface of computing systems over the last years and with increased speed in recent times. Apart from graphical user interfaces with touch features and multiple sensors, recently voice recognition technology is making a breakthrough.

Conversational agents with natural language understanding and machine learning allow it to maintain quite reasonable conversations in a very natural way without the user having to follow strict predefined commands. Voice assistants like Amazon Alexa, Google Assistant or Siri embodied in smartphones or smart speakers are entering the life of many users. From getting information (weather, traffic, news, etc.) to automating the home (lights, music, plugs, etc.), a wealth of use cases is coming up. This opens also interesting new opportunities for education that have not been fully explored yet.

MOOC (Massive Open Online Course) platforms like edX or Coursera showed the world that technology was ripe for more learning scenarios that had not been harnessed before. Cloud computing as the basis for video hosting, interactive quizzes, forums, and embedded tools allowed bringing educational experiences around the world. Their openness has brought new opportunities to disadvantaged populations. MOOCs are massive, but they are also personal. Learners can view videos at their own pace, do quizzes when they want, but can education be made even more personal?

Voice assistants are personal assistants in the sense that they allow learners to be involved in a useful learning conversation. In the literature, there exist some initiatives

A. Tatnall and N. Mavengere (Eds.): SUZA 2019, IFIP AICT 564, pp. 99–106, 2019.
https://doi.org/10.1007/978-3-030-28764-1_12

of the use of conversational agents for education. The web site for Google Assistant [1] references many agents developed for educational purposes. Often, they just cover small goals. The work of Demetriadis et al. [2] uses conversational agents to interact together with learners in MOOC discussion forums. Our approach differs from the one of Demetriades in the sense that our assistant should be used in a one-to-one conversation with each learner, rather than being an additional partner with a multitude of learners in a forum.

2 Java-PAL

We have developed an educational program on the edX platform with a series of three MOOCs to learn programming in Java. The program is available both in English [3] and in Spanish [4]. Combined they have had close to half a million registrations in several runs so far. Learners have come from all over the world: 210 countries have been reported. Apart from the rich resources already offered through the platform, we wanted to offer the learner an additional learning experience through a voice assistant.

Java-PAL is an application with which students learn about the basic concepts of Java programming shown in the first of our three Java MOOCs. One of the main purposes of Java-PAL is to offer our learners concepts of Java programming based on what they have already studied [5, 6]. Java-PAL is programmed with Actions on Google. A prototype is available on smartphones and also on smart speakers like Google Home. Later on, we envisage to improve the present version with videos to be shown on devices like Google Home Hub and compatible devices.

3 Design Principles

Apart from the technical design decisions, which are described elsewhere [5, 6], we want to focus in this paper on some basic underlying design decisions that we have followed for Java-PAL. Usage modes of a web-based learning tool is quite different from one based on voice interactions.

In this paper, we summarize some principles we have inferred from our present experience. Figure 1 shows 5 of the 6 design principles:

- User-Friendliness with a Quality Conversation. A quality conversation is essential to engage the learner. We want to encourage the learner to be comfortable with the assistant and continue exploration. Style and content of the conversation have to be properly designed. Among others, messages of encouragement should be considered for the persona underlying the assistant.
- Overview for Conceptual Navigation. When learning about one concept, we want to offer the learner related concepts. Therefore, an underlying concept map is useful in order in order to connect to related concepts.
- Flexibility with Several Interaction Modes. Along the same lines, we want to allow the learner to be able to have different exploration modes. Such can be the direct request for the explanation of a concept, or for an example of a concept.

Alternatively, the learner should be able to let the assistant take the initiative and pose questions.

– Personalization to Learner Preferences. The assistant should be aware of each specific learner and their history and preferences to personalize the interaction individually.

– Adaptation to Device Affordances. Due to the proliferation of devices with different features, it is key to recognize the affordances and deliver the best experience in the context of the affordances available.

Fig. 1. 5 design principles

Apart from the first principle, a quality conversation, the other four represent adaptation to different aspects. The learner preferences principle adapts to the learner, the device affordances principle adapts to the device, the conceptual navigation principle adapts to the topic under study, and the interaction mode principle adapts to the mood and need at each moment.

There is a sixth principle. Such a tool is never the definitive one. A tool has to be maintained, adapted, evolved to changing specifications and insights. Evolvability and extensibility need to be considered from the very beginning of the design process. This takes us the principle No. 6.

– Extensibility for Future Evolution. Although we have designed our assistant initially for the teaching of Java, we should be able to adapt it to other MOOCs by changing content as easily as possible. Also, new devices, new usage modes, new pedagogies, etc. could all imply the evolution of our conversational agent.

Let's analyze these principles in closer detail.

3.1 User-Friendliness with a Quality Conversation

In a similar way as there are theories to design a user-friendly GUI (graphical user interface) [10], a VUI (voice user interface) needs to follow some guidelines. Grice [11] defines four proposals to maximize several aspects of a conversation. The assistant should maximize the amount of information provided (maxim of quantity) at each interaction, but only to the level that is relevant (maxim of relevance). It should also communicate clearly (maxim of manner) and cooperate with the user (maxim of quality). The assistant should engage with the user in a cooperative conversation.

When designing a conversational agent, it is necessary to give it a persona, a personality. It is very important not to design a cold relationship between learner and assistant, but to have one which is warm and welcoming. May the learner fail often or give all answers right, scheduling messages of encouragement is always right. Misunderstandings need to be handled well, time-outs be well thought of, in summary, the flow of conversation needs to be right.

3.2 Overview for Conceptual Navigation

In contrast to studying with the MOOC, where the learning sequence plays a preeminent role, we expect the usage of Java-PAL to be more sporadic, exploratory and playful. The learner might want to jump from one concept to a related one. For example, if the user is learning about expressions we can suggest to look at the concept of variable or at different kinds of operators, because they have a direct relationship. Or if the learner doesn't fully understand the concept of a statement, we can recommend him to look at concepts such as conditional statement and repetition.

The concepts and the relationships between them can be defined with a concept map. Our first approach was to use existing terminology that can be found in ontology literature, such as the work in [7] or [8], but it was difficult to establish the relationships between the concepts in which our Java MOOC is based on. Moreover, the main purpose of the application is not related to the kind of relationship between the concepts, but with the existence of a relationship itself. Thanks to the ontology defined (see Fig. 2), we are able to offer the learners related concepts based on their educational needs.

Fig. 2. Ontology of concepts

3.3   Flexibility with Several Interaction Modes

Learning that happens through dialog (also called dialogic learning [9]) has been proved to be more effective than education based on monologs. Learners take a more active role when they are involved in a conversation. We also wanted to provide our assistant with more than one mode of operation. Offering the learner different operation modes can make the dialog more refreshing and fluent.

There is a first mode where users can ask for definitions or examples of Java concepts that they need for clarification and understanding, or just the ones related to the questions they are not able to answer correctly. In this mode, users take the initiative of asking anything, but then the assistant can lead the teaching conversation offering related concepts. Then there is a second mode, where the assistant takes the initiative, and asks learners questions related to the concepts studied, to check their knowledge. Finally, we found it interesting to have a feedback mode for self-development, where learners will be given the results of their performance during the quizzes, so they can know their strong and weak points, while also giving some encouragement and congratulations.

There are also some extra interesting features that we considered important to make the Java-PAL more appealing to the end users. They will be able to change some personalized settings, like the name to be called and the number of questions they would like to be asked. We wanted our Java-PAL to be able to adapt to possible or future changes in the users requirements; we are opened to listen to the users feedback, and add some other properties in the next versions.

3.4   Personalization to Learner Preferences

Personalized learning provides each learner with different specific user experience depending on many different parameters that conform a user model [12]. Personalization can help to improve the learning process. This learner profile can be obtained by different means: (1) the users introduce their preferences, feelings, behaviours, etc. directly, e.g. with a form; (2) there is an automatic detection of these features through students' interactions with the learning platform.

Adaptive learning for hypermedia systems can adapt the contents or the presentation [12]. In our voice assistant we are mainly focused on the personalization of contents, specifically in the adaptation of questions to students and in the adaptation of the recommended resources if a student fails a question. The personalization can be provided taken into account a user model (e.g., a basic one might only be based on the student knowledge on different skills) and the specific contents and their relationships (given by a proposed ontology).

The student model can include interactions from different platforms (e.g., by the Learning Management System but also with the voice assistant) and the data from different sources can be combined to detect some student feature. An ontology might also be used to provide interoperability at the semantic level among these different systems.

The content model given by the ontology provides some extensibility and interoperability at the semantic level. Concepts that are used in different platforms (e.g., in a MOOC or in a voice assistant) have a common meaning and relationships with other concepts based on the proposed ontology.

3.5   Adaptation to Device Affordances

Voice assistants are increasingly being integrated into a larger number of devices. Traditionally, voice assistants have been used only through desktop/laptop computers or mobile devices (smartphones, tablets), where the user has a screen to facilitate oral communication, including images or videos when needed, and a keyboard, to write in case there is a misunderstanding in the communication between user and voice assistant.

However, 2018 was the year of smart speakers (and a turning point for voice assistants), with Google Home, Amazon Echo or Apple HomePod at the fore-front.

These devices only allow an oral communication, since they do not bring any built-in screen or keyboard, forcing to simplify the communication between user and assistant. The next generation of smart devices will once again incorporate a screen, as is the case with Google Home Hub, allowing richer interactions between voice assistant and user.

But that is not all, there are hybrid situations in which the main source of communication with a voice assistant may be an oral conversation, but accompanied by small visual indications. This would be the case while driving in the car, as much visual information can turn into a distraction and cause loss of contact with the road, but small visual indications can help to better understand and follow the oral conversation.

All in all, a voice assistant for education must take into account the device with which the learner works, and its context, and adapt its interactions accordingly. For example, in an educational environment where the user gets questions, explanations, and examples from a smart speaker connected to a voice assistant, these need to be short and concrete, without the possibility of attaching an explanatory image or video. Nevertheless, in other contexts, in which it is possible to include visual support, more complex questions, explanations and examples can be used.

3.6   Extensibility for Future Evolution

Extensibility refers to the fact that a minimum number of changes should be done in order to make the application to work in other contexts, e.g., to other courses of a different domain, including new sources of data or with courses with different questions.

The voice assistant application should be as extensible as possible. There will be a part of the application that will be common. There will also be some parts of the application that should be replaced depending on the context.

The common parts include: (1) the semantic models with the ontologies that can model the user or even the contents if they are in the same domain; and (2) some algorithms for adaptation and personalization.

Among the changing parts are the ontology (it should be adapted to the domain but the defined relationships should be used in any contexts), the own questions and the annotations of the different resources (questions and contents).

4   Conclusion

As Anant Agarwal, CEO of edX, says, education will be omni-channel. Learners will want to use multiple devices that are synchronized to offer a convenient learning experience. Laptops and smartphones each have their specific features and moments for which they are the best fit. Now voice assistants have entered the scene with their limitations and promises offering an interesting complement to the existing landscape.

We have presented in this paper some decisions that have guided the design of a voice assistant for learning Java. We believe that voice assistants can be an important added value to existing learning methods and that we are just scratching the surface of what is possible with voice-operated applications.

Acknowledgments. This work has been partially funded by FEDER/Ministerio de Ciencia, Innovaci´ony Universidades - Agencia Estatal de Investigaci´on/Smartlet project (TIN2017-85179-C3-1-R). In addition, this work has been partially funded by the e-Madrid-CM project with grant No. S2018/TCS-4307, which is funded by the Madrid Regional Government (Comunidad de Madrid), by the Fondo Social Europeo (FSE) and by the Fondo Europeo de Desarrollo Regional (FEDER).

References

1. https://assistant.google.com/explore/c/3/?hl=en-US. Accessed May 2019
2. Demetriadis, S., et al.: Conversational agents as group-teacher interaction mediators in MOOCs. In: Learning with MOOCs 2018, Madrid, Spain, pp. 43–46. IEEE (2018)
3. Kloos, C.D., et al.: Introduction to Java Programming, professional certificate program in English, edX. www.edx.org/professional-certificate/uc3mx-introduction-java-programming. Accessed May 2019
4. Kloos, C.D., et al.: Introducción a la programación en Java, professional certificate program in Spanish, edX. www.edx.org/es/professional-certificate/uc3mx-introduccion-a-la-progra macion-en-java. Accessed May 2019
5. Aguirre, C.C., Kloos, C.D., Alario-Hoyos, C., Muñoz-Merino, P.J.: Supporting a MOOC through a conversational agent. Design of a first prototype. In: 20th International Symposium on Computers in Education (SIIE), Cádiz, Spain, pp. 1–6. IEEE (2018)
6. Kloos, C.D., Catalan, C., Muñoz-Merino, P.J., Alario-Hoyos, C.: Design of a conversational agent as an educational tool. In: Learning with MOOCs 2018, Madrid, Spain, pp. 27–30. IEEE (2018)
7. John, S.: Development of an Educational Ontology for Java Programming (JLEO) with a hybrid methodology derived from conventional software engineering process models. Int. J. Inf. Educ. Technol. **4**(4), 308–312 (2018)
8. Boyce, S., Pahl, C.: Developing domain ontologies for course content. Int. Forum Educ. Technol. Soc. **10**(3), 275–288 (2007)
9. Flecha, R.: Sharing Words: Theory and Practice of Dialogic Learning. Rowman & Littlefield, Lanham (2000)
10. Nielsen, J.: Designing Web Usability: The Practice of Simplicity. New Riders Publishing, San Francisco (1999)
11. Grice, H.P.: Logic and conversation. In: Cole, P., Morgan, J. (eds.) Syntax and Semantics, vol. 3, pp. 22–40. Academic Press, Cambridge (1975)
12. Brusilovsky, P.: Methods and techniques of adaptive hypermedia. User Model. User-Adap. Interact. **6**(2–3), 87–129 (1996)

Institutional Project-Based Learning: Evidence from a Multi-actor e-Government Reform

Endrit Kromidha$^{(\boxtimes)}$ (iD)

University of Birmingham, Birmingham, UK
e.kromidha@bham.ac.uk

Abstract. This study contributes by providing a conceptual framework around learning in public administration reforms. Large e-government projects through which reforms are introduced often involve multiple organisations, they are complex, require a careful consideration of power and have a long institutional impact on society. Project-based learning (PBL) and institutional theory from public administration studies form the theoretical framework this study builds upon. Findings suggest that learning in public administration reforms in the context of a developing country is characterised by strategic, constructive and reflective practices that follow each other in cycle along project implementation stages. The unit of analysis in this study is project organisations instead of students or employees where project-based learning has been traditionally applied, making the contributions of this study unique and relevant not only for project managers, but also for policy makers, local policy leaders and international organisations.

Keywords: Public sector · Project-based learning · Institutional theory · e-government · Developing country

1 Introduction

Learning in the public sector can be a painful, but necessary process that happens between imitation and innovation [35]. There has been a growing interest in organizational learning in the public sector [12] as an approach to continuous improvement, knowledge acquisition, and creation. While Finger and Brand [12] argue that public sector agencies should be transformed into learning organizations, they provide little evidence of how this happens in practice.

Recently there is a shift towards participatory public decision-making [20, 39] and open innovation [11]. Other innovation models in the public sector domain have become more focused by taking a closer look at projects [1], their risk management [19], agile configuration [6] and even investments [2]. The complexity of multiple overlapping projects has been followed by research on semantic models of shared knowledge management [43]. These approaches are extended even to user cantered models for rural development through e-government projects [26]. Policy intervention models in support of e-government for developing countries have also been attempted [5] by taking a best-practice perspective.

© IFIP International Federation for Information Processing 2019
Published by Springer Nature Switzerland AG 2019
A. Tatnall and N. Mavengere (Eds.): SUZA 2019, IFIP AICT 564, pp. 107–116, 2019.
https://doi.org/10.1007/978-3-030-28764-1_13

Such previous studies, however, take for granted and do not say much about the learning process that takes place during most e-government innovation projects. This study intends to address this gap by adapting an institutional theory perspective on project-based learning perspectives to explore the following research question: How does institutional learning happens in internationally assisted e-government reforms for development?

2   Institutional Theory and Project-Based Learning in e-Government

According to March and Olsen [27–34] an institution can broadly be described as an enduring collection of rules and practices around structures of meaning and resources [29]. Institutionalizing not only policy implementation changes, but also the very process that institutionalized them is a major issue of governance that often relates to project-based learning.

Although institutions are often resilient to change, they can be designed, especially in a political context, influenced by actors and preferred solutions in collective public choices [8, 9]. Interregional institutional learning is the next level where learning is presented along a cycle of encoding, conceptualization, operationalization, and experimentation between regions [14], a framework that differs little from an explanation of social exchanges [41]. More research in this later direction considers the transfers of power among e-government project actors [23] and adaptive power of social-ecological systems towards change, and conflict resolution [13]. Many of these studies are informed by the ideas of New Public Management (NPM) that tries to use business management concepts in the public sector context [10]. They conclude that learning in public administration reforms is not a simple transfer of knowledge from those who know more to those who know less, but rather a complex process dispersed among adaptation, exchanges, transformation, intermediation and acceptance.

Project-based learning (PBL) on the other hand focuses on learning around and from projects based on five criteria: centrality, questioning, constructive investigation, autonomy and realism [40]. A key principle of PBL is learning by doing [3]. The model has been successfully applied not only in classroom settings but also in workplaces to solve problems through learning projects [38]. Learning in workplace settings is characterised by a combination of organisational and individual spaces and processes [15, 16], taking a reflective and contextual approach [17]. Although PBL has traditionally been applied to classroom settings, there is scope for the model to be adapted to any project setting, building on existing research on learning in organisational settings. However, what is different in the context of e-government public sector reforms is the involvement of multiple and often temporarily-connected organisations connected by power relationships and institutional forces [23, 24]. The unit of analysis for learning in this case should be the project and the involved stakeholder organisations instead of one organisation and its employees or the teacher and student relationship in classroom settings.

PBL suggests that technology can support students and teachers as they work on projects to sustain motivation and thought [3]. These would be desirable outcomes in any e-government project reform aiming to institutionalize new practices among all project stakeholders and citizens. However, creativity, technology innovation and in general change presents a number of challenges and risks that in organizational settings are controlled through organizational structures [18], but building such learning organisations that can facilitate the smooth implementation of innovation and change projects is not easy [21]. Research on learning in public administration is limited and often around organizational culture, but there is some recognition of the relationship between projects and learning [25]. However, when multiple public and private organisations are involved like in the case of e-government project reforms present another level of complexity where institutional forces in that case replace the organisational structures mentioned early.

To unfold and explore PBL through the lenses of institutional theory this study aims to propose a conceptual framework that can capture both the project-based learning interactions, and the more longitudinal relationship among project actors beyond a specific project itself. This is necessary to reconcile the differences between the two approaches, PBL being short-term and contingency focuses, and institutional theory being long-term focused.

3   The Case Study Methodology

The case study evidence [44] for this interpretivist analysis [42] is based on the implementation of the electronic register of civil status in Albania. The multi-actor project was assisted by international donors such as the European Union, the Organization for Security and Cooperation in Europe, and Statistics Norway. This research was part of larger research project, conducted in 2010–2012, a period when the project was fully implemented and managed by the government of Albania, and the international donors.

This study started with a careful documentary review [4], analysing 74 documents consisting of national information and communication technology strategies, government programmes, project related documents, legislation, and final project reports. The review of these public materials allowed a better understanding of the projects to design the semi-structured interview strategy and questions.

The primary empirical evidence for this study was collected through semi-structured interviews [22] as part of a larger project on the institutionalisation of e-government reforms in developing countries. In total 16 interviews were conducted with government officials, top and middle project managers from the various organisations involved. This includes a focus group with 4 front and back-office employees of the General Directorate of Civil Status, the leading organisation responsible for the e-government project reform.

The documentary review and semi-structured interviews focused on three main areas informed by the earlier discussion on PBL and institutional theory: 1. The project implementation process, 2. Their role in it, 3. Institutionalization of practices and learning on an individual and organizational level. These three broad themes formed the basis for the coding structure and analysis of the findings [36] presented in the following section.

4 Findings

The development and modernisation of the National Register of Civil Status was a very important learning process for all parties involved. The first and most obvious element was coded in the analysis of data as 'learning from abroad', referring to all the know-how brought by the international assistance, imported from outsourcing foreign companies, and lessons learned from world best practices. The reason is clearly given by a specialist in the Department of Strategy and Donors Coordination in the Council of Ministers as follows:

"It is also a security issue I would say, because if someone has tried it before, we don't need to experiment. It has a standard. Now you find the funds, you take it and treat it the same way. You don't start from A but from Z and you are sure."

This statement highlights the security of implementing proven project practices, expressing confidence on the ability of Albanian authorities and users to adapt the lessons learned and changes to local needs. In this case, local parties had to make use of their experience with the old system and combine such lessons learned with a ready-given new National Register of Civil Status. Speaking in these practical terms, one of such lessons adapted in Albania were, for example, the adaptation of manuals used for the electronic register of civil status or addresses, as a specialist who worked for the General Directorate of Civil Status explains:

"But for as far as the technical part is concerned, I can say as I said before, there was a manual based on which we were working. So, a model of work was created, based on the examples of similar work models in Europe."

Local authorities were involved to create these manuals, contributing with their experience, but the 2.5 million Euros of assistance for the project came from the European Union. What appears like learning from best practices for the government, translates into enforced changes for the users. Here are two examples that support this argument. The first is a quote from an interview with a representative of the National Agency of Information Society, talking about the adaptation of e-government stages, their methodology, and evaluation in Albania:

"We have seen and analysed how Europe monitors this. [...] We have analysed these, we have tried to adjust them for our country, and this is easy for as long as you monitor the situation by monitoring the web page, because when we want to look at use, then we have to conduct surveys with the users."

Trying to understand how end-users learn the use of new systems, or even learning from them, appears difficult from her words. Instead, as many other best practices in Europe, they end up with an easy but less accurate top-down approach based on assumptions.

The second example is from a representative of the Department of Strategy and Donor Coordination in the Council of Ministers. He talks on the importance of top-down communication to promote strategies or otherwise lessons learned, and to-be-implemented reforms like the modernisation of National Register of Civil Status:

"Part of our system of integrated planning is a strategy of communication which is also on the web site. It explains how all our objectives are promoted and how it is monitored."

Learning from and about citizens appears to be a bigger challenge for the government, than it was for end-users to become used to the new system. Indeed, objectives are developed and promoted from top to bottom, but there is no strong evidence of a parallel bottom-up approach.

The government of Albania sees a learning challenge related to the education and literacy levels. This is how a representative of the Ministry of Innovation and Information Technology explains this situation:

"The strategies in our field of information society are, how to say this, even if 20% of population will absorb them only, that is a great step, because these strategies are related not only to information technology, but also to education. Education has a great influence. But for the time it takes for the new generation to finish school and enter our cycle of policy-making, it takes at least a cycle of 10 years."

The time constrains to achieve such long-term goals tend to justify the current approach of enforced changes and adaptation. Thus, enforced fast-track learning of the electronic National Register of Civil Status appears to have been the norm during the project implementation stage. The bottom-line in terms of transfers of knowledge and learning is the utilitarian view of a project coordinator from OSCE, the donor agency, focusing on the end results:

"The system is in place and it works. [...] Regular investment into human resources are needed in terms of training, in terms of latest know-how, latest developments."

The interview where this statement was taken happened only a few months before the OSCE assistance was officially and ultimately over for this project in Albania. All the local and foreign staff like the interviewee in this case was dismissed. The system clearly works, but beyond the clear reporting picture presented by the OSCE's representative, an official of the General Directorate of Civil status has a more critical approach to the control of expertise and knowledge by the assisting third parties:

"Since OSCE started, it is helping us with trainings, financing trainings for our staff, to take over the system of the civil status, because still the system is under the control of the Austrian party. We are simply users. To acquire the knowledge to administer the system ourselves, they offer, OSCE offers support for our trainings."

Local authorities and citizens have learned how to use the electronic National Register of Civil Status. The question is whether the Albanian structures are capable of managing and further developing the system, or international assistance was and will always be indispensable. A representative of the assisting agency, OSCE, leaves the responsibility for such decisions with the Albanian parties by giving the following answer about dissemination of experiences and learning:

"Success stories implemented by Albania are ready to be multiplied in different countries, there is no doubt. So again, there are some lessons learned. Look what works, share that, see what doesn't work, what are the mistakes, inform partners about that and ask them to adjust it"

Calling the project a success story is related to its potential to be successfully disseminated elsewhere, but it is exactly the part on "inform partners about that and ask them to adjust it" that the Albanian specialist before doesn't like. The OSCE representative talks but is still sceptical about the learning and development of local capabilities in Albania. The former Albanian technician on the other hand perceives this policy as undermining his jobs' independence and creating a sense of dependency on international assistance.

It is clear from the evidence in this study that learning from international practices and assistance has been adapted successfully in Albania. The National Register of Civil Status was a success story in this sense being easily institutionalized among end-users. However, to preserve and advance the progress achieved so far, the policy-makers must learn how to learn from citizens and understand them better. While the top-down learning has been institutionalized and disseminated, this bottom-up approach has not yet been fully integrated in the Albanian public administration.

5   Discussion

Operationalizing the findings of this study, the following conceptual framework based on PBL and institutional theory is proposed to have a better understanding of learning stages in e-government innovation projects.

This diagram summarizes the key lessons about institutional learning from this study. A key lesson learned is that embedding the institutional knowledge into the people and not only in the system and technology being implemented is crucial to e-government project implementation as evidenced also by Chung et al. [7]. However, for the institutionalization of such reforms, learning should focus on local acceptance, as well as capabilities for the development and maintenance of the systems. Building on existing knowledge on organizational culture and learning in public administration [25], institutional learning is explained better through the PBL approach.

This study shows that although institutionalizing the sustainability of reforms often starts with the technical assistance and involvement of the donors, it is finally shaped by the local managers and end-users. Needs and vision of the key actors are what guide the procurement and management of resources. Implementation of reforms in this regard is supported by training on accredited practices proposed by the intervention of change enablers, their expert knowledge, and most importantly some positive political will. Learning actors can be divided in two groups: supporters and resisters, influenced by the costs and benefits resulting from the change. The integration and dissemination of learning among other structures, and furthermore its institutionalization seems to depend more on their ability to coordinate their actions than on the needs of end-users (Fig. 1).

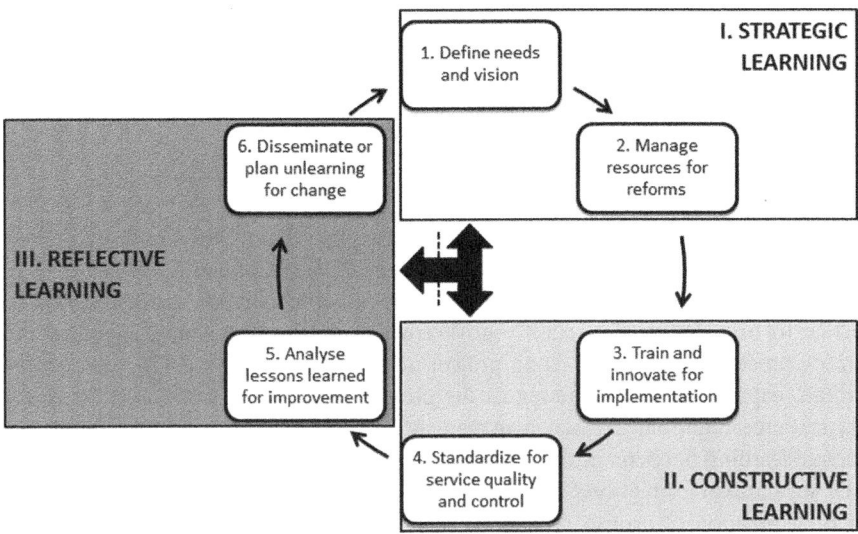

Fig. 1. Institutional learning cycle e-government innovation projects

This study shows that although institutionalizing the sustainability of reforms often starts with the technical assistance and involvement of the donors, it is finally shaped by the local managers and end-users. Needs and vision of the key actors are what guide the procurement and management of resources. Implementation of reforms in this regard is supported by training on accredited practices proposed by the intervention of change enablers, their expert knowledge, and most importantly some positive political will. Learning actors can be divided in two groups: supporters and resisters, influenced by the costs and benefits resulting from the change. The integration and dissemination of learning among other structures, and furthermore its institutionalization seems to depend more on their ability to coordinate their actions than on the needs of end-users.

Information technologies assist learning to be embedded into the very systems and automated procedures the people using them must perform, acquiring a momentum of their own. This is typical on an operational level. Yet, it is exactly this automation of learning we see in e-government reforms that raises technology above human reflection and critical thinking, thus putting at risk further development and innovation.

Unlearning appears to be one of the most difficult elements to accept and consider in the public sector, especially if it has to be applied on so-called modern structures like e-government reforms. Yet, it is a necessary process for the recognition of learned practices and validation of lessons learned. Unlearning on the other hand is a difficult but necessary process that allows further change and development in e-government reforms [37]. Without it most structures are limited within their constructive learning stage of short-term solutions to immediate problems, automation and institutionalization of practices that tend to become irrational with time and development in other sectors.

Undoubtedly, there has been a marked improvement in the efficiency and performance of service delivery in the two case studies. The key question here is the extent to which it can be replicated in other public sector organizations, particularly in those agencies that deliver less definable outputs or whose front-line staff have considerable discretion.

6 Conclusion

Reflecting on the definition of institutions given by March and Olsen as enduring collection of rules and practices around structures of meaning and resources [29], it is possible to conclude that project-based learning should become an institutionalized practice for successful multi-actor e-government reforms. This study identified three learning processes happening along project implementation stages. The first, strategic learning, happens in the beginning of the project when needs and vision are aligned with resource requirements and management to carry out the work. Secondly, constructive learning happens in the process of training people and upgrading technology while standardizing practices. Thirdly, reflective learning relates to analysis, reporting and dissemination of project outcomes, preparing the path for another cycle starting with strategic learning.

Large e-government reform projects involving multiple actors and their transformative power constitute the unique context of this study. It is in such environments where the contingency approach suggested by project-based learning can be combined with the longitudinal focus of institutional theory to re-conceptualize learning beyond classroom and organization boundaries.

Future research on multi-actor projects should pay more attention not only to learning processes related to humans, but also to machine learning capabilities of the innovative technologies we continue to implement.

References

1. Becker, J., Algermissen, L., Niehaves, B.: A procedure model for process oriented e-government projects. Bus. Process Manag. J. **12**(1), 61–75 (2006)
2. Becker, J., Bergener, P., Kleist, S., Pfeiffer, D., Räckers, M.: Evaluation of ICT investments in public administrations based on business process models. In: Wimmer, M.A., Scholl, H.J., Ferro, E. (eds.) EGOV 2008. LNCS, vol. 5184, pp. 124–135. Springer, Heidelberg (2008). https://doi.org/10.1007/978-3-540-85204-9_11
3. Blumenfeld, P.C., Soloway, E., Marx, R.W., Krajcik, J.S., Guzdial, M., Palincsar, A.: Motivating project-based learning: sustaining the doing, supporting the learning. Educ. Psychol. **26**(3–4), 369–398 (1991)
4. Bunn, F., Trivedi, D., Alderson, P., Hamilton, L., Martin, A., Iliffe, S.: The impact of Cochrane systematic reviews: a mixed method evaluation of outputs from Cochrane review groups supported by the UK national institute for health research. Syst. Rev. **3**(1), 125 (2014)
5. Chauhan, R., Estevez, E., Janowski, T.: A model for policy interventions in support of electronic governance. Paper presented at the Proceedings of the 2nd International Conference on Theory and Practice of Electronic Governance, pp. 199–205 (2008)

6. Chen, J., Wang, D., Pan, S.L.: Understanding organizational agility development for Government–a process model of resource configuration. University of Queensland, Australia (2011)
7. Chung, H., Lee, G., Kuo, R.: Determinants of public servants' intention to adopt e-government learning. Rev. Public Pers. Adm. **36**(4), 396–411 (2016)
8. Dunleavy, P.: Democracy, Bureaucracy and Public Choice: Economic Explanations in Political Science. Longman, London (1991)
9. Dunleavy, P., Margetts, H., Bastow, S., Tinkler, J.: New public management is dead–long live digital-era governance. J. Public Adm. Res. Theor. **16**(3), 467–494 (2006)
10. Eakin, H., Eriksen, S., Eikeland, P.O., Øyen, C.: Public sector reform and governance for adaptation: implications of new public management for adaptive capacity in Mexico and Norway. Environ. Manag. **47**(3), 338–351 (2011)
11. Feller, J., Finnegan, P., Nilsson, O.: Open innovation and public administration: transformational typologies and business model impacts. Eur. J. Inf. Syst. **20**(3), 358–374 (2010)
12. Finger, M., Brand, S.B.: The concept of 'learning organisation' applied to the transformation of the public sector. In: Easterby-Smith, M., Araujo, L., Burgoyne, J. (eds.) Organizational Learning and the Learning Organization: Developments in Theory and Practice, pp. 130–156. Sage Publications Limited, London (1999)
13. Folke, C., Hahn, T., Olsson, P., Norberg, J.: Adaptive governance of social-ecological systems. Ann. Rev. Environ. Resour. **30**, 441–473 (2005)
14. Hassink, R., Lagendijk, A.: The dilemmas of interregional institutional learning. Environ. Plann. C **19**(1), 65–84 (2001)
15. Illeris, K.: A model for learning in working life. J. Workplace Learn. **16**(8), 431–441 (2004)
16. Illeris, K.: The Fundamentals of Workplace Learning: Understanding How People Learn in Working Life. Routledge, New York (2010)
17. Järvinen, A., Poikela, E.: Modelling reflective and contextual learning at work. J. Workplace Learn. **13**(7/8), 282–290 (2001)
18. Kazanjian, R.K., Drazin, R., Glynn, M.A.: Creativity and technological learning: the roles of organization architecture and crisis in large-scale projects. J. Eng. Tech. Manag. **17**(3–4), 273–298 (2000)
19. Kefallinos, D., Lambrou, M.A., Sykas, E.: An extended risk assessment model for secure E-government projects. Int. J. Electron. Gov. Res. (IJEGR) **5**(2), 72–92 (2009)
20. Kim, J.: A model and case for supporting participatory public decision making in e-democracy. Group Decis. Negot. **17**(3), 179–193 (2008)
21. Kim, J., Wilemon, D.: The learning organization as facilitator of complex NPD projects. Creat. Innov. Manag. **16**(2), 176–191 (2007)
22. King, N., Horrocks, C.: Interviews in Qualitative Research. Sage, Thousand Oaks (2010)
23. Kromidha, E.: Transitions of power in multi-actor information system projects. Int. J. Project Manag. **35**(8), 1587–1596 (2017)
24. Kromidha, E., Córdoba-Pachón, J.: Discursive institutionalism for reconciling change and stability in digital innovation public sector projects for development. Gov. Inf. Q. **34**(1), 16–25 (2017). https://doi.org/10.1016/j.giq.2016.11.004
25. Mahler, J.: Influences of organizational culture on learning in public agencies. J. Public Adm. Res. Theor. **7**(4), 519–540 (1997)
26. Malhotra, C., Chariar, V.M., Das, L.K.: User centred design model (G2C2G) for rural e-governance projects. Int. J. Electron. Gov. **2**(4), 378–401 (2009)
27. March, J.G., Olsen, J.P.: Rediscovering Institutions: The Organizational Basis of Politics. Free Press, New York (1989)
28. March, J.G., Olsen, J.P.: Democratic Governance. Free Press, New York (1995)

29. March, J.G., Olsen, J.P.: Institutional perspectives on political institutions. Governance 9(3), 247–264 (1996)
30. March, J.G., Olsen, J.P.: The logic of appropriateness - advanced research on the Europeanisation of the nation-state. ARENA - Centre for European Studies, University of Oslo, Oslo, Norway (2004)
31. March, J.G., Olsen, J.P.: Elaborating the "new institutionalism". In: Rhodes, R.A.W., Binder, S.A., Rockman, B.A. (eds.) The Oxford Handbook of Political Institutions, pp. 3–20. Oxford University Press, Oxford (2006)
32. March, J.G., Olsen, J.P.: The new institutionalism: organizational factors in political life. Am. Polit. Sci. Rev. 78(3), 734–749 (1984)
33. March, J.G., Olsen, J.P.: The institutional dynamics of international political orders. International Organization, 52(4, International Organization at Fifty: Exploration and Contestation in the Study of World Politics), pp. 943–969 (1998)
34. March, J.G., Olson, J.P., Olsen, J.P.: Organizing political life: what administrative reorganization tells us about government. Am. Polit. Sci. Rev. 77(2), 281–296 (1983)
35. Metcalfe, L.: Public management: from imitation to innovation. Aust. J. Public Adm. 52(3), 292–304 (1993)
36. Miles, M.B., Huberman, A.M.: Qualitative Data Analysis: An Expanded Sourcebook. Sage Publications, London (1994)
37. Pan, G., Pan, S.L., Newman, M., Flynn, D.: Escalation and de-escalation of commitment: a commitment transformation analysis of an e-government project. Inf. Syst. J. 16(1), 3–21 (2006)
38. Poell, R.F., der Krogt, V., Ferd, J., Wildemeersch, D.A.: Solving work-related problems through learning projects. Int. J. Lifelong Educ. 17(5), 341–351 (1998)
39. Reddick, C.G.: Citizen interaction and e-government: evidence for the managerial, consultative, and participatory models. Transform. Gov.: People Process Policy 5(2), 167–184 (2011)
40. Thomas, J.W.: A review of research on project-based learning. The Autodesk Foundation, San Rafael, California (2000)
41. Vurro, C., Dacin, M.T., Perrini, F.: Institutional antecedents of partnering for social change: how institutional logics shape cross-sector social partnerships. J. Bus. Ethics 94, 39–53 (2010)
42. Walsham, G.: Interpretive case studies in IS research: nature and method. Eur. J. Inf. Syst. 4 (2), 74–81 (1995)
43. Wimmer, M.A.: Implementing a knowledge portal for e-government based on semantic modeling: The e-government intelligent portal (eip. at). In: Proceedings of the 39th Annual Hawaii International Conference on Paper presented at the System Sciences, HICSS 2006, vol. 4, p. 82b (2006)
44. Yin, R.K.: Case Study Research: Design and Methods, 4th edn. Sage Publications, London (2009)

Integrating ICT in Pre-service Teacher Education in Zanzibar: Status, Challenges and Opportunities

Umayra El Nabahany$^{(\boxtimes)}$ ⓘ and Said Juma$^{(\boxtimes)}$ ⓘ

State University of Zanzibar, SUZA, Zanzibar, Tanzania
{umayra.al-nabhany, said.juma}@suza.ac.tz

Abstract. The notion of integrating ICT in education has proven to provide various solutions to educational issues. Preparing pre-service teachers for ICT integration has been crucial in many teacher training colleges and universities. The present paper with preliminary data findings explores the status, challenges and opportunities that exist in the integration of ICT tools in pre-service teacher education at the State University of Zanzibar. This was a mixed study that employed both qualitative and quantitative methods. However, the major approach used was quantitative. Initial findings indicate that despite SUZA having its own updated Learning Management System (LMS) and ICT tools and infrastructures, there are still many challenges related to infrastructures, readiness, ICT skills and comfortability in integrating ICT tools in teaching and learning. In addition, the paper explores the many opportunities that are available at the State University of Zanzibar in the integration of ICT in education particularly in pre-service teacher education.

Keywords: ICT · Learning · Teaching · Pre-service teachers · Teacher education · Zanzibar

1 Introduction

The integration of Information and Communication Technology (ICT) in pre-service teacher training has been gaining currency worldwide since the advent of the 21st century. Research suggests that effective use of ICT can enhance teaching and learning among pre-service teachers [1, 2, 14]. Preparing pre-service teachers for ICT integration has been crucial in many teacher training colleges and universities [3, 4]. [5] argue that pedagogical knowledge and content knowledge are not enough to make teachers effective. Teachers need to be trained to integrate ICT with pedagogy and content into teaching through a combination of knowledge of technology. Separate courses on ICT may not be enough for an effective ICT integration in teacher education [6]. Such a course needs to be accompanied with other strategies such as e-learning policy; and an institutional strategy to improve and encourage the use of ICT technologies in teaching and learning [7].

In Tanzania, an extensive research has been done on the use of ICT for teaching and learning among university students in Tanzania [8]. However, there are regional

© IFIP International Federation for Information Processing 2019
Published by Springer Nature Switzerland AG 2019
A. Tatnall and N. Mavengere (Eds.): SUZA 2019, IFIP AICT 564, pp. 117–124, 2019.
https://doi.org/10.1007/978-3-030-28764-1_14

variations as well as differences in uptake technology integrations at institutional levels. For example, little is known about the exact capacity of SUZA academic staff to integrate ICT for pre-service teacher education. Furthermore, it is not clear what are the perceived challenges and opportunities of integrating ICT in pre-service teacher education. Thus the present study was set to explore SUZA's ICT capacity and the process of integrating ICT into pre-service teacher education. In the remaining parts of this paper, we first present the background and context of the study followed by the purpose of the study, the study objectives, research questions, study design and conceptual framework. We then proceed with the description of the methodology of the study and presentation and discussion of the findings from both the quantitative and qualitative data. Finally we provide some recommendations which may have a number of practical implications for future practice in the study context.

2   Background and Context of the Study

This research explored the process of integrating ICT into pre-service teacher education in Zanzibar – a semi-autonomous part within the United Republic of Tanzania. The study was conducted at Tunguu campus (located in the South Region) and Nkrumah campus (located in the Urban West Region) of the State University of Zanzibar.

The State University of Zanzibar (SUZA) is one of the youngest universities in the region, but by far one of the fastest growing in the region. SUZA has 6 schools at the moment namely School of Natural and Social Sciences, School of Education, School of Kiswahili and Foreign Languages, School of Continuing and Professional Education, School of Health and Medical Sciences, and School of Business. New schools in the pipeline include School of Petroleum and Engineering, School of Computing, Communications and Media, School of Agriculture and School of Tourism Development.

School of Education gets a majority of students studying to be teachers compared to any other school at SUZA per year. For instance, data from Department of Quality Assurance indicate that in 2016/17 the number of registered students for Bachelor's degree only was 396, out of that number 216 were students taking education courses. The School also offers some programmes to students taking other degrees particularly from the School of Natural and Social Sciences and School of Kiswahili and Foreign Languages. Majority of students specializing in education programmes have limited ICT literacy skills compared to those in other specializations.

The university has been striving to ensure proper teaching and learning environments for the 21st century learners at SUZA. Academicians are constantly trained to create teaching and learning content that integrates technology. The university has put the infrastructure and facilities such as computer labs with access to the internet and Wi-Fi access across the university. A Learning Management System (LMS) has been used since 2011 with the assistance from partner university of Copenhagen through a Building Stronger University Project. A number of courses at SUZA are utilizing the LMS through Blended Learning and E-Learning teaching approaches. Additionally, the university has successfully initiated a Centre for Digital Learning which records and airs teaching programmes to help the students across Zanzibar. The university is currently developing a first ever Kiswahili Massive Open Online Course (MOOC) which will soon be available online for the learners. Moreover, the university has created an Open Educational Resource (OER) guideline as well as ICT policy which is followed at the university.

Currently, more than 300 courses are available on the Learning Management System even though they are not fully utilized due to many challenges. These challenges are related to both to course instructors preferring face to face mode of teaching as well having insufficient IT skills which is a major requirement to utilize online platform fully. In a survey carried out by [9], it was noted that there were difficulties in the preparation of teachers to integrate technology in the classroom due to the following reasons: (1) many teachers, while having access to technology in school, said they do not make use of them in teaching. (2) the majority of teachers are not ready to use and create the resources for teaching and learning using technology particularly those related with the use of the computer. (3) most of the activities carried out with the computer affect their physical and mechanical use, rather than the integration of technology into the curriculum.

Students on the other hand, apart from having basic IT skills needed to use the Learning Management System, they are still not motivated to use the LMS for their courses. The poor internet connections, insufficient access to ICT tools also make it difficult for SUZA to fully integrate technology in teaching and learning.

3   Purpose of the Study

To explore the use and integration of ICT into pre-service teacher training at the State University of Zanzibar.

3.1   Objectives

To achieve the aforementioned purpose, the study was guided by three objectives:

1. To examine the use of ICT in pre-service teacher education
2. To explain the current status and challenges of integrating ICT in pre-service teacher education and
3. Put forward a framework to help SUZA integrate ICT in learning and teaching for pre-service teachers.

3.2   Research Questions

To reach these objectives, the study attempted to answer three research questions namely:

1. What ICT resources are accessible to the preservice teachers at SUZA?
2. How/to what extent do the pre-service teachers at SUZA use the available/accessible ICT resources?
3. What are the constraining factors for ICT integration among pre-services teachers at SUZA?

4. What are the constraining factors for ICT integration among lecturers in pre-service teacher training?
5. What framework can be designed for ICT integration amongst pre-service teachers at SUZA?

3.3 Study Design

The study aimed to gain a deep insight and intensive analysis of the use of ICT among the University students. Thus, it employed a case study design [10, 11]. The State University of Zanzibar was selected as a case study to gain an in depth understanding of the integration of ICT into the pre-service teacher training. The study therefore did not aim to compare or generalise its findings to other Universities or similar institutions.

3.4 Conceptual Framework

We have adopted [5] conceptual framework on integration of technology into teachers' pedagogical knowledge. [5] added technology (e.g. projector, mobile phone, iPad) on Shulman's Pedagogical Content Knowledge and proposed the concept of Technological Pedagogical Content Knowledge (TPCK), which is concerned with use of technology for teaching and learning specific contents. The framework includes a complex interplay among four constructs namely (1) Pedagogical Content Knowledge; (2) Technological Pedagogical Knowledge; (3) Technological Pedagogical Content Knowledge and (4) Technological Content Knowledge. In this framework, [5] maintain that teacher education should enable teachers to have an understanding of how technology influences pedagogy and content. In the same vein, [12] emphasizes that 'The goal of teacher education is not to indoctrinate or train teachers to behave in prescribed ways, but to educate teachers to reason soundly about their teaching as well as to perform skilfully' (p. 13).

In this framework the main argument is that mere presence or introduction of technology in educational institutions such as schools or universities is not sufficient. Of more importance is how the technology is integrated and used to enhance teaching and learning among teachers.

The TPCK framework assumes that 'learning environments that allow students and teachers to explore technologies in relationship to subject matter in authentic contexts are often useful' (Ibid, p. 1045).

3.5 Data, Data Collection Instruments and Study Participants

Both primary and secondary data were used in this study. Primary data included both qualitative and quantitative data which were mainly collected through a survey method. Three online questionnaires were used to collect data from the pre-service teachers (N = 123, f = 86, m = 37); Heads of department from the School of Education and the School of Natural and Social Sciences (N = 4, f = 1, m = 3); and Lecturers (N = 6, f = 3, m = 3). The students were either provided with iPads or asked to use their smartphones to access the online questionnaire. The lecturers and the heads of department respondents used their laptops, smartphones or desktop computers to respond to the questionnaires.

3.6   Data Analysis

We used Microsoft Excel and Tableau Desktop 2018 to analyse the quantitative data from the Google Forms. Tableau, provides an easy and faster drag-and-drop approach to visual analysis of Excel spreadsheet data that was obtained through Google Forms. For the qualitative data we used Thematic Content Analysis [13].

4   Findings

4.1   Existence of ICT Policy

The heads of departments were asked to respond whether SUZA has its own written statement on the use of ICT. Only one respondent knows about the existence of the policy and the rest do not know. This suggests that even if the policy statement might exist, it is not known to other heads of departments.

Using ICT for Pedagogical Purposes
The data has shown that only one respondent out of 4 knows about written statement specifically about the use of ICT for pedagogical purposes. Three of the respondents indicate that there is no such policy at SUZA and one does not know if it exists or not.

Integrating ICT in Teaching
When the lecturer respondents were asked if they integrate ICT tools in their teaching, four of the respondents said yes and two indicated to do that sometimes. For those who answered yes to integrating ICT tools in their teachings, their reasons were: "It is easy especially by using social media, it is easy to engage the student directly in the learning process."; "It simplify my teaching seeing several examples from YouTube"; "There are limited Knowledge of ICT programs". And for those who said they sometimes integrate ICT tools in their teaching, their reasons were: "During preparation, searching materials and in classroom instructions become easier".

Search the Internet to Collect Information
Majority of the respondents 5 out of 6 indicated that they use internet almost or everyday to search for information online while 1 respondent out of 6 does this several times in a month. Interestingly, when asked on the frequency of using computers to create blogs or discussion forums for students, one respondent indicated to use that once in a week and 5 of the respondents indicated to have never done that.

Challenges of Integrating ICT Tools in Teaching at SUZA
The respondents were asked to mention challenges if there are any that are likely to be faced by SUZA academic staff in integrating ICT tools in their teaching. The answers given included poor network; many of the students are not conversant with computer; students are not motivated to use LMS, many of them prefer social media like

Facebook; sometimes internet is so slow; unreliable electricity; and shortage of few resources such as computers.

Opportunities in Integrating ICT Tools in Teaching at SUZA

The respondents indicated that there are several opportunities can make integration of ICT tools in teaching easier. The opportunities mentioned included presence of LMS, and availability of power; getting materials from other universities; awareness amongst staff on the need for ICT integration and the presence of ICT experts around all the SUZA campuses.

ICT Tools and Comfortability of Using Them

Data show that of all the surveyed respondents, the majority of the pre-service teachers (99%) have access to one or more tools of ICT technologies for learning. Smartphones and laptops were the most popular ICT tools that are owned and used for learning amongst the pre-service teachers. Data show that 97 (78.9%) own and use smartphones. With regard to comfortability of using these ICT tools, many of the respondents were comfortable whereby 56 (45.5%) felt very comfortable with using ICT tools for learning, 33 (26.8%) felt a little comfortable, 31 (25.2%) felt fairly comfortable, and only 3 (2.4%) were not comfortable at all.

Skills of Using ICT Tools

The respondents were asked to mention whether they have enough skills in using the ICT tools in their studies. Many of them (60.2%) said that they do not have enough skills while only 39.8% claimed to have enough ICT skills for their studies.

Access and Connection to Internet While at SUZA

The findings reveal that 86% of the pre-service teachers have access to internet while at SUZA. The most popular source of connection according to the majority (111) of the respondents (90.2%) is SUZA Wi-Fi while mobile data was mentioned as the second most common source of connection to internet.

Using IT Technologies in the Classroom Environment

The respondents were asked to give their views about using IT technologies in the classroom. There were differing responses on this theme. Many of them acknowledged the importance of ICT for improving teaching and learning but also raised several concerns such as:

"ICT services in SUZA especially school of Kiswahili are very poor. We had no access to LMS in whole first year, and in this year only one lecturer used it";

"Not all the instructors of SUZA are interested in using ICT because some of them don't have the skills towards ICT and they don't want to use the resources." "The lecturers should try to use simple terms and should not speak too first during the lectures because ICT needs more practice than theory. Of more importance is also the need for those responsible to repair the computers which are not working."

These study findings reveal the actual current situation regarding the use and integration of ICT into pre-service teacher training at the State University of Zanzibar. Generally, the findings show that there is very little integration of ICT due to various factors. The findings also indicate the shortage of various ICT equipment to enhance teaching and learning at the University. These findings may contain important implications for improving the use of ICT technologies in order to enhance teaching and learning of the pre-service teachers at the study context.

5 Concluding Remarks and Recommendations

Integration of ICT into pre-service teacher training at the State University of Zanzibar has still got a long way to go despite several initiatives taken. Both students and the staff have reported a number of challenges which hinder effective ICT integration. These include unreliable internet services, shortage of ICT facilities like computers, having staff who are unmotivated to integrate ICT in their teaching methodologies, and few opportunities of ICT training for the students. In addition, the existing ICT policy is not adequately shared to the staff members. This study has focused on the integration of ICT in pre-service teacher training. We posit according to [5] framework that effective pre-service teacher preparation should be cognizant of the need to integrate ICT in the pre-service teacher training. Both pre-service and in-service teacher need to be empowered to effectively integrate ICT in their teaching. Thus, pre- service teachers should start to experience how such integration can be done right from their teacher training institutions rather than experiencing it as an add on when they begin their career in schools.

Based on the study findings, we put forward some recommendations which may contribute to improve the process of integrating ICT into pre-service teacher training.

The ICT policy should be shared to all staff. This will help to ease an effective and collaborative implementation of the policy. It is also worth considering the need to review the ICT policies to keep abreast with rapid pace of technological advancement. For a more effective integration of ICT into the pre-service teacher education, SUZA may wish to consider preparing ICT guidelines for integration of ICT in teaching and learning with clear implementation plan and sufficient will to support the implementation from the University Management.

As the study findings have indicated a shortage of ICT facilities including computers, there is, therefore, a definite for SUZA to enhance availability and accessibility of technological facilities for both the students and the staff. Greater efforts are needed to ensure the School of Education prioritizes technologies and infrastructures to be used by all pre-service teachers at the University and their prospective schools during their practice teaching in schools.

Ensuring appropriate ICT systems, services (e.g. increasing broadband access) and support for the students and the staff should be a priority. This should include continuing professional development opportunities of teachers and academicians in ICT integration for teaching and learning.

Another important practical implication of the study findings is that there is a need for developing a policy about using social networks (e.g. Facebook, WhatsApp etc.) in teaching and learning to avoid unintended and unethical use of the networks amongst both students and the academics. In addition, the academicians who integrate ICT tools in their teaching (e.g. using LMS, making their courses online) can be motivated through promotion or other ways to encourage them to integrate ICT into their teaching methodology.

References

1. Tondeur, J., Van Braak, J., Sang, G., Voogt, J., Fisser, P., Ottenbreit-Leftwich, A.: Preparing pre-service teachers to integrate technology in education: a synthesis of qualitative evidence. Comput. Educ. **59**(1), 134–144 (2012)
2. Farjon, D., Smits, A., Voogt, J.: Technology integration of pre-service teachers explained by attitudes and beliefs, competency, access, and experience. Comput. Educ. **130**, 81–93 (2019)
3. Kisalama, R., Kafyulilo, A.C.: Developing pre-service teachers' technology integration competencies in science and mathematics teaching: experiences from Tanzania and Uganda. Makerere J. High. Educ. **3**(2), 99–113 (2011)
4. Harrington, R., Rhine, S.: Digital tools for accelerating preservice teacher effectiveness. In: Pre-Service and In-Service Teacher Education: Concepts, Methodologies, Tools, and Applications, pp. 926–955. IGI Global (2019)
5. Mishra, P., Koehler, M.J.: Technological pedagogical content knowledge: a framework for teacher knowledge. Teach. Coll. Rec. **108**(6), 1017 (2006)
6. Tondeur, J.: Enhancing future teachers' competencies for technology integration in education: turning theory into practice. In: Seminar.net, vol. 14, no. 2, pp. 216–224 (2018)
7. Dahms, M.-L., Zakaria, H.L.: Institutional capacities in E-learning and problem based learning at universities and university colleges in Tanzania and Ghana. Department of Development and Planning, Aalborg University (2015)
8. Mbalamula, Y.S.: Role of ICT in teaching and learning: influence of lecturers on undergraduates in Tanzania. Education **4**(22), 24–25 (2016)
9. James, P.T.J.: Mobile-learning: Thai HE student perceptions and potential technological impacts. Int. Educ. Stud. **4**(2), 182–194 (2011)
10. Creswell, J.W.: Mapping the field of mixed methods research. J. Mixed Methods Res. **3**(2), 95–108 (2009)
11. Bryman, A.: Social Research Methods. Oxford University Press, Oxford (2008)
12. Shulman, L.: Knowledge and teaching: foundations of the new reform. Harvard Educ. Rev. **57**(1), 1–23 (1987)
13. Clarke, V., Braun, V.: Thematic analysis. In: Michalos, A.C. (ed.) Encyclopedia of Quality of Life and Well-Being Research, pp. 6626–6628. Springer, Dordrecht (2014). https://doi.org/10.1007/978-94-007-0753-5
14. Parkman, S., Litz, D., Gromik, N.: Examining pre-service teachers' acceptance of technology-rich learning environments: a UAE case study. Educ. Inf. Technol. **23**, 1–23 (2018)

Enhancing Virtual Learning by Improving the Learning Environment and User Experience

Nicholas Mavengere$^{(\boxtimes)}$ and Mikko Ruohonen

University of Tampere, Kalevantie 4, 33014 Tampere, Finland
{nicholas.mavengere,mikko.ruohonen}@tuni.fi

Abstract. Learning is an essential virtue in a dynamic environment. Technologies offer both opportunities and challenges to learning. The global nature of the environment today calls for virtual learning, which offers dimensions, such as, convenience, time and cost factors. This research seeks to promote virtual learning experience by improving the learning environment and user experience. The research is based on a total virtual learning experience of a masters' level information and communication technology for development (ICT4D) class at the University of Tampere. A survey was conducted at the mid-course stage to assess the virtual learning experience and propose ways to improve learning process. The assessment included how well the virtual environment and pedagogy promoted quality learning, that is, constructive, collaborative and conversational learning. The research seeks to promote quality learning by improving the learning environment and participants' virtual learning experience. That is, context is embraced to map the learning process that suits the learners and study contents. The results of this study included highlight of pedagogical techniques and technological tools that fit the learners' and study content requirements to foster learning in a virtual environment.

Keywords: Virtual learning · User needs in virtual learning ·
Context in virtual learning · Virtual learning review · Quality learning

1 Introduction

The advances in technologies, for example, mobile and cloud based technologies offers opportunities for enhancing learning. The need to embrace innovative teaching practices to enhance the learning process by adopting new technologies and pedagogical practices has been called for, some time now. For example, twenty years ago Leidner and Jarvenpaa [3] advocated for information technology (IT) use to improve business management school. However, the continuously changing technology and educational practices mean that this call for research to improve the learning process will always be required. In addition, factors such as globalization are also influencing the educational environment. In fact, virtual learning in different set ups, such as blended and wholly virtual approach, has been widely adopted.

The advantages of virtual learning have been well documented. For example, Chou and Liu [1] noted the potential of virtual learning in eliminating barriers and increasing

© IFIP International Federation for Information Processing 2019
Published by Springer Nature Switzerland AG 2019
A. Tatnall and N. Mavengere (Eds.): SUZA 2019, IFIP AICT 564, pp. 125–134, 2019.
https://doi.org/10.1007/978-3-030-28764-1_15

flexibility, convenience, student retention, individual learning, convenience, currency of material and feedback. However, there are also related disadvantages, such as, possibility of participants' feeling isolated thus leading to anxiety and confusion thus reducing learning effectiveness. Therefore, it is important to embrace virtual learning to try to maximize the benefits gained, as well as to reduce the negative impacts [5]. One way of doing that, is in understanding context and students' needs as users of the virtual learning environment. Oxford dictionary defines context as the circumstances that form the setting for an event and in terms of which it can be fully understood. In this research context refers to the circumstances that form the setting of virtual learning course, such as, learning model, students' virtual learning experience and study contents. This study seeks to highlight ways in which context and user needs are considered in mapping pedagogical practices and technological tools in pursuit of quality learning. Quality learning is elaborated in the next section, theoretical background. Thus, the research question is; how could context and user needs to promote quality learning in virtual learning?

The research is based on a total virtual learning experience of a masters' level information and communication technology for development (ICT4D) course hosted at the University of Tampere. A survey was conducted at the mid-course stage to assess the virtual learning experience and propose ways to improve learning process. Details of the course and survey are in the methodology section below. The research seeks to promote quality learning by considering context and user needs. That is, context is understood to map the learning process that suits the learners and study contents. The results of this study include highlight of pedagogical techniques and technological tools that fit the learners' and study content requirements to foster learning in a virtual environment. These pedagogical techniques and technological tools that promote quality learning are proposed in this study. Such techniques and tools has to fit the learning context, for instance, in the ICT4D course adoption was a result of the mid-course virtual learning review. Hence, context is argued to be reviewed and thereafter recommendations on specific pedagogical techniques and technological tools to be adopted. For instance, mid-course review could be way to draw appropriate measures for virtual learning.

The next section elaborates the theoretical basis of this research. For example, qualities of learning also referred to as quality learning in this research is elaborated, as well as, the learning models. After that, the methodology section, describes the ICT4D course the survey conducted. Then, the research findings are highlighted, followed by discussion and conclusion.

2   Theoretical Background

We should always strive for the best. There are fundamental aspects of learning, referred to as quality learning which we should always seek to achieve. These are the cornerstones which technology could aid to build upon to foster the learning process. Ruokamo and Pohjolainen [4] suggested the following qualities of learning;

1. Active - Learners' role in learning process is active; they are engaged in mindful processing of information and they are responsible for the result.
2. Constructive - Learners construct new knowledge on the basis of their previous knowledge.
3. Collaborative - Learners work together in building new knowledge in co-operation with each other and exploiting each other's skills.
4. Intentional - Learners try actively and willingly to achieve a cognitive objective.
5. Contextual - Learning tasks are situated in a meaningful real world tasks or they are introduced through case-based or problem-based real life examples.
6. Transfer - Learners are able to transfer learning from the situations and contexts, where learning has taken place and use their knowledge in other situations.
7. Reflective - Learners articulate what they have learned and reflect on the processes and decisions entailed by the process.

These learning qualities were evaluated in the survey, which was conducted in the ICT4D course. This was done in order to adopt technological tools and pedagogical practices that promote the above-mentioned qualities of learning. Please see methodology section below for more information about the survey.

Jarvenpaa and Leidner [3] suggested that "the effectiveness of information technology in contributing to learning will be a function of how well the technology supports a particular model of learning and the appropriateness of the model to a particular learning situation". Therefore, it is important to draw the specific learning model and ways to effectively use the learning technologies. Table 1 illustrates some learning models, please note this is not exhaustive but highlights some of the models.

Table 1. Summary of learning models adopted from Jarvenpaa and Leidner [3]

Model	Basic premise	Goals	Major assumptions	Implications for instruction
Objectivism	Learning is the uncritical absorption of objective knowledge	Transfer of knowledge from instructor to student Recall of knowledge	Instructor houses all necessary knowledge Students learn best in isolated and intensive subject matter	Instructor is in control of material and pace Instructor provides stimulus
Constructivism	Learning is a process of constructing knowledge by an individual	Formation of abstract concepts to represent reality Assigning meaning to events and information	Individuals learn better when they discover things themselves and when they control the pace of learning	Learner-centered active learning Instructor for support rather than direction
Collaborativism	Learning emerges through shared	Promote group skills-communication,	Involvement is critical to learning	Communication oriented

(continued)

Table 1. (*continued*)

Model	Basic premise	Goals	Major assumptions	Implications for instruction
	understandings of more than one learner	listening, participation Promote socialization	Learners have some prior knowledge	Instructor as questioner and discussion leader
Cognitive information processing	Learning is the processing and transfer of new knowledge into long-term memory	Improve cognitive processing abilities of learners Improve recall and retention	Limited selective attention Prior knowledge affects level of instructional support needed	Aspects of stimulus can affect attention Instructors need feedback on student learning
Socioculturism	Learning is subjective and individualistic	Empowerment Emancipatory learning Action-oriented, socially conscious learners with a view to change rather than accept or understand society	Anglos have distorted knowledge and framed information in their own terms Learning occurs best in environments where personally well known	Instruction is always culturally value laden Instruction is embedded in a person's everyday cultural/social context

In the ICT4D course is based on the constructivism model and its derivations, that is, collaborativism and cognitive information processing. This is in line with Ruokamo and Pohjolainen [4] who argued that constructivism is increasingly an essential theory in the research of technology-based learning.

3 Methodology

The University of Tampere hosted an international virtual course with participants from Finland, Germany, and South Africa. The course topic was Development 2.0, that is, Information Communications Technologies for Development 2.0. The course comprised of 33 participants who had diverse virtual learning experience as illustrated in Fig. 1. About 50% of the participants had 5 or more times of virtual learning experience.

A survey was conducted at the middle of the course. The objectives in conducting the survey included reviewing the virtual learning experience for the class and adopting measures, pedagogical, technology tools and practices to enhance virtual learning. The Fig. 3 below illustrates the virtual experience in the first half of the course. This figure is a normal curve, which illustrates above satisfactory view to the virtual experience in the class, with 57% regarding the experience as very good.

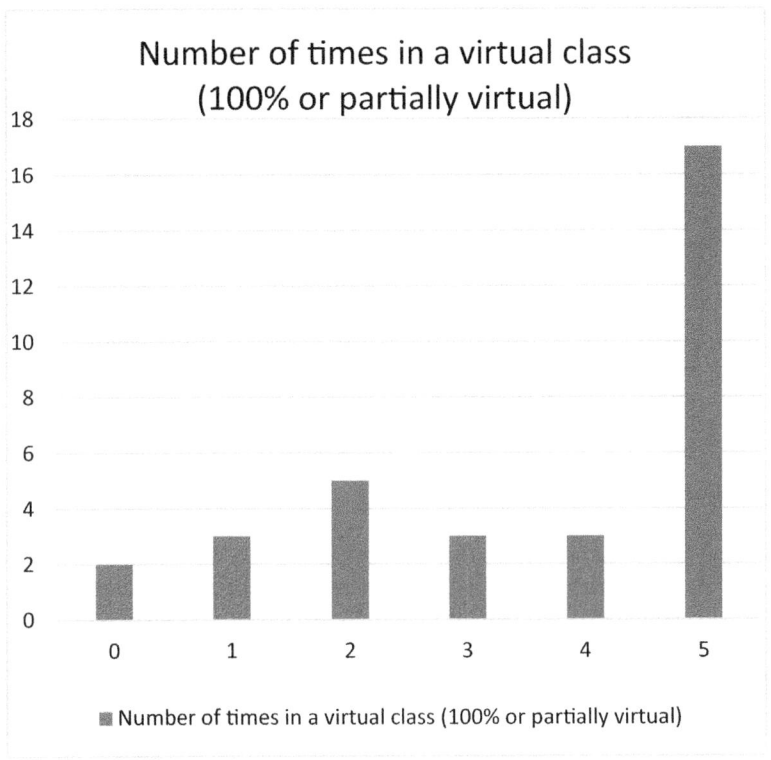

Fig. 1. Virtual learning experience

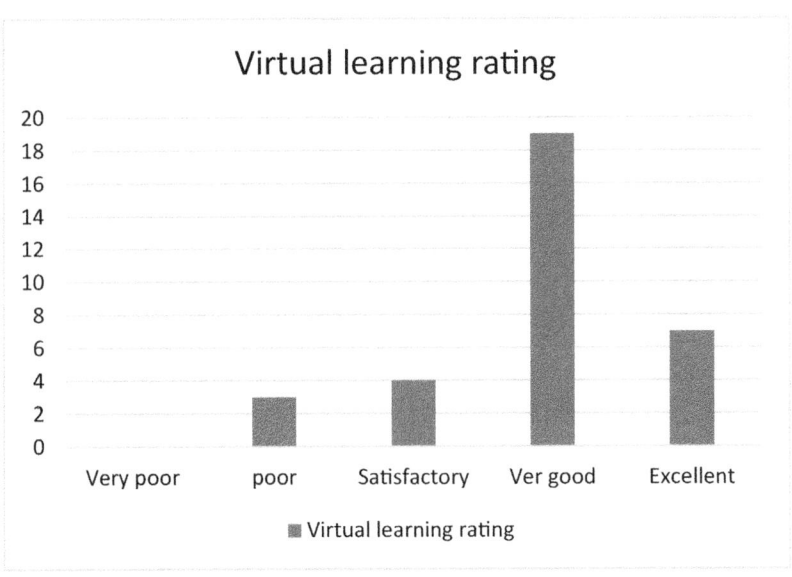

Fig. 2. Virtual learning experience rating

Figure 2 illustrate that the virtual learning experience was very good but the qualitative review showed that there were some specific gaps which needs to be addressed. For instance, several participants highlighted the need for more interaction, as shown in the quotes below,

"I would prefer the learning to be more interactive. Now communication is rather one sided and only between the course teacher and the participant".

"I appreciate the strict deadline which I have to abide by, though I failed once, since it offers me with a structured guideline to follow the course so I can regularly schedule my time to think about the topic. In contrast, I would have preferred an occasional group chat platform (due to varying study schedules of all the participants) that is more conducive to dynamic interaction amongst us, rather than individual reflection, although the latter is prerequisite to the former".

Thus, some measures to improve the virtual learning experience were implemented. These are described in the next section.

4   Results

The types of material used in the first half of the course were assessed to determine their suitability to the virtual learning environment. Figure 3 below illustrates how the learners evaluated the material. All the material were generally valued quite high except books.

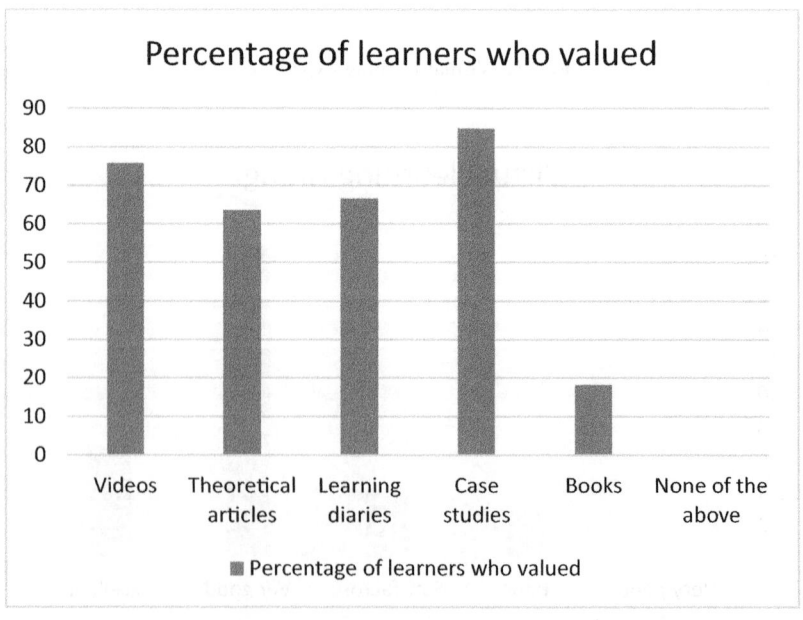

Fig. 3. Evaluation of material types used in virtual learning

There were also technology applications that were proposed for adoption in the course. Figure 4 shows learners' acceptance rate of new applications adoptions. Online discussion forum is most desired for adoption as one student noted "online discussion where we even allow to raise question and put opinion".

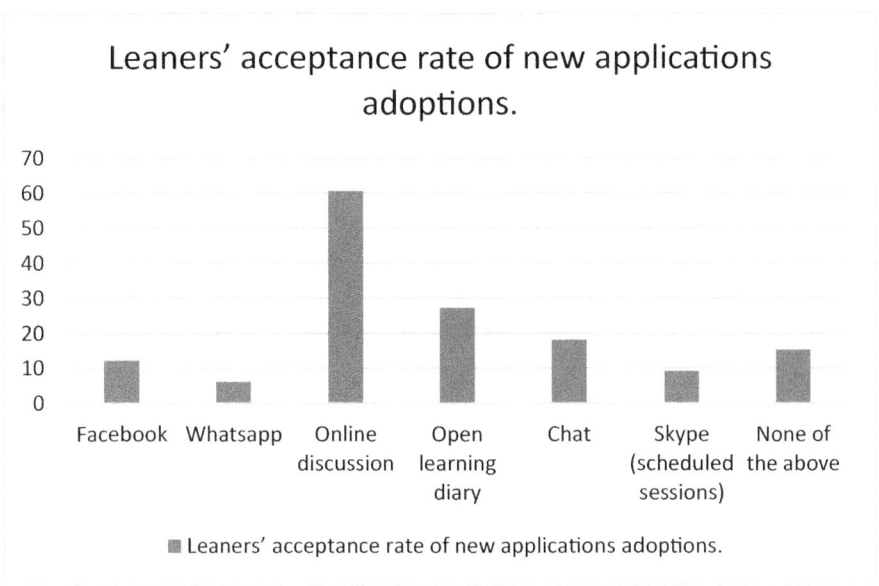

Fig. 4. Leaners' acceptance rate of new applications adoptions.

Assessment techniques are also evaluated as shown in Fig. 5. Learning diary and essay were the most preferred assessment techniques. All the other assessment techniques are below 50%.

The qualities of learning proposed by Ruokamo and Pohjolainen [4] were also evaluated as shown in Fig. 6. Only two qualities of learning namely constructive and contextualized are above 50%. This means that efforts, in terms of pedagogy and supporting technologies, needed to be enforced in pursuit of the quality learning, these are highlighted in the next section, discussion.

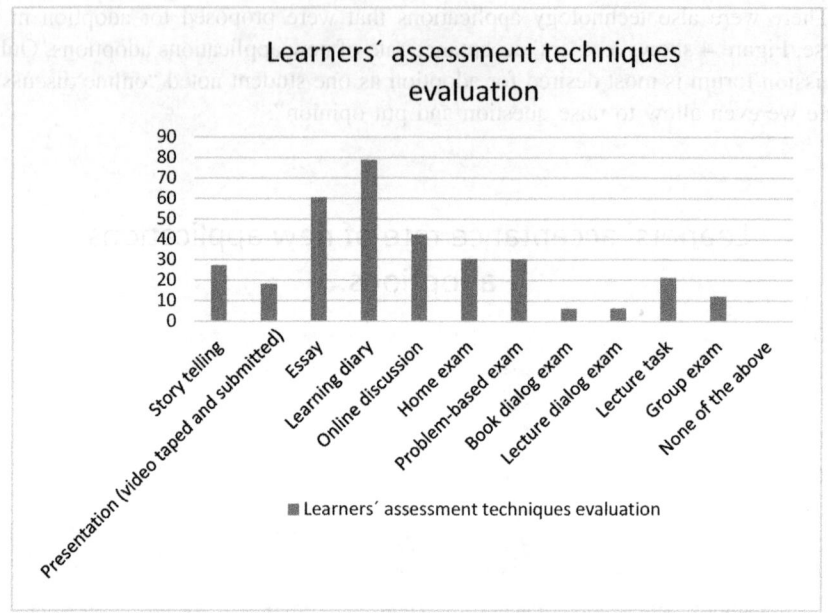

Fig. 5. Learners' assessment techniques evaluation

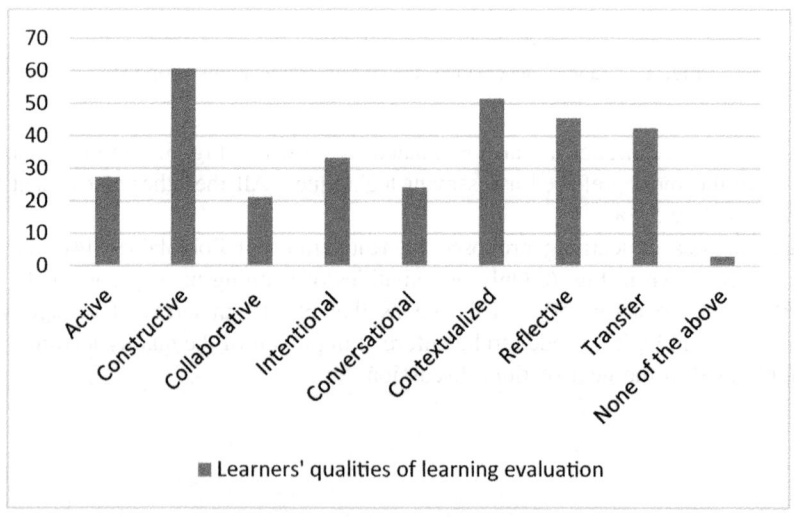

Fig. 6. Qualities of learning evaluation

5   Discussion

The constructivist model of learning perceives learning as "the formation of abstract concepts to represent reality; learning is that which "decentrizes" the individual from the material. Learning is reflected in intellectual growth that leads to scientific reasoning, abstract thought, and formal operations" [3]. Thus constructivist model centers learning on the learner and advocates for a learning environment that forces learners to discover things themselves unlike when instructed. In the ICT4D course activities, such as, open learning diary encourages participants to share their experience in constructing meaning of the study contents. This relates to the cooperative model of learning or collaborativism. In addition, the ICT4D course also included group work to develop a wiki of a book, Frugal Innovation by Navi Radjou and Jaideep Prabhu. Halvorson et al. [2] advocated for active and participatory learning.

Table 2. Pedagogical technique and technological tools that promote qualities of learning

Quality of learning	Pedagogical techniques promoting	Technological tools promoting
Active	Group discussions	Online chat rooms
Constructive	Group book summary	Wiki
Collaborative	Team work	Video-conferencing
Intentional	Open leaning diaries	Discussion forum
Contextual	Case studies	Wiki
Transfer	Peer and self-assessment workshops	Gamification
Reflective	Essays	Discussion forum

Table 2 illustrates examples of pedagogical practices and technological tools that were adopted in the ICT4D course to promote quality learning. It is important to highlight that context and user needs were assessed which lead to the adoption of these pedagogical practices and technological tools. One important pedagogical practice that promote most of the qualities of learning is formulating groups and actively promote group work. This will encourage interaction within the participants and create atmosphere where participants could learn from each other. This is important in virtual learning environment which has high risk of participants feeling isolated. There are many different ways to integrate discussion forums, for instance, participants initiated forums promote intentional learning.

6   Conclusion

The integration of technology to promote learning will always be a burning issue because of the potential offered by the ever-evolving technologies. In addition, technology offers virtual learning possibility, which has advantages of convenience and flexibility. This research advocates for understanding the context and user needs to foster quality learning. Excellence should always be sort in learning, thus this research highlights attempts in pursuit of quality learning, that is, active, constructive, collaborative, intentional, contextual, transfer, reflective learning.

References

1. Chou, S., Liu, C.: Learning effectiveness in a Web-based virtual learning environment: a learner control perspective. J. Comput. Assist. Learn. **21**, 65–76 (2005)
2. Halvorson, W., Crittenden, V., Pitt, L.: Teaching cases in a virtual environment: when the traditional case classroom is problematic. Decis. Sci. J. Innov. Educ. **9**(3), 485–492 (2011)
3. Leidner, D.E., Jarvenpaa, S.L.: The use of information technology to enhance management school education: a theoretical view. MIS Q. **19**(3), 265–291 (1995)
4. Ruokamo, H., Pohjolainen, S.: Pedagogical principles for evaluation of hypermedia-based learning environments in mathematics. JUCS – J. Univ. Comput. Sci. **4**(3), 292–307 (1998)
5. Jonassen, D., Howland, J., Marra, R., Crismond, D.: Meaningful Learning with Technology, 3rd edn. Pearson Merrill Prentice Hall Publishing, Upper Saddle River (2008)

Teachers' Perception on Using Kio-Kit to Enhance Teaching and Learning STEM Subjects in Zanzibar

Raya Idrissa Ahmada(✉) ⬤, Ali Abdulla Abdulla⬤,
Said Ali Said Yunus⬤, and Maryam Jaffar Ismail⬤

The State University of Zanzibar, P.O. BOX 146, Zanzibar, Tanzania
{raya.ahmada,ali.abdulla,said.yunus,
maryam.ismail}@suza.ac.tz,
https://www.suza.ac.tz

Abstract. In the current situation, teachers are encouraged to use interactive, student-centered approaches than using traditional approaches that mainly focus on 'chalk and talk'. Student-centered approaches, also learner-centered, involve methods of teaching that shift the focus of instruction from the teacher to the student. When these approaches are powered by technology, they can doubly enhance teaching and learning. The most current technology that gains popularity in Africa in teaching and learning process is the Kio-Kit technology which promised to improve the quality of teaching and learning. It is a digital education toolbox which contains different forms of digital contents to help students in their learning process. The box contains 40 Kio tablets in which students use them to access the contents available in the Kio-Kit box. This paper aims to discuss the perception of using this type of technology from school teachers who have been trained intensively to use them to enhance the teaching and learning of STEM subjects. During the exploration, we confirmed that Kio-Kit technology enhances teaching and learning and helps the students gain necessary skills for the 21st century digital era. The results also reveal STEM teachers' readiness to use the Kio-Kit technology in the classroom. Further, the paper describes the challenges encountered during the exploration of Kio-Kit in classroom and some suggestions are proposed.

Keywords: Kio-Kits · Digital classroom · ICT · Student-centered learning · STEM for Success · Zanzibar

1 Introduction

With the developments and application of Information and Communication Technologies (ICTs) in education sector, the digital technology has transformed the teaching and learning processes. These changes have been brought forward by the advent of various digital technologies that keep on emerging every now and then. The study by Mashhadi and Kargozari [1] concluded that digital technology if used appropriately, it can develop better understanding of basic concepts provided for learning.

© IFIP International Federation for Information Processing 2019
Published by Springer Nature Switzerland AG 2019
A. Tatnall and N. Mavengere (Eds.): SUZA 2019, IFIP AICT 564, pp. 135–144, 2019.
https://doi.org/10.1007/978-3-030-28764-1_16

Currently, there are various forms of digital technologies used to support teaching and learning process such as e-learning platforms like Moodle, Blackboard, Schoology, and Social Medias platform which include services such as Facebook, WhatsApp, and Google Class to mention few.

The teachers should make sure that they encourage students to use ICT as a supplementary tool with the traditional mode of education. The new technologies should make the students learn more and more and not otherwise. This is very important as because technology can be a distraction in education. General view show that students may misuse the technology by wasting most of their time to communicate with friends on social networks and playing online games.

In their study, Forzani and Leu [2] argue that all students must start learning new literacies skills early if they are to gain the skills they will need as adults. This indicates the importance of various skills gained as a result of using technologies in education.

Most of the technologies require the Internet access or other form of connectivity to access different contents available online. Kio-Kit is a digital learning solution engineered in Africa which came as a toolbox with educational contents within it, connectivity and charging capabilities [3]. It has been plotted with features to make it easy to be used in schools in the emerging markets, most of which has poor connection to the Internet and power cut problem. Mark [4] stated that "the thinking behind the Kio-Kit was to narrow the huge educational gap that exists between schools that have access to books, internet and general access to learning content and those that do not."

2 Motivation for the Study

The study is part of preliminary results extracted from the STEM FOR SUCCESS ZANZIBAR (S4SZ) project, which is a two-year collaborative project between the State University of Zanzibar (SUZA), Milele Zanzibar Foundation (MZF) and Forum for African Women Educationists (FAWE)[1]. The main goal of the project is to help students especially girls in STEM related field to perform better in their studies, increase their interests and have a clear understanding of STEM subjects and STEM career path right in their early years of studies.

Technology usually provides numerous tools that can be used in and out of the classroom to enhance student learning. In this way, technological tools can dramatically increase student learning, enhance student engagement as well as help teachers come out with creative activities and tasks in teaching their students, Kio-Kit being in the list.

In 2018, the S4SZ project invested about 5 Kio-Kits. Each box has a set of 40 resilient tablets that comes with a server pre-loaded with contents in different categories to help students in English language, literacy in both English and Kiswahili, numeracy, science and general knowledge. Since the Kio-Kit comes with full infrastructure, it is suitable in Zanzibar context where the Internet access is not reliable and the number of

[1] The authors gratefully acknowledge the contributions of Wellspring Philanthropic Fund (WPF), Milele Zanzibar Foundation (MZF) and the State University of Zanzibar (SUZA) for supporting the S4Sz initiative in many ways including integrating technology.

textbooks is limited as compared to the number of available students in classes, especially in rural schools.

The Kio-Kit consists of a solid waterproof plastic box, containing 40 toughened tablets in it. Inside the box, there is a server which stores the all the learning materials which are shared to all students' kio-tablets using wireless technology [5]. The box comes with 40 slots to place the kio-tablets after use, and once they are placed they can be charged through the box. To ensure security, the box can also be locked with the tablets inside it and it is very heavy that it is not easy for someone to run away with it.

This digital classroom technology (Kio-Kit) was proposed to be used in Zanzibar classroom to enhance teaching and learning process and promote student-centered approaches in 15 selected schools both in Unguja and Pemba. Hence, a two-day training was conducted to all selected teachers from secondary schools working on of different STEM subjects from the selected schools, in which nine (9) schools from Unguja and six (6) schools from Pemba were involved in the study.

Seventy-five (75) teachers were trained from fifteen (15) selected schools which were part of S4SZ project. The schools involved lower secondary STEM classes (Form one & Form two). Each school brought 5 teachers (4 STEM subject teachers and 1 head teacher), in other words 60 STEM subject teachers were trained intensively, and 15 headteachers participated in the training for coaching and supporting purposes. The training was conducted in three teacher centres (Centre A, B & C).

Different activities were prepared for them to understand how they can use Kio-Kit to enhance teaching and learning and moving from "frontal teaching" and "chalk and talk" style of teaching to student-centered approach, in which students' interaction and engagement are highly practiced, making learning relevant and fun.

After the two-intensive day training and exploration of the Kio-Kit box, a further exploration was made to understand teachers' perception on the use of Kio-Kit in enhancing teaching and learning STEM subjects. This is very crucial to know, as the teachers are expected to utilize the technology to the fullest to explore more creative ways of making education interactive, fun to motivate the students, change their mindset on STEM related subjects in order to improve learning.

3   Objectives

The study objectives were as follows: -

1. To highlight how Kio-Kit was planned to be used for enhancing teaching and learning STEM subjects in Zanzibar lower secondary classes (Form One and Form Two)
2. To analyse teachers' perception of using Kio-Kits from those teachers who has been trained to use it in order to improve their teaching and learning
3. To identify challenges encountered during the exploration and the use of Kio-Kit in classroom situation
4. To propose the way forward for technology enhancement in teaching and learning process as expected.

4 Methodology

Since Kio-Kit is a new technology to the most of the teachers participated in this study, the main aim was to find how far they perceive this technology, and to accomplish that aim different factors were considered during the study.

4.1 Study Design

To obtain rich and detailed information needed to document how teachers were exploring and using Kio-Kit for teaching, both qualitative and quantitative data were collected. At each teacher's centre (A, B and C), an online survey was given to both STEM teachers, Headteachers or Assistant Headteachers to complete it to check technology familiarity and uses. STEM teachers were selected based on the assumption that the successful integration of technology can transform STEM classes.

4.2 Data Collection

The data were collected from a two days intensive training on the Kio-Kit technology for the STEM teachers teaching Form I and Form II classes from both Unguja and Pemba (Zanzibar). A manual for Kio-Kit for teachers was prepared and used in the training as a guide. The manual was broken down into eight (8) modules explaining what a Kio-Kit is, why it is used, how it works and how it can be integrated into the classroom situation. In addition to that, the teachers were also asked to explore the relevance and applicability of the contents available in the Kio-Kit.

After the training the link to the questionnaire which was prepared using Google Form was shared to both the participants who participated in the training. The teachers were encouraged to fill the form by sending several reminders through WhatsApp.

4.3 Participants

Out of sixty (60) STEM trained teachers, thirty-five (35) responded to the online questionnaire, twenty-one (21) of them were male and fourteen (14) were female. From these, eight (8) were Physics teachers, eight (8) were Mathematics teachers, nine (9) were Chemistry teachers, seven (7) were Biology teachers and the remaining three (3) were from Engineering discipline. 15 Headteachers were not included in the survey. During the training the teachers were observed and then were given the online questionnaires to respond. Teachers' participation was voluntary.

5 Results and Discussion

Data were collected and analysed by the STEM Kio-Kit technical team. Google form was used to collect and analyse them. The data were gathered into two main categories, the first part asked about teacher's profile with information including gender, school, subject specialization, teacher's experience and role. The second part consisted of main questions on the perception of using Kio-Kit in classroom and the challenges of using this technology with an extra space provided for any additional comments. The following were cited to depict teachers' perception on using Kio-Kit to enhance Teaching and Learning STEM subjects in Zanzibar.

5.1   Teachers Personal Information

In terms of gender, 35 out of 75 teachers from the 15 schools who participated the training responded, in which 60% being male and 40% were female.

The study also went further to know the teaching experience of the participants. As shown in Fig. 1. Teaching experience of STEM teachers Below, the results reveals that majority of the teachers (44%) have experience of about 1 to 5 years in teaching, while 24% fall under the category of 6 to 10 years of working experience, 9% of teachers have experience of 11 to 15 years while 21% among them fall under 15 to 20 years of experience and about only 2% were having more than 20 years of working experience.

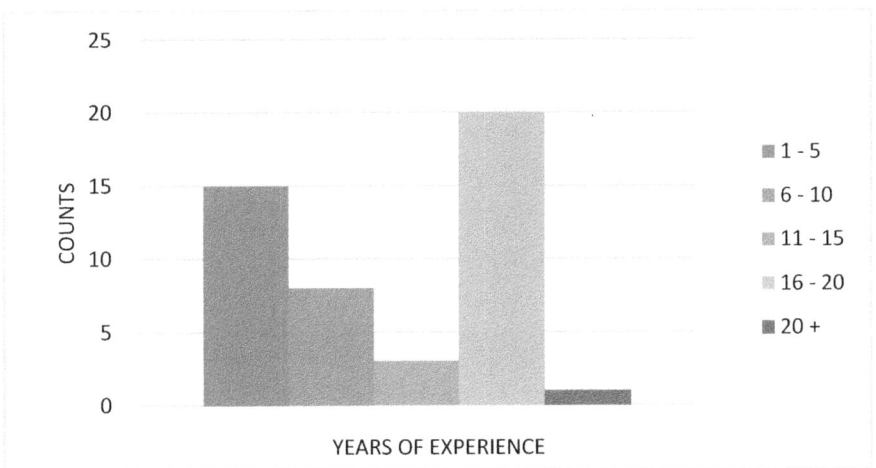

Fig. 1. Teaching experience of STEM teachers

Moreover, the teachers were asked to mention their subjects of specialization in relation to STEM subjects. The results showed that, 21.2% of teaches Biology subject, 21.2% are Chemistry teachers, 24.2% are Physics teachers, 24.2% are Mathematics teachers and the remaining 9.1% come from Engineering and Technology subjects (Fig. 2).

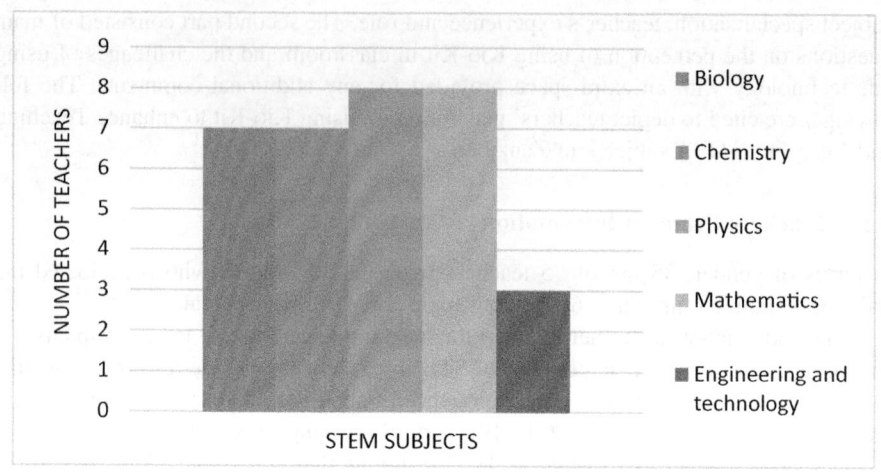

Fig. 2. Subject of specialization of STEM teachers

Most of the teachers who participated in the training were subject teachers (82.9%) while only 8.6% were head teachers, 2.9% were assistant head teachers, 2.9% class teachers and the remaining 2.9% were section leaders (Fig. 3).

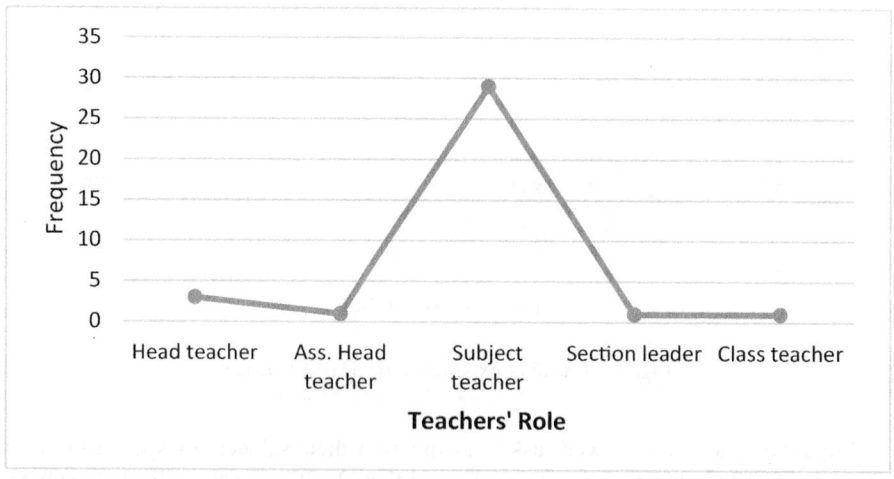

Fig. 3. Teacher's role

5.2   Teachers' Perception on Using Kio-Kit in Teaching and Learning

In order to measure the perception of the teachers on the use of Kio-Kit, different criteria have been used to check the degree of their perceptions on using this new technology as shown in Fig. 4.

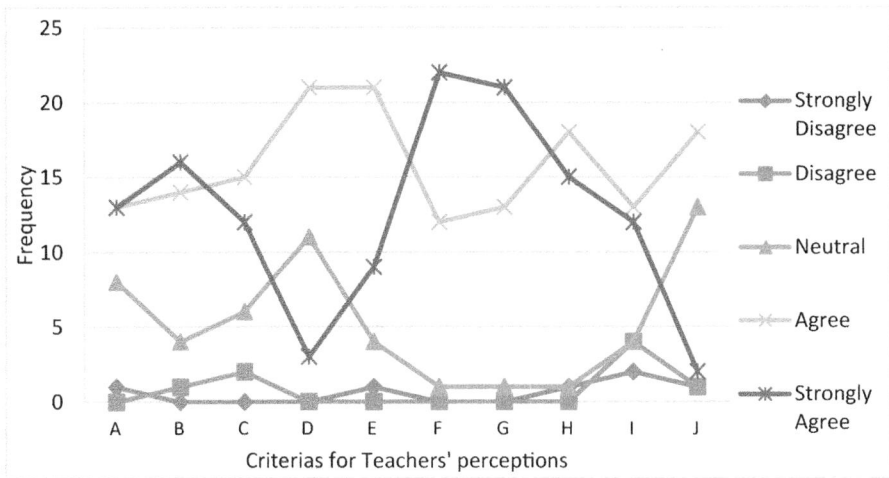

Fig. 4. Teachers' perception on the use of Kio-Kit

The perception criteria used in Fig. 4 are defined using the letters as tabulated in Table 1 below.

Table 1. Criteria used to measure teachers' perception on using Kio-Kit technology

Letter	Criteria
A	Improve students' attendance
B	Improve teachers attendance
C	Pedagogical shift in classroom
D	Increase engagement with the local community
E	Improve information literacy skills in students
F	Increase students interaction and participation
G	Provide new knowledge and skills to student
H	Give more opportunities for students to learn
I	Involve all types of learners in learning process
J	Improve student English literacy

Improve Student Attendance

Majority of the teachers agreed that the use of Kio-Kit technology in the classroom will improve students' attendance. 74.2% strongly agree on this, while only 2.9% disagree, the remaining 22.9% were neutral. The idea is also supported by the study conducted by Mundy [6] who summarised that teachers perceived a significant increase in the student engagement, student excitement as well as student acceleration of learning.

Improve Teachers Attendance

85.7% of the participants agreed that the use of Kio-Kit technology in the classroom will improve the attendance of the teachers in the class.

Pedagogical Shift in Classroom

Out of the teachers who responded, 80% support that the use of Kio-Kit technology in classroom will transform the teaching in schools. The remaining 20% were neutral and none of them disagree on this. The use of technology in education has changed the learning process due to the introduction of new features in the pedagogy such as collaborative learning and rapid access of information. Various new learning theories have been proposed such as heutagogy and paragogy as mentioned by Popovici and Mironov [7].

Increase Engagement with the Local Community

The findings show that 68.6% of the teachers agree that the use of Kio-Kit technology will boost students' participation in the classroom, while 31.4% of them were neutral.

Improve Information Literacy Skills in Students

Information literacy skills in students are perceived to improve by the use of Kio-Kit in the classrooms by 80% of the teachers. Only 2.9% of them disagree and the remaining 17.1% were neutral.

Increase Students' Interaction and Participation

Most of the teachers agree on the increase of students' interaction and participation. 91.4% agree fully to this, 5.7% were neutral and only 2.9% disagree. It is obvious, as Kio-Kit like any other digital technology will provide features such as collaborative learning, multitasking as well as rapid information access.

Provide New Knowledge and Skills to Students

The study revealed 97.1% of the teachers agree that students will gain new knowledge and skills to students, the remaining 2.9% were neutral while none of them disagree. Kay et al. [8] commented that middle and secondary students who were introduced to web-based learning tools in their classes gain a hands-on learning experience and was able to practice new skills.

Give More Opportunities for Students to Learn

The study also revealed that 94.3% of the teachers agree that the use of Kio-Kit in classroom will give more opportunities for the students to learn, 2.9% were neutral while 2.9% disagree.

Involve All Types of Learners in Learning Process

71.4% of the teachers perceived that the integration of this new technology in their classes will involve all types of learners in the learning process, 11.4% of them were neutral and the remaining 17.1% disagree on the following point.

Improve Student English Literacy

In this study 57.1% of the teachers agree on the improvement of student English literacy, 37.1% were neutral, 5.8% while disagree. The study made by Cheng [9] exposed that all the teachers who participate in the study appreciated the use of technology in enhancing teaching and learning English due to the presence of various online materials that will enable them together with their students to cope well with this situation.

6 Challenges of Using Kio-Kit in Classroom

In addition to the above points, the teachers were asked to mention if they may encounter any challenges in using this kind technology during their classroom. The overarching challenge for most of the teachers was on time management on introducing the lesson to class and the use of Kio-Kit. While most of them claim that it was very difficult for them to manage time as it is a new method introduced to them, others relate time management to the time it takes for the resources found in the Kio-Kit to be displayed.

Another major concern is on the large number of students in most of Unguja and Pemba Schools. The distribution of the Kio tablets will be very difficult for them since only 40 kio-tablets available, which is different from the real scenario currently facing many schools which has very large classroom and many students at a time.

Further, the teachers also mentioned that student's concentration might be another challenge, since they can concentrate on other contents apart from what the teacher wants them to view, as there is no any form of control on the teachers' side.

Other challenges mentioned including lack of teachers with competence in using current technologies, and most of them suggested more training to the teachers. Some teachers also pointed out that some teachers are resistant to use the new technologies in their classes, and they prefer the traditional way of teaching due to their experience. Most of them also mentioned about the available contents in the Kio-kit which to some extent is not relevant for the chosen group of students (Form one and Form two students). Lastly, some teachers dictate that English is a problem to most of their students, and they are afraid the students may fail to follow the given instructions and navigate through various contents available in the Kio-Kit.

7 Conclusion

As we have seen above, Kio-Kit technology is one of the digital technologies that can be used in classroom to improve or enhance teaching and learning, especially in countries where there is no adequate infrastructure such as internet access and the like. Allowing young students to use current technologies afford them the opportunity to explore and giving them more opportunity to learn by themselves and improve their critical thinking skills, which are the most important skills needed in the 21st century workplace. Results from the teachers demonstrate that the use of Kio-Kit technology have many positive impacts on students' performance as well as teachers' technical know-how despite the few challenges that has been stated earlier. It is safe to argue that with some improvements, commitment and dedication, the use of this technology is of importance for the preparation of the students in the technological era.

References

1. Mashhadi, V.Z., Kargozari, M.R.: Influences of digital classrooms on education. Proc. Comput. Sci. **3**, 1178–1183 (2011). https://doi.org/10.1016/j.procs.2010.12.190
2. Forzani, E., Leu, D.J.: New literacies for new learners: the need for digital technologies in primary classrooms. Educ. Forum **76**(4), 421–424 (2012). https://doi.org/10.1080/00131725. 2012.708623
3. Hoyles, C., Noss, R., Kent, P.: On the integration of digital technologies into mathematics classrooms. Int. J. Comput. Math. Learn. **9**(3), 309–326 (2004). https://doi.org/10.1007/ s10758-004-3469-4
4. Hack and Craft Homepage. https://hackandcraft.com/insights/articles/brck-kio-kit-revolutionising-education-africa/. Accessed 14 Mar 2019
5. ITU News: The Kio Kit: a digital learning solution engineered in Africa for the world, 27 March 2018. https://news.itu.int/the-kio-kit-african-solution-digital-learning/. Accessed 14 Feb 2018
6. Mundy, M.-A., Kupczynski, L., Kee, R.: Teacher's perceptions of technology use in the schools. Sage Open **2** (2012). https://doi.org/10.1177/2158244012440813
7. Popovici, A., Mironov, C.: Students' perception on using eLearning technologies. In: The 6th International Conference "Education Facing Contemporary World Issues", 7–9 November 2014
8. Kay, R., Knaack, L., Petrarca, D.: Exploring teacher's perceptions of web-based learning tools. Interdisc. J. E-Learn. Learn. Objects **5**, 527–550 (2009)
9. Cheng, S.-C.: Teachers' perceptions on the use of digital tools in English teaching and learning (2018)

Challenges and Opportunities of Managing Social Media Generated Records in Institutions of Learning: A Case of the Midlands State University, Zimbabwe

Shephard Pondiwa[(✉)] and Margaret Phiri[(✉)]

Midlands State University, Gweru, Zimbabwe
pondiwas@gmail.com, phirisisa@gmail.com

Abstract. The management of institutions of learning largely depends on the way their records are managed. Social media use and management of records created on social media is a subject that has raised a number of issues that require academic research to focus on. It has become inevitable for organizations and institutions of learning to embrace the use of several social media platforms in their conduct of business. The paper explores how the Midlands State University (MSU) in Zimbabwe has embraced the use of social media in the conduct of official business and how this has affected teaching and learning. The study employed a case study approach that used questionnaires and semi structured and structured interview questions. This research views social media generated records as records which must be managed well as they are part and parcel of the institution's assets and that if they are not properly managed this affects the provision of education. The paper is informed by the continuum concept. The objectives of the study were to identify the social media platforms used at the Midlands State University, challenges and opportunities brought in by social media as a learning platform as well as a communication platform. The study also aimed to develop a model that can be used to integrate social media generated records into the main records management system since such integration is key to the proper management of institutions of higher learning.

Keywords: Social media · Records management · Midlands State University

1 Introduction

Records are a vital tool that is used in the management of institutions of educational institutions. There has been an increase in the use of social media records for official business transactions in institutions of higher learning and other organizations in Zimbabwe. Apart from MSU, Social media is also used in other state universities such as Chinhoyi University of Technology (www.cut.ac.zw), University of Zimbabwe (www.uz.ac.zw) Great Zimbabwe University (www.gzu.ac.zw) Bindura University of Science Education (www.buse.ac.zw) and Zimbabwe Open University (www.zou.ac.zw) among others. Teachers colleges and polytechnics have also adopted the use of social media generated records to communicate with their stake holders as well

A. Tatnall and N. Mavengere (Eds.): SUZA 2019, IFIP AICT 564, pp. 145–156, 2019.
https://doi.org/10.1007/978-3-030-28764-1_17

disseminate study material to students. This has gone a long way in changing the way institutions conduct teaching and learning as well as the way they do business and socializing. Mavengere and Ruohonen [10] state, "Technology use in the tertiary education sector is of immense importance for educational development in Africa". In Zimbabwe social media use has been adopted as part and parcel of this drive to use technology for both academic and social use. The use of social media has come with challenges particularly in the area of the records management. These challenges include identification of authorship, control of data on social media, appraisal of these records as well the capture of content from social media records into records management systems.

The Midlands State University is one of the 13 state universities in Zimbabwe. It was established by the Midlands State University Act in 1999. The Midlands State University (MSU) has nine faculties, namely Arts, Education, Law, Commerce, Natural Resources Management and Agriculture, Social Sciences, Mining and Mineral Processing Engineering, Medicine and Science and Technology. These faculties use social media generated records in one way or another in the conduct of business. The use of social media records for doing official business at the Midlands State University is a relatively new development for example Facebook was first used at Midlands State University for doing official business in 2013. WhatsApp, Twitter, YouTube and Instagram were first used for official business in 2014 by the Midlands State University. Prior to the adoption of the use of social media, Midlands State University had been creating both paper and electronic records in its conduct of business. These records were and still continue to be managed using a hybrid records management system. This is a system in which some records are kept in their paper form while others are kept in the electronic form. Nakpodia [12] describes a hybrid records management system as one that makes use of records in both electronic and paper form.

In his speech at a Results Based Management workshop at Kadoma Ranch Motel from 19–21 December 2018, the Vice Chancellor of MSU indicated that there are challenges with regard the way the university is communicating on social media. The Herald of 3 January 2019 carried a story titled "MSU dismisses fees hike story" In this article the institution emphasised that what had circulated on social media regarding an increase in fees was not true. The Registrar commented, "The institution has its channels of communication which include its website, social media platforms and mainstream media" (Herald 3 January 2018). On 17 January 2018 the MSU Registrar released a statement to refute social media reports that claimed that MSU had failed to pay for licences of Turnitin, an anti-plagiarism software that is used to cheque plagiarism in students assignments and projects (Herald 17 January 2018). The use of social media in institutions of learning has grown tremendously and such records created on these platforms need to be managed well as there are key to the smooth running of these institutions.

2   Theoretical Background

This study is influenced by the continuum theory developed in 1990 by Frank Upward. It states that record keeping processes should be put in place before the records are created. This is to say record keeping requirements such as policies, systems, processes, social mandates and laws should be put in place first before records are created. The continuum concept is also based on the idea that records are not only created to serve the interests of future archivists or historians but they are created to serve immediate operational needs [1, 2]. Shepherd and Yeo [14] also state that Archivists and Records Managers need to be involved together with Information Systems Designers in the creation of records keeping systems. Social media has of late been used as a means to deliver educational content. In as much as social media is indeed transforming education delivery and reshaping learning and teaching activities we cannot ignore the need to capture properly records created, used and maintained on social media platforms. This can effectively be done if learning institutions employ the use of the continuum concept in managing such records. The records continuum model encourages a participatory nature starting from the design phase whereby Archivists, Records Managers and Systems Designers all take part in the designing of the system that manages records from creation to disposition. This implies that the records that are created on social media platforms can be prospered managed if there is collaboration between record managers and archivists. Such well managed records positively impact the way learning institutions are managed. Thus the continuum theory was relevant to this study in that it appreciates the need to properly manage records from creation to disposal. Kemoni [7] observed that the continuum model is widely accepted for managing records both in paper and electronic form. The model is relevant to the study in the sense that it appreciates records starting from their creation up to disposal. It also becomes very relevant in that social media records are created in the electronic format and as such they can be managed using the continuum model.

3   Methodology

Through a case study of the Midlands State University, the study employed a qualitative methodology with an interpretivist paradigm to do an in depth analysis of the challenges and opportunities that are faced in the management of social media generated records and how this impacts on the management of institutions of learning. A case study is an empirical inquiry that investigates a contemporary phenomenon in depth and within its real-life context, especially when the boundaries between phenomenon and context are not clearly evident.

The design helped the researchers to have a clear picture on how the MSU staff, students and other stakeholders perceive their experience regarding the use of social media and how it impacts on the principles of records management. The researchers employed the use questionnaires and interviews to obtain information from the informants.

The study targeted a total of 50 participants comprising of staff members and students. Forty of these are people who are employed by the Midlands State University and they generate and use social media records in their day to day activities. Ten students were also part of the sample as they are in some cases consumers of the material posted on social media platforms.

3.1 Interviews

The researchers used both structured and unstructured interviews to solicit information from the entire population. According to Cohen et al. [3] interviewing is "a valuable method for exploring the construction and negotiation of meanings in a natural setting". Interviews are a relevant instrument in qualitative research. Structured and semi structured interview questions were used to get information from key informants such as Faculty Administrators, records clerks and managers and lecturers. Interviews enabled the researchers to get firsthand information from both students and staff members that create and use social media records.

3.2 Questionnaires

The research used questionnaires to examine the challenges that users and creators of social media records at MSU face. The researchers distributed 30 questionnaires to staff members who work closely with social media records. Members were purposively selected. 10 questionnaires were distributed to students who were randomly selected as they came to register for the new semester.

4 Results

4.1 Social Media Platforms Used at MSU

This research revealed that there are several media platforms that are used at MSU for both personal and official university business. Questionnaire respondents (staff) were asked which social media platform they used the most to do official university business and the results are shown in the Table 1 below:

Table 1. Social media usage at MSU

Type of social media platform	Frequency	Percentage
Facebook	4	13.3
WhatsApp	20	66.7
Twitter	2	6.7
YouTube	3	10
Instagram	1	3.3

4.2   Challenges of Managing Social Media Records

There are many challenges that are associated with the use of social media generated records. This study revealed that MSU has faced the following challenges in creating, using and managing social media generated records:

Lack of Policy Regulating Creation, Use and Maintenance of Social Media Records

Records should be managed according to authorised policies. Mulati and Wasike [13] posit, "A policy is a governing principle, plan or course of action which guides the operation of a given entity" A Records management policy can also be described as an authoritative statement of intent to manage records in an appropriate and suitable manner for as long as they are required for business purposes. Existing records management laws (especially in Zimbabwe) do not accommodate social media records. In the absence of such recognition, social media records may be deleted before their time or permanently retained unnecessarily. In Zimbabwe there is no University that has a social media policy that addresses the way social media generated records should be managed. Even though The Midlands State University has a records Management policy, it does not explicitly cater for social media generated records and this has created problems in the way such records are managed. Many scholars have emphasized on the importance of a comprehensive records management policy. Kabata advances that most organisations do not take the management of social media records seriously as they take a sweeping approach to the management of their records. The absence of a social media policy at MSU is evidence that what Kabata claims is common in most institutions. Latham [9] emphasizes the need for a policy that regulates the management of records including digital records. He argues that a records management policy is essential in the management of institutional records in that it spells out what should and what should not be done. It is intended to form the initial framework or principles which express how records should be managed within the organization. It is therefore essential that the creation, management and disposal of records at MSU be guided by policy. This will make it easy for the integration of social media generated records to be integrated into the main hybrid system. This is in line with ISO 15489-1 (2016) which states that managing records should encompass taking appropriate effort to protect their authenticity, reliability, integrity and usability ISO 15489-1 (2016). Ihejirika et al. [16] posit that in some institutions social media is used in the promotion of academic material and content such as library material. This paper argues that if MSU wants to do the same this has to be guided by policy.

Anecdotal evidence used in this study revealed that the absence of policies that regulate the use of social media generated information has made it very difficult for the Midlands State University to manage the records generated from such platforms. 97% of administrators interviewed admitted that they were using social media in the conduct of official university business but they were not being guided by any policy.

The study revealed that there is great use of social media platforms outside business hours and in most cases use their personal social media accounts to do university business. This has resulted in confusion as there are multiple communication channels which do not usually address an issue in the same way. Various stakeholders have been given different versions of the same issue thereby creating confusion.

While the University is run by a committee system, there is no committee dedicated to the management of social media generated information. There is however a Website committee but its duties are only restricted to what appears on the official MSU website (www.msu.ac.zw) This absence of a committee to regulate the use of social media has resulted in a number of challenges as officers have posted and removed post about the institution as they wish. The responsibility to post and remove items on Facebook, twitter and WhatsApp is left in the hands of two officers who work in the Information and Publicity Office. When asked how they chose what to post on social media platforms they indicated that they used their discretion to select what to post. This has an impact on the way such institutions conduct their business and the way such issues affect stakeholders such as students.

What Constitutes a Social Media Record?

Results from this study indicated that it is difficult to identify what constitutes a record on social media platforms. The situation is worsened by the rate of accumulation of social media records. The accumulation rate is very rapid such that organizations may be unable to identify the elements that constitute an authentic record like content, context, structure and associated metadata. This problem was found to very common at all the MSU campuses by this study. ISO 15489-2016 describes a record as information created, received and maintained as evidence and as an asset by an organization or person, in pursuit of legal obligations or in the transaction of business. So while there is confusion among users on what is a record, it must be noted that the ISO 15489-(2016) definition qualifies social media information to be records. It is therefore necessary for institutions to note that what they create on social media qualify to be defined as records and as such these records can be used as evidence of a transaction or conversation. Duranti [4] argued, "We consider a record to be a document made or received in the course of activity. As it takes part in some action, it is seen as evidence of it, that is, as its mirror and proof. The value of such evidence, in terms of validity and weight, depends on the RELIABILITY of the record. A record is considered reliable when it can be treated as a fact in itself, that is, as the entity of which it is evidence".

Ownership and Control of Social Media Data

The study revealed that it is not clear as to who owns information that is on social media. The information generated on social media is usually managed by third parties and the organization or individuals who use or create it may not have total control on such records. These third parties usually have too much influence on how the information is created, circulated or kept. They may choose to terminate their services and users have no control over that. The host company may choose to use the information for purposes other than that which the creators intended to use it for. This is possible because most social media platforms provide a generic "terms of service" agreement for all customers.

The researchers also found out that records created through the use of social media tools residing on third-party servers pose serious challenges such as proprietary file formats, tools to capture information, frequency of capture, questions regarding the boundaries of a record, and concerns over the ability to maintain the 'context' of the record. Social media has contributed in the creation of records that are born digital. Digital creation has allowed organizations to create records and provide information in a variety of new formats, but has also presented challenges to recordkeeping processes. The variety of applications and platforms used to create, transmit, and store records may complicate how organizations manage, retain, and retrieve their records because it is not certain, for example whether the devices and applications organizations currently use to create and retain digital records will be viable over long periods of time and ensure enduring access to information.

Lack of Technical Skills to Manage Social Media Generated Records

Another challenge with regards the use of social media records is to do with technical skills to manage such records. People who manage such records require constant training so that they are better able to capture, manage and preserve them to ensure long-term access to such records. Out of the 10 Staff members interviewed at MSU, only 2 (20%) had technical skills to manage social media generated records. The rest indicated that they only used social media and were not able to capture and preserve content. (80%). This has an impact on the way the institution manages its social media records in that most of the valuable records that are created on social media platforms end up been mismanaged due to lack of technical skills to capture and preserve social media content.

90% of questionnaire respondents indicated that they were not aware of any technical courses that they could undertake to ensure the proper management of records generated on social media. This is an indication that a lot needs to be done in the area of capacitating members of staff at the Midlands state university so that they can be able to manage social media generated records well.

Confidentiality

The confidentiality of records held by an institution or its employees is of paramount importance for as long as such records influence decision making within the institution. Social media compromises confidentiality. Information shared on most social media platforms contain personally identifiable information that includes work locations, employment information, education, hobbies and photos. In the traditional records management context such information ought to be managed properly to ensure appropriate confidentiality. However, with social media platforms such confidentiality is not always certain as it is possible to harvest information even in instances whereby particular organizations are not responsible for creation. This is compounded by the fact that most social media platforms are collaborative in the sense that a post on Facebook may contain links from YouTube. This presents challenges during capture if the techniques used to capture these records cannot encapsulate the whole record, [5, 8] 90% of interviewed people admitted that they were aware that the use of social media such as Facebook, Twitter and WhatsApp among others was not very safe as confidential information can be shared in social media groups and thereby compromising the confidentiality of such information.

Capture of Social Media Content

The capturing of the content of records that have been created by any organization is of paramount importance. Records are dependent upon the availability of the contextual information which confirms their relationship to administrative and operational activities (World Bank 2004). For that reason, it is necessary to make sure that the content of all records is captured correctly. Capturing records created by social media is one of the most paramount activities that record creators, managers and archivists should be able to do professionally. NARA posits, "Social media content capture is an emerging topic that has not consolidated around standards for capture" ISO 15489 stresses that managing records encompasses creating and capturing records to meet requirements for evidence of business activity. It also involves taking appropriate action to protect their authenticity, reliability, integrity and usability as their business context and requirements for their management change over time.

This means that as records are generated through the social media platforms it is necessary to capture their content. This is not an easy task as it involves a lot of work and commitment. Kaplan [6] argues that the retention of social media records can be very difficult, especially those that are frequently updated. In order to possess the necessary characteristics of public records, records must be captured or filed in the official recordkeeping system. The Midlands State University does not have clear strategy on how they will capture information emanating from social media. Records are created used and disposed without capturing their content for posterity. Capturing the correct content of social media records is essential in the management of institutions of learning as it enhances transparency and accountability.

Authenticity of Social Media Records

Authentic records are the cornerstone of sound management of institutions of learning. A record must have basically four characteristics which are content, form, context and structure [14] it is when a record has these characteristics that it can be said to be authentic. This is quite important in that if the authenticity of a document is doubtful then it may not need to be integrated into a records management system. Rogers posits, "The assessment and protection of the authenticity of digital records and data are recognized as fundamental issues for the records' current use as well as for their long term preservation and dissemination." The idea of record authenticity is codified in ISO 15489-1:2016, the international records management standard as follows: "An authentic record is one that can be proven to be what it purports to be, to have been created or sent by the person purported to have created or sent it, and to have been created or sent at the time purported".

Durant [4] gives a detailed explanation of what record authenticity is by stating:

Legally authentic documents are those which bear witness on their own because of the intervention, during or after their creation, of a representative of a public authority guaranteeing their genuineness. Diplomatically authentic documents are those which were written according to the practice of the time and place indicated in the text and signed with the name(s) of the person(s) competent to create them. One factor that has proved very problematic at MSU and many other institutions regarding the authenticity of digital records is that they are vulnerable to unauthorized or inadvertent change and loss.

Some institutions have adopted the use of digital signatures to protect the authenticity and integrity of electronic documents. The use of digital signatures ICA Committee on Archival Legal Matters summed up the importance of authentic records by stating that authentic documents are "reliable not only at the moment when they are created but remain reliable for a long time to come".

Several media generated records about the Midlands State University have been circulated on WhatsApp. The authenticity of some of the circulated documents is questionable as in most cases one can end up with several versions of the same story. The 2018 MSU graduation ceremony was 'postponed' several times in social media platforms. This resulted in confusion as to which date was the correct graduation date. Research also indicated that some students circulated fake news or fake notices on some social media groups claiming that lecturers had cancelled lectures.

Appraisal of Social Media Records

Social media records, like any other records should be appraised Miller and Roper [11] define appraisal as "the process of determining the value of records for further use, for whatever purposes and the length of time for which that value will continue". In an attempt to explain appraisal, Yiotis explains that, "Appraisal is done in order to determine which institutional activities create records that provide a true image of society". The inability to appraise social media records results in misguided decisions by the institution. Appraisal has posed many challenges to records managers and archivists. In most cases when there are various versions of a document or record, it can be difficult to know the authentic version. This poses problems and makes it extremely difficult to integrate such records. This problem is compounded by the fact that most institutions have no control as to who posts on social media and when can information be posted. This has resulted in many versions of the same story being posted and commented on official sites. Thus to a larger extent one can argue that the use of traditional methods in the appraisal of records needs some revisiting in order to take into account changing contexts and formats in which these records are formed.

Lack of Appropriate Gadgets to Access Social Media Platforms

The adoption of the use of social media records by officials in the Midlands State University such as lecturers and administrators has been done on the assumption that all the students have a gadget that connects to the internet and can support social media platforms. Lecturers have posted learning material and assignment questions on social media yet 33% of the interviewed students indicated that they had challenges accessing such information as they did not have the appropriate gadgets such as smartphones and laptops. With 72% of Zimbabweans being said to be living in poverty smartphones are one of the luxuries that most students go without and such the use of social media for activities such as lesson delivery can turn out to be disastrous.

5   Opportunities for Midlands State University Presented by the Use of Social Media Records

In spite of the various challenges that are associated with the use of social media there are also a number of opportunities which come with the adoption of social media. In the case of Midlands State University which has adopted a multi campus system social media has enhanced quick information sharing across campuses and affiliate colleges. Social media has also allowed easy communication with stakeholders and potential stakeholders of the university allowing fast and easy dissemination of information with the same effect as mass media or even better. This has enabled the university to frequently update its stakeholders of the various developments taking place in the university in an endeavour to maintain transparency and accountability which is enshrined in its mission statement. Compared to mass media such as radio and tele-vision the use of social media is far more affordable and quick.

The core business of Midlands State University is teaching and learning and in this regard the adoption of social media has allowed lecturers to constantly communicate with their students updating them of any developments and distribute learning material. This at least decreases the chances of students being surprised by impromptu lectures and in-class examinations or tests. 90% of the lecturers interviewed indicated that they had used social media in one way or another. Some interviewees explained how convenient social media platforms were in terms of knowledge sharing amongst themselves as professionals and also in some cases between themselves and the stu-dents. Social media has also allowed the university's students to be able to share information amongst themselves and keeping abreast with the latest findings and researches in their field of study. Students can organise group discussions arrange researches and communicate findings on social media platforms (Fig. 1).

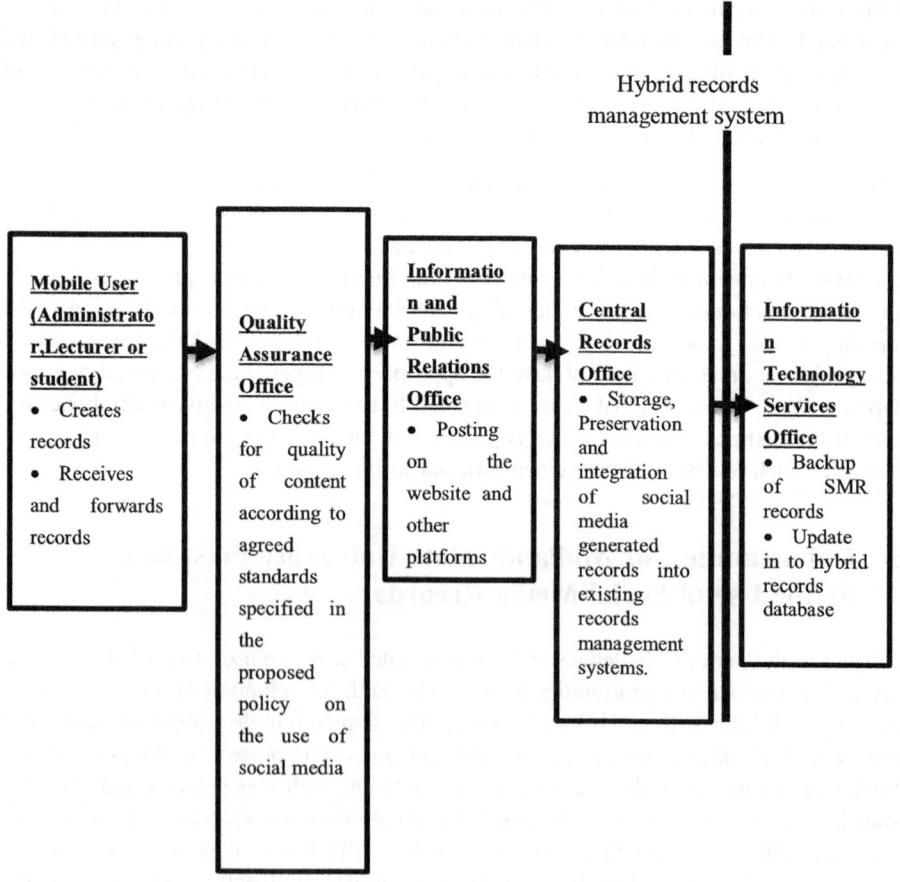

Fig. 1. Social media records integration model

The above model proposes that MSU employees and in some isolated cases students using social media records to do official business should do it in a manner that is regulated as shown by the model. The model will operate well if there is a social media policy that regulates the way social media generated records are created, used and disposed. Vuori [15] argues that social media has the potential to give institutions competitive advantage over those that may not use it.

6 Conclusion

This study has shown that the Midlands state university has adopted the use of social media in the various business activities. The use of social media has been done without following any policy and as such the records created out of such transactions have not been properly integrated into the main records management systems. Apart from the challenges that have been discussed in this paper, MSU can take advantages of opportunities that exist in the field of social media and gain competitive advantage through taking advantage of the fact that social media has reduced the world into one global village and as such knowledge sharing has been enhanced. However, the use of social media needs to be done in line with policies. MSU can also take advantage of the fact that social media has been widely accepted by user within and outside the university as 'official' communication platforms and utilise the model that the researchers developed to be used as a model to integrate social media generated records.

References

1. Atherton, D.P.: Computer aided learning and design in control education (1985). https://doi.org/10.1177/014233128500700201. Accessed 02 Feb 2019
2. Bantin, P.C.: Electronic Records Management, A Review the Work of a Decade and Reflection on Future Directions: Encyclopedia of Library and Information Science (2002)
3. Cohen, L., Mannion, L., Morrison, K.: Research Methods in Education, 5th edn. Routledge, London (2007)
4. Duranti, L.: Preservation of Integrity of Electronic Records. Klewer Academic Publishers, Netherlands (2000)
5. Ginsberg: Retaining and Preserving Federal Records in a Digital Environment: Background Issues for Congress (2013). https://fas.org/sgp/crs/misc/R43165.pdf. Accessed 04 Mar 2019
6. Kaplan, A.M., Haenlein, M.: Users of the world, unite! The challenges and opportunities of social media. Business Horizons (2016)
7. Kemoni, H.N.: Theoretical framework and literature review in graduate management research (2008). http://findarticles.com/p/articles/ml_7002/ls_2_18/al_n31877456/. Accessed 16 Jan 2019
8. Kim, K.: Social media and records management challenges (2012). https://www.slideshare.net/foipop/social-media-and-records-management-management-challenges-2012-0917m-14359486. Accessed 10 Mar 2019
9. Latham, R.: Managing Web 2.0: Tasmanian Archive and heritage office. State Records Guideline, no. 18, Tasmania (2012)

10. Mavengere, N.B., Ruohonen, M.J.: Using open source software for improving dialog in computer science education - case Mozambique university. In: Tatnall, A., Kereteletswe, O. C., Visscher, A. (eds.) Information Technology and Managing Quality Education, 9th IFIP WG 3.7 Conference on Information Technology in Educational Management, ITEM 2010 Kasane, Botswana, 26–30 July 2010

11. Millar, M., Roper, L.: Managing Hospital Records: A Study Programme. International Records Management Trust, London (1999)

12. Nakpodia, E.D., Dafiaghor, F.K.: Lateness: a major problem confronting school administrators in Delta State, Nigeria (2011)

13. Mulati, N., Wasike, J.: Assessment of Hybrid Records Management Systems at Mount Kenya University, Kenya International Journal of Science and Research (IJSR) ISSN (Online): 2319-7064 Index Copernicus Value (2015): 78.96 | Impact Factor (2015): 6.3 (2015)

14. Shepherd, E., Yeo, G.: Managing Records: a Handbook of Principles and Practice. Facet Publishing, London (2003)

15. Vuori, V.: Social media changing the competitive intelligence process: elicitation of employees' competitive knowledge, Thesis for: Doctor of Science in Technology (Ph.D.) Tampere university (2011)

16. Ihejirika, K.T., Anne Gouldin, A., Calvert, P.: How social is your social media? Managing social media marketing in academic libraries (2018). http://creativecommons.org/licenses/by/4.0. Accessed 31 May 2019

Antecedents of Sustainable Vocational Education and Training in ICT in Global South Countries

Javier Osorio[✉] and Julia Nieves

Universidad de Las Palmas de Gran Canaria,
35017 Las Palmas de Gran Canaria, Spain
javier.osorio@ulpgc.es

Abstract. The topic of sustainability is another component of the complex issue of fostering effective vocational education and training (VET) initiatives in information and communication technologies (ICT) in Global South countries. There is no workable model of VET for Development, and simple, symptomatic solutions are no longer suitable. This paper attempts to summarize some drivers that can be considered as antecedents of this issue. They conform part of the big picture that arises when addressing long term, structural proposals. The prism of sustainability has been included as a complementary lens with which to look at it. Sustainability can serve to either shed some light on the issue or, alternatively, add some uncertainty and pressure, with the result of making it even more complex.

Keywords: Vocational education and training · VET ·
Information and communication technologies · ICT ·
Global South · Sustainability

1 Introduction

The development of vocational education and training (VET) in many Global South countries is a complex issue. In fact, it is a complex issue all around the world, but in the case of low-income countries it faces additional challenges because of the lack of available educational and technological resources. The task of interpreting and unravelling the picture of all variables and circumstances that converge when designing and developing VET initiatives, especially in Global South countries, appears to be a difficult one. Analysis and recommended courses of action have been raised by national governments, regional organisations (Southern African Development Community - SADC, Union of South American Nations - USAN) and global institutions (OECD, UNESCO); often with the only result being that the big picture becomes even more complicated. The objective of this paper is to re-examine the issue of VET initiatives in Global South countries under the prism of sustainability which, as a general concept, can potentially influence it both internally and externally.

Most of the arguments for explaining the differences in educational development between the Northern and Southern hemispheres tended to focus on the endemic lack of resources allocated to the educational arena in Global South countries. Another

© IFIP International Federation for Information Processing 2019
Published by Springer Nature Switzerland AG 2019
A. Tatnall and N. Mavengere (Eds.): SUZA 2019, IFIP AICT 564, pp. 157–166, 2019.
https://doi.org/10.1007/978-3-030-28764-1_18

reason has been the low level of social-economic development, which serves as a constraint to the virtuous loop that links educational and economic improvement. The mirror of the Global North - where no doubt arises when justifying the link between education and economic development as the key to success - may promote the view that the formulae that apparently fits well in one part of the world can also work equally well everywhere else. Within this landscape, during the last thirty years another agent has irrupted becoming a major protagonist: information and communication technologies (ICT). The nature of this actor, heavily demanding of huge investments for it to be incorporated into the educational arena, has been supposed to be both a source of opportunity that allows educational processes to be aligned in countries of both hemispheres and, at the same time, a threat because of the costly nature of technology. The acquisition of ICT may, eventually, permit resources that could be allocated to other social or economic initiatives to be deferred. However, some research has showed that the focus on technology is not a key driver in educational improvement [1], thus providing a way to challenge the globally accepted paradigm of technology as a key factor in educational improvement.

Because of the complexity of the problem, we advocate for continuing the research on the variables and topics involved, to the extent where most of the big picture can be depicted. Although knowing the global blueprint does not mean that a solution or set of solutions can be outlined, at least it can encourage one to avoid symptomatic, short-term solutions and seek for structural ones instead. The organisation of this paper follows the proceeding structure. The first section addresses some outstanding variables and their implications in VET development programmes. The second section addresses the issue of taking into consideration sustainability as a filter that can also influence VET development. The third section offers some examples of recommended courses of action proposed by researchers and institutions aligned with sustainability principles. The paper concludes with some final thoughts about the implications for sustainable vocational education and training in ICT in Global South countries.

2   An Approach to the Big Picture

An important number of papers and contributions dealing with the topic of VET in Global South countries address the issue from different but complementary perspectives, contributing towards shedding light on the problem. Most of them propose courses of action to face the issue and achieve better results. The general perception is that the task appears complex because of the high number of variables involved, and that single solutions are ineffective. Next, several of those variables are briefly described, without the pretence of being exhaustive.

2.1   The Information Technology Utopia

[2] categorised the ambitious policy rhetoric contained within the launch of project documents by governmental bodies and international institutions as examples of the 'magical properties' that policymakers attach to the new technologies in education, where the most extended assumption is that more technology equals more learning. The

large number of newer and more resource-demanding initiatives that have arisen as part of the reform agendas to bring ITC into the educational setting seem to have become little more than a hardware distribution operation [3]. Despite more than two decades of research indicating the absence of any direct causal link between investment in education technology and improved learning outcomes, a remarkable number of policy statements from government officials still show their perception about the strong relationship between ICT and the quality of learning [4]. The political rhetoric does little to recognise that the relationship between technology and the classroom has always been a complex one. [5] highlighted the small amount of research that has taken place to investigate the relationship between ICT, classroom practice and learning outcomes. [1], in their analysis of ICT investment in schools in the USA and the impact upon student learning outcomes, have shown that no clear causal link exists between ICT investment and improved educational performance; indeed, their analysis confirms that socio-economic status (SES) has a far higher significance than connectivity and how many computers are in the classroom, even when equipment is available to students on a one-to-one basis. Some small overall student performance gain is evident in high-SES schools, but these gains are almost completely absent from low-SES schools, where other social and educational factors are of much more significance. [6–8], have promoted an alternative view and commented on how idiosyncratic and dependent upon local conditions ICT implementation is. For instance, a UNESCO survey [9] acknowledged the small impact that ICT investment has had on education in the Middle East.

Across the world, governments have spent hundreds of millions of dollars on providing schools with ICT equipment and broadband connectivity [10]. The extent to which this significant investment is having any impact on innovative teaching and learning and the development of twenty-first-century skills is rather more limited. There is no automatic link between computers in the classroom and the development of the skills expected of an autonomous, self-directing learner. Another issue related to the generalised perception of technology as a central agent in education improvement is raised in low-resource environments, whereas the critical attitudes of teaching staff about technology development can, in turn, negatively influence the attitudes of recipients. In such environments, the complaints of teaching staff about the technology available locally, the electricity supply, the irregular connectivity, the bugs in their operating systems, or the age of their computers, can lead to a decrease in the amount of pride stakeholders take in their own resources [11].

There is an extant literature on ICT adoption that recognises availability and accessibility in developing countries as key factors. The literature reflects the efforts to promote the use of ICT in education in Global South countries as a component of the political will to modernise education, but funding continues to be, at large, a major constraint [12]. Since the late 1990s, based on private initiatives and sponsorships from non-governmental organisations (NGOs), several projects have aimed to equip schools with computer equipment (computers, video projectors and Internet access) and teacher training in the use of ICT. The situation among countries is different; for instance, [12] reports that visits to 46 educational institutions in the Republic of Burkina Faso and Democratic Republic of Congo, on their own, highlight the fact that certain states do not have sufficient resources to provide state schools with computer rooms. This situation contrasts with the evidence that only a few studies that focus on the impacts of ICT on national development that can inform ICT policy and decision-making in Africa exist [13].

2.2 The Complexity to Develop Effective Institutions in Global South Countries

Although the neoliberal paradigm advocates for reducing as much as possible the intervention of public bodies in the economic and, even, the educational setting, a rather majoritarian consensus exists regarding the importance of institutions in promoting the development of their communities. Institutions symbolise the formal structures, informal rules and norms that govern the behaviour and expectations of different states [14]. The role of institutions in economic growth has been widely studied by researchers and has evolved over time. An institution often displays two sides of the same coin in the sense that it can either facilitate or delay development and economic growth depending on how it is structured in terms of decision-making. Good institutions have been known to promote economic growth in three major ways [15]: (a) they create environments conducive to protecting property rights; (b) they constrain the actions of the 'elite' (on the contrary, 'poor' institutions promote the vested interests of elites to the detriment of the majority); and (c), they provide the population with investment opportunities in economic activities. [16] and [17] provide empirical evidence to show that an economy with a good system of accountable government and a peaceful political terrain provides environment conducive to poverty reduction. On the side of growth, [18] and [19] demonstrate that government effectiveness positively and significantly affects Africa's economic growth, and one catalyst for economic growth is the existence of political institutions of limited government.

For [20] developing effective institutions in Sub-Saharan Africa (SSA) has been particularly complicated. Several impediments deter these institutions' efficiency. They include a proliferation of underdeveloped and ineffective institutions that make numerous African countries a high risk and unattractive environment for investors; poor political institutions that lead to economic mismanagement through kleptocratic dictatorships and political instability; weak social capital and social polarisation in SSA that prevents the intergroup cooperation necessary for economic development and leads to polarisation, which increases the risk of conflict; and finally, inadequate state capacity to reform or invest in institutions that promote economic development. Although not generalisable, [21] add another underlying reason, arguing that in developing countries public institutions often fail to provide services on an equal scale to all citizens, leading to what they call 'political marginalisation'. Abounding on this issue, they consider that areas with higher concentrations of marginalised citizens are likely not benefitting from the distribution of public goods. Political marginalisation usually occurs in areas with little influence in the political outcomes of democratic processes [21].

2.3   International Institutions' Role in Global South VET Initiatives

Several international institutions, such as the UNESCO and UNICEF, have a long tradition of collaboration in education transformation and improvement in Global South countries Rather recently, an institution as the OECD, established initially as an instrument for increasing the development of advanced economies, has shown interest in educational improvement in developing countries. This institution promoted a strategy - the OECD skills strategy, launched in 2012 [22] - which provides a policy framework that guides countries on how to invest in skills for creating jobs and boosting economic growth, in the context of the global economic crisis. The main objective was to transform countries into internationally competitive high skills economies. In the policy framework of the OECD, education and training policies should contribute to these strategies by [22]: (a) developing the relevant skills for the knowledge economy; (b) incentivising the participation of inactive individuals in the labour market through retraining and up-skilling; and (c) fostering entrepreneurship and supporting employers in the creation of highly skilled jobs. Given the renewed global interest in the skills sector of the education and development field, and the scarcity of solid alternative policy frameworks at a global level, it is reasonable to expect that a substantial number of stakeholders, including donors and governments in developing countries, will use the OECD skills strategy as a policy guide [23].

The OECD skills strategy policy framework rests on the OECD's traditional economistic focus on education and the primacy of human capital orthodoxy [22, 23]. The central premise of human capital theory is that investment in education and training is a key driver of economic growth [24–26]. More education and training will contribute to the development of individuals' skills, which has been associated with both higher individual earnings and growing societal wealth [27]. It may be interesting to note that the Better Skills report makes repeated reference to the situation of jobs and skills in 'emerging economies' and 'middle income countries', which are cited more than fifteen times in the report [22]. The report also makes explicit reference to the situation in West, East and Central Africa [22]: 41. The OECD skills strategy clearly sees skills as the key to tackling inequality and promoting social mobility because, 'investing in skills is far less costly, in the long run, than paying the price of poorer health, lower incomes, unemployment and social exclusion - all of which are closely tied to lower skills' [22]: 18. Undoubtedly, from this perspective, these premises advocate for a wide development of VET initiatives.

3   The Lens of Sustainability

Most ICT sustainability issues in developing countries are related to ensuring the continuity of ICT projects, so as to develop ways in which to alleviate the challenges associated with the use of ICT [28]. Among the challenges faced by ICT initiatives in Global South countries are: limited access to infrastructure, limited formal education, insufficient training and capacity building, financial and political constraints, and social and cultural challenges [28]. Sustainability focusses on two views of analysis, that is, the sustainability of ongoing ICT access, independent of specific technologies or projects, and the sustainability of development results through ICT-enabled develop-ment - e.g., education, health, empowerment, etc. [29]. ICT sustainability can be cat-egorised into social and cultural, institutional, economic, political, and technological sustainability, which should be developed harmoniously in order to promote the overall ICT project sustainability [29].

However, another side of sustainability, which has been explored less, is that related to the link between expectations and real professional opportunities for those involved in VET programmes. No policy framework on education policies can aspire to provide better welfare opportunities if it operates in a context of high unemployment rates and low-paid jobs [22, 23]. Additionally, problems in the supply of skills can be due to poor information on the needs of the market and/or to the low capacity of education and training systems to respond to these needs. An informed educational planning initiative would ensure that the supply of skills is sufficient, in terms of both quantity and quality, to meet the current and emerging needs of the markets. Even in the case that education systems cannot satisfy the needs of the local markets, the availability of this information would allow governments to develop their own strategy to attract talent from abroad. In a global knowledge economy, governments are not merely encouraged to facilitate internal mobility among local labour markets; importing skills and talent from outside the country is also seen as very effective solution for dealing with the skills-shortages of national economies [23]. In other words, developed countries can become the magnet economies for highly skilled jobs. It is under this perspective that it is worth applying the prism of sustainable education and learning over the big picture: is it fair to attract talented and skilled workers from developing countries towards magnet economies, thus possibly meaning that they will never contribute to the well-being of the communities which made the effort to provide them with those skills?

This question could shed new light to the view of the big picture or, alternatively, make it even more complex. A first matter of concern would arguably be the interest for lower income countries to spend their money in VET development policies knowing that a portion of skilled trainees would eventually leave their communities in seek of better opportunities in magnet economies. A second concern, just obviating the implications of the first one, is that the reality of the economy, contrary to what human capital theories would argue, is characterised by a rapid expansion of the global supply of skills and the incapability of the demand to follow this pace and to generate enough highly-skilled jobs for this highly skilled population. As a consequence of this imbalance between the supply and demand for skills, countries will need to deal with the social discontent produced by the false promise of education and skills, as well as the social problem of growing unemployment and underemployment among trained professionals. A final consideration under the prism of sustainability in education and training, with implications for the dominant paradigm, which advocates continuous economic growth, is that relating to the current 'productivist' model of development. This model influences the social-educational system downward, thus focusing educa-tional policies towards the objectives of continuous economic growth, as if no other alternatives could be feasible and/or desirable. If, as it seems, this paradigm of con-tinuous economic growth is accepted as the driving force for development and social welfare, then it is necessary to study its environmental repercussions. The investment and use of information technology has potentially negative environmental implications. These implications need to be addressed if the well-being of future generations is not to be compromised. The type and magnitude of the negative impacts of ICT on the environment should also be studied from the perspective of sustainability. Consequently, policies aimed at minimising environmental damage ought to be developed in parallel with VET initiatives.

4 Recommended Courses of Action

As stated at the beginning of this paper, no easy solution can be provided for improving the development and effective success of VET initiatives in ICT in Global South countries. To pretend such a task would, very likely, only lead to symptomatic solutions, thus deferring the design and implementation of structural solutions with long-term beneficial outputs. Instead, some general guidelines to address root problems - proposed by various researchers - are summarised below; an integrated view might be the key to start unrevealing the big picture.

Regarding the ICT utopia in education, [3]: 723 argues that for educational technology to have an impact in classrooms as dramatic as it has been credited with having on the streets, through social networking, a more fundamental shift in thinking about education is required. The development of the 21st Century skills for employability that the youth of today are said to need in order to succeed in a globalised employment marketplace will not be achieved simply by more or less successful computer hardware distribution strategies and improved connectivity in schools. [11] summarise the lessons learned from the UNICEF's Child-Friendly Technology Framework programme in eleven countries around sub-Saharan Africa and offer some best practices guidelines: (a) Don't Get Distracted by Devices or Upgrades: with the goal of moving away from technology as the focus of improvements in education, emphasising rather the importance of well-designed user experiences as the key to holding stakeholder's attention and engagement into the learning process; (b) Offline, No-tech Activities are a Critical Foundation for Technology Initiative Success: for every lesson and every step in curricular progression, there should be a complimentary robust offline component, which can be completed when the infrastructure is non-cooperative or available; (c) Always Consider the Teacher as a Primary Beneficiary: the experience of UNICEF's Child-Friendly Technology Framework showed that teachers were the hinge upon which programme success was leveraged; (d) Partners Create Sustainability: a way to highlight the benefits of promoting collaboration or support from NGOs, local governments and companies so as to succeed in connecting classroom initiatives, thus fostering long term collaboration; (e) Budget Yourself Out of Business, with the aim of including the wider community as actors that can collaborate in generating connections, prompting students to reach out for resources even in the case of educational funding ends; and (f) Monitoring and Evaluation, in order to better adjust the scarce resources to enhance field demands.

As regards the problems derived from the need to develop effective institutions, [30] argue for adopting a microeconomic approach that explicitly takes political and bureaucratic incentives and constraints into account. Such an approach can provide a fruitful, and complementary, way forward. They conclude that innovations in the measurement of performance and ability in education and health open up ways to influence the political economic equilibrium. A number of researchers have pointed out some institutional ingredients that can contribute to accelerating the effectiveness of Institutions to foster economic growth. Among them, well-defined property rights [31], the effectiveness of interest groupings [32], political stability and credibility [33], control of corruption [34], regulatory and bureaucratic quality [35], avoidance of the coexistence between weak institutions and powerful industrial groups [36], strong and adequate political institutions [37], and [38] the illustration that the investment rate is positively correlated with per capita GDP growth when accountability is taken into account.

Under the vision of VET programmes as a means to develop skills in the workforce, the OECD skills strategy [22] stresses that investing in skills is just the first step; successful skills policies also need to ensure that available skills are used effectively so that no investment is wasted. Despite the fact that in the short term a 'skills surplus' may develop, in the long term investing in the skills supply will always pay off because it can help to transform the kinds of employment on offer in such economies, as employers can more easily recruit skilled workers who, in turn, improve the quality of the work that they do.

5 Final Thoughts

At first glance, taking into consideration the contributions of the academic community, it could be argued that a developing country, with good institutional quality and good regulations, lack of corruption, good intellectual property laws, a stable democracy and/or rule of law, etc., would be able to attract internal or external investments in educational ICT and, coupled with good government policies - including the promotion of VET initiatives -, could eventually lead to technology readiness and a high level of professional ICT usage. From this point on, there can also be a direct relationship between ICT development and levels of human development and economic growth. However, this apparently straightforward route map, has demonstrated that it does not adhere to any simple or fluid set of activities. In any case, under the hypothesis of Global South countries having developed their full capacity to promote effective educational, and consequently, VET initiatives, the challenge of sustainability as a complex issue surrounding any model of vocational education and training for development still remains.

Far from the neoliberal imaginary with which policies from the Global North are imbued, as a prospective conclusion about the ITC utopia in Global south countries, it could be stated that for promoting the development of twenty-first-century skills amongst students, the strength of local traditions and social-economic status are of much greater importance. The recognition that the problem is not (only) in the supply of skills, implies that education systems cannot address skills problems alone and a more coordinated national strategy is needed. Furthermore, as [39] argued, there is still no workable model of vocational education and training for development. As a final point of consideration, it could be worth stressing that most of the above discussion focuses on topics and concerns that have little to do with engagement in debates about skills for sustainable production and consumption.

References

1. Warschauer, M., Matuchniak, T.: New technology and digital worlds: analyzing evidence of equity in access, use, and outcomes. Rev. Res. Educ. **34**(1), 179–225 (2010). Mar.
2. Jensen, C.B., Lauritsen, P.: Reading digital Denmark: IT reports as material-semiotic actors. Sci. Technol. Hum. Values **30**, 352–373 (2005)
3. Lightfoot, M.: Education reform for the knowledge economy in the state of Sangon. Compare: J. Comparative Int. Educ. **45**(5), 705–726 (2015)
4. Law, N., Pelgrum, W.J., Plomp, T.: Pedagogy and ICT Use in Schools Around the World: Findings from the IEA SITES 2006 Study. Springer, Berlin (2008)
5. Sutherland, R., et al.: Transforming teaching and learning: embedding ICT into everyday classroom practices. J. Comput. Assist. Learn. **20**, 413–425 (2004)
6. Apple, M.W.: Are we wasting money on computers in schools? Educ. Policy **18**, 513–522 (2004)
7. Cuban, L.: New technologies in old Universities (2001)
8. Monahan, T.: Globalization, Technological Change, and Public Education, 1st edn. Routledge, New York (2005)
9. Stamboliyska, R.: Information technologies and education in the Arab World. Nature Middle East (2013)
10. Selwyn, N.: Education in a Digital World: Global Perspectives on Technology and Education. Routledge, New York (2012)
11. Calhoun, E., Calhoun, N.: Using technology to shift education paradigms in low-resource environments. Stab. Int. J. Secur. Dev. **3**(1), 21 (2014)
12. Thibeault, E.: Décryptage de l' usage des TIC au Burkina-Faso et en République démocratique du Congo Accès, pratiques et compétences des étudiants ICT' s use a alysis i Bu ki a -Faso and Democratic Republic of Congo Access, practices and students competences, no. Ea 4071, pp. 1–20 (2013)
13. Bankole, F.O., Mimbi, L.: ICT Infrastructure and It's Impact on national development: a research direction for Africa. African J. Inf. Syst. **9**(2), 77 (2017)
14. Luiz, J.M.: Institutions and economic performance: Implications for African development. J. Int. Dev. **21**, 58–75 (2009)
15. Acemoglu, D., Robinson, J.A.: Why Nations Fail: The Origins of Power, Prosperity and Poverty, 1st edn. Crown, New York (2012)
16. Chong, A., Calderón, C.: Causality and feedback between institutional measures and economic growth. Econ. Polit. **12**, 69–81 (2000)
17. Tebaldi, E., Mohan, R.: Institutions and poverty. J. Dev. Stud. **46**, 1047–1066 (2010)
18. Anyanwu, J.C.: Factors affecting economic growth in Africa: are there any lessons from China? African Dev. Rev. **26**, 468–493 (2014)
19. Mijiyawa, A.G.: Africa's recent economic growth: what are the contributing factors? African Dev. Rev. **25**, 289–302 (2013)
20. Manda, D.K., Mwakubo, S.: Institutions and service delivery in Africa: an overview. J. Afr. Econ. **22**(Suppl. 2), 4–15 (2013)
21. Blimpo, M.P., Harding, R., Wantchekon, L.: Public investment in rural infrastructure: some political economy considerations. J. Afr. Econ. **22**(Suppl. 2), ii57–ii83 (2013)

22. OECD: Better Skills, Better Jobs, Better Lives A Strategic Approach to Skills Policies (2012)
23. Valiente, O.: The OECD skills strategy and the education agenda for development. Int. J. Educ. Dev. **39**, 40–48 (2014)
24. Schultz, T.W.: Investment in human capital. Am. Econ. Rev. **51**(1), 1–17 (1961)
25. Denison, E.F.: Sources of postwar growth in nine Western Countries. Am. Econ. Rev. **57**, 325–332 (1967)
26. Becker, G.S.: Human Capital: The Concise Encyclopedia of Economics. Columbia, New York (1964)
27. Hanushek, E.A., Woessmann, L.: Do better schools lead to more growth? Cognitive skills, economic outcomes, and causation. J. Econ. Growth **17**, 267–321 (2012)
28. Pade-Khene, C., Mallinson, B., Sewry, D.: Sustainable rural ICT project management practice for developing countries: investigating the Dwesa and RUMEP projects. Inf. Technol. Dev. **17**(3), 187–212 (2011)
29. Hietanen, O.: Indicators of sustainable development. Futura **21**(2), 6–7 (2002)
30. Bold, T., Svensson, J.: Policies and institutions for effective service delivery: the need of a microeconomic and micropolitical approach. J. Afr. Econ. **22**(Suppl. 2), 16–38 (2013)
31. Knack, S., Keefer, P.: Institutions and economic performance: cross country tests using alternative institutional measures. Econ. Polit. **7**, 207–227 (1995)
32. Olson, M.: The Rise and Decline of Nations: Economic Growth, Stagflation, and Social Rigidities. Yale University Press, New Haven (2008)
33. Barro, R.J.: Economic growth in a cross-section of nations. Q. J. Econ. **106**, 407–443 (1991)
34. Mauro, P.: Corruption and growth. Q. J. Econ. **110**, 681–712 (1995)
35. Keefer, P., Knack, S.: Why don't poor countries catch up? A cross-national test of an institutional explanation. Econ. Inq. **35**, 590–602 (1997)
36. Lane, P.R., Tornell, A.: Power, growth, and the voracity effect. J. Econ. Growth **1**, 213–241 (1996)
37. Nissanke, M., Thorbecke, E.: Introduction: globalization–poverty channels and case studies from Sub-Saharan Africa. African Dev. Rev. **20**, 1–19 (2008)
38. Diop, A., Dufrénot, G., Sanon, G.: Is per capita growth in Africa hampered by poor governance and weak institutions? An empirical study on the ECOWAS countries. African Dev. Rev. **22**, 265–575 (2010)
39. McGrath, S.: Vocational education and training for development: a policy in need of a theory? Int. J. Educ. Dev. **32**(5), 623–631 (2012)

The Role of Computer Science Education for Understanding and Shaping the Digital Society

Ralf Romeike[(✉)]

Freie Universität Berlin, Königin-Luise-Street 24-26, 14195 Berlin, Germany
ralf.romeike@fu-berlin.de

Abstract. In the omnipresent discussion on the role of ICT in education, the contribution of computer science education is often mentioned, but not always understood. This paper discusses the relation between ICT education and computer science education and the benefits of understanding the fundamental concepts and ideas of Computer Science (CS). Computer science is a dynamic and highly innovative science, whose products make a significant contribution to the development of the so-called "Digital Society." How should computer science teaching be adapted to the continuous technical further developments? Based on the outcomes of several research projects, this paper will outline how innovations in computer science can be taken up in order to improve the teaching of computer science. i.e., the topic of "databases" will in future offer a broader perspective on how to deal with data in the sense of "data management". Agile methods, which are known from professional software development, can support learners and teachers, despite difficult school conditions, to better achieve the objectives in project based teaching. Programmable microcontrollers extend the view of computers as standing on a desktop towards ubiquitous embedded or also cyber-physical systems, which enable new and motivating approaches for the design of computer science lessons in the context of physical computing. As a target perspective, pupils should be able to understand the phenomena of the "digital society", but also to be involved in the design of them in accordance to their needs.

Keywords: Computer science education · Digitalization

1 Introduction

It was the year of 2016 in which the term "digitalization" had arrived in the education debate and dominated the debates under the keyword "digital education". In Germany, the discussion was fueled not least by the fact that the Standing Conference of the Ministers of Education and Cultural Affairs (KMK) made the digitalization of society a focal topic and presented a strategy for "Education in the Digital World" [11]. Although more and more people are now interested in digital media and want to use it in educational processes, the question of what "digitalization" actually is still leads to uncertainty among many teachers. Although the results of digitalization are obvious - digital media are omnipresent and influence all conceivable everyday processes - their

© IFIP International Federation for Information Processing 2019
Published by Springer Nature Switzerland AG 2019
A. Tatnall and N. Mavengere (Eds.): SUZA 2019, IFIP AICT 564, pp. 167–176, 2019.
https://doi.org/10.1007/978-3-030-28764-1_19

causes, fundamentals and further application and design possibilities are still a mystery for many people. Although word has got around that digital "something has to do with 0 and 1", in fact this description can neither explain digitalization nor estimate its effects and possibilities.

In his book "More than 0 and 1", Honegger [4] puts it in a nutshell: digitalization in the narrower sense refers to the transformation of analogue (i.e. infinitely variable continuous) data into digital form, i.e. form that can be reproduced on digits and thus processed by computers. As a result, data from all areas of life that can be digitilized can now be automatically recorded, stored, processed, transmitted and disseminated at low cost. The associated enormous increase in the availability of information results in far-reaching opportunities and challenges for society. The basis and driving force of digitalization is computer science. An understanding of its fundamentals, ideas and principles is therefore necessary if one wants to understand and help shape the function, opportunities and development of digital media. The aim of this article is to use the discussion on digital education to show what contribution computer science education can make to understanding the digital world and thus also to offer starting points for ICT education.

2 Digitalization

The extent of the "digital revolution" will be illustrated by a simple example (cf. [15]): Imagine sitting in the top row of Berlin's Olympic Stadium at 12 noon and from a magical cloud "dripping" into the (waterproof) stadium - just one drop per minute, but the volume of the drop doubles every time. The stadium's gonna be full up sometime. But how long can we take and watch the play? After 1 min 2 drops fall, then 4 drops, then 8 drops, then 16 drops and so on. After 45 min the Olympic stadium is still 93% empty, but we don't have time for a nap anymore - only 4 min later the stadium will be full. We also find such exponential growth in the information technology development of the last 50 years. Computers, for example, double their performance every two years, and the volume of data on the Internet grows just as rapidly. We also seem to get used to the developments very quickly: smartphones, navigation systems, the Internet and portable computers have already changed everyday habits massively, even though just about 10 years ago the iPhone was the first smartphone to be sold on a massive scale. Today, it's hard to imagine that Facebook recently had no significance and that the mobile Internet was only just starting out. If one considers the further development of Internet services such as MySpace, StudiVZ or Second Life[1], it becomes clear that it is hardly foreseeable which concrete technologies will be relevant in the coming years. Analogous to our introductory example, it is now perhaps 12:45 pm. We seem to be facing enormous, hardly foreseeable changes due to digitalization, but the development will not be over at 12:49 pm. Just a few years ago, ICT education researchers also discussed how Second Life, for example, could be opened up for ICT education. Flashing back, it can be described as regrettable how much energy, lifetime and money

---

[1] These Internet services had millions of users at times, but are largely irrelevant today.

has been invested in the processing of extremely short-term trends and how little the education system has ultimately profited from them.

In the field of school informatics, experiences with less sustainable approaches have also been made. The worldwide failure of information technology related education since the 1980s has repeatedly shown that if the technical and social developments driven by computer science are reduced to the use and application of tools and the discussion of their effects, success can only be achieved in the short term (cf. [1]). Such knowledge and acquired skills were often simply obsolete when pupils left school. Computer science education addresses the problem of short-living skills by orienting itself towards fundamental ideas and principles of the reference discipline of computer science.

3   Fundamental Ideas and Principles of Computer Science

Why is a school subject "computer" or "digital media" not a good idea? For the same reason that there is no subject "pocket calculator" in school: Educational processes that focus primarily on the application and discussion of current media and tools lead to directly applicable and useful skills, but these are quickly obsolete. For this reason, school refers to the underlying scientific disciplines, so that pupils first acquire basic competences and, building on this, application skills. For example, in the subjects of physics, chemistry and mathematics, the principles, fundamental ideas, methods and working methods of the respective science are to be conveyed, so that an understanding of the specialist tools, problems and solution strategies develops from this. Computer science education is also based on fundamental ideas (cf. [14]), concepts and principles of computer science. This will be illustrated in the following using the example of word processing.

For example, let's take the present text and try to double the line spacing between the two lines below this line. People who are mainly proficient in using word processing systems typically try to achieve the goal by marking the two lines and setting the "Line spacing" option to "double line" in the menu bar. The result of this action, however, turns out differently than expected: Not only are the two marked lines separated from each other, but further lines above and below are also displayed as double lines. In computer science education, pupils at lower secondary level learn the concepts that explain this phenomenon: In word processing systems, different types (classes) of text elements must be distinguished, such as characters and paragraphs, each of which has its own properties (attributes); "line spacing" is an attribute of the Paragraph class. If a line of the paragraph affected by the selection is assigned the attribute value "double line", this applies inevitably to all lines of the paragraph. This concept can be applied to various word processing systems (e.g. MS Word, Open Office, Latex). The consideration of the underlying classes and attributes also helps in the efficient handling and understanding of other software applications. Empirical studies have shown that the teaching of such conceptual basics leads to more sustainable competences than functional-application-oriented teaching ("user training"), which focuses solely on user skills [18].

But what are the ideas and principles behind digitalization? Let us first consider the human senses of seeing and hearing. With a transmission rate comparable to about 1 Mbit/s, the eyes offer the fastest connection of the outside world to the brain. But how can visual information be digitized and processed in the computer? Typical topics in the subject area deal with image processing products such as Photoshop, image formats such as JPEG or the storage space requirement of an image in the memory of the digital camera in megabytes. These are also terms which can be assigned to the application skills and which can change quickly. One principle that comes to bear here is the way in which visual information is represented and thus digitally captured. There are two main procedures to be distinguished here: The acquisition of visual information pixel by pixel in the form of a pixel graphic is known from digital cameras. Associated with this are, for example, phenomena of increasing blur and staircase effects when enlarging the image as well as high memory requirements when displaying in high quality. These phenomena typically do not occur when enlarging letters and logos in poster printing. This is due to the fact that in these cases the visual information is efficiently represented as vector graphics. The overall picture is described by the underlying geometric objects (e.g. lines, ellipses, fill patterns), so that the overall object can be "drawn" in any size, similar to "painting by numbers". The principles behind these two processes are not limited to the digitization of visual information. Music, for example, is represented with comparable methods. Analog audio signals are digitized by sampling and storing a sample (according to the sampling rate). As with pixel graphics, information is lost and the larger the sample size, the greater the memory requirements - and thus the higher the quality. Comparable to vector graphics is the MIDI format, in which especially instrument type, pitch, duration and volume (comparable to notes) are described, so that music can be generated from them. We do not only find these processes underlying digitalization in information technology. Sampling is used in all possible application contexts, e.g. in opinion polls or any other surveys; the representation of facts by modelling key factors is a typical scientific approach. These examples clearly show that the core and contribution of computer science, and thus also of computer science education, is not limited to the creation and application of computers and computer software, but above all focuses on the development of creative solution strategies. These strategies always precede the implementation of automated processes using computers (see also Sect. 6).

Strategies for processing large amounts of data have recently become known as Big Data. How these can be used and which competences pupils can acquire to understand Big Data, to deal with data and to use them will be examined in the following.

4 Big Data - Understanding, Managing, Benefiting

Without an understanding of how data and information are obtained, an understanding of Big Data is hardly possible. An understanding of how large amounts of data are stored and processed seems equally important. In the "digital society", for example, the relevance of conscious and reflected handling of data for each individual has greatly increased. Through the ubiquitous networked digital systems, we generate and use data multiple times a day and make decisions about our data. In social media, data is exposed or protected, phone book contacts and other data on the smartphone are synchronized with servers and across devices, personal and business data on computers and in the cloud must be protected from loss and unauthorized access. Quasi incidentally, we permanently leave behind metadata (e.g., the GPS location or radio cell of the smartphone, origin, browser type and – settings for Internet surfing or Tweet location and language, but also the background color used on Twitter are stored and evaluated by the relevant service providers), mostly without being aware of it. As the volume of data grows rapidly, so does the speed at which data is generated and transferred (velocity) and the bandwidth of data types and sources (variety). These three properties are the core characteristics of Big Data.

Big Data is also highly relevant for ICT education. Interfaces to information technology also become clear. For example, Tulodziecki [16, 17] refers to a teaching example developed by our Research Group, in which the pupils use and further develop an IT system for the analysis and evaluation of data streams and get to know the basics of data management and big data. Tulodziecki [17] makes it clear that central questions of ICT education can and should also be dealt with on the basis of these computer science related questions. In the teaching example, pupils learn to evaluate and visualize data from the Twitter data stream and to gain new insights ([8], see Fig. 1). They encounter potential dangers of Big Data, but will also get to know the opportunities and possibilities when using and evaluating public data sources. To this end, they acquire skills in data analysis (classification, clustering and association), metadata analysis, real-time analysis of data on the Internet and monitoring.

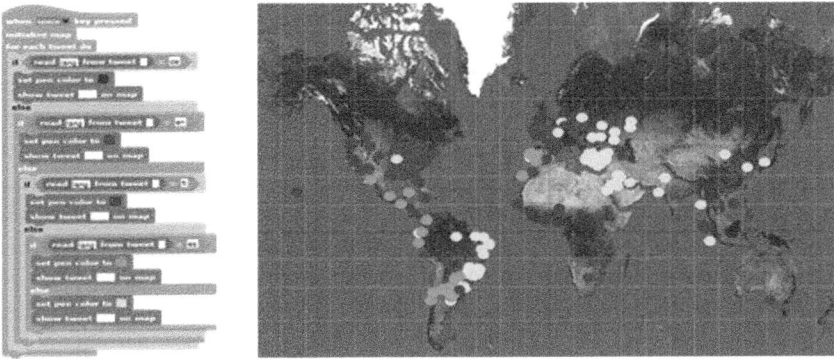

Fig. 1. Visualization of Twitter metadata using the block-based programming language Snap!.

5 Perspectives on Phenomena of a "Digital World"

Since 2016, the cooperation between the fields of ICT education and computer science education has intensified and led to a common perspective which constructively underpinned the discourse on digital media in Germany. In February 2016, the seminar "Informatics and School" took place at Schloss Dagstuhl. It dealt with the relationship between computer science education and "digital education" and continued a constructive interdisciplinary discourse between representatives of computer science, computer science didactics, media pedagogy, ICT education, politics, schools and business. As a result of the seminar, the joint "Dagstuhl Declaration: Education in the Digital Networked World" [7] was published, which provides a promising approach for further discourse. Digital education should therefore look at the phenomena, artefacts, systems and situations of the "digital world" encountered by pupils from an application, socio-cultural and technological perspective. In the following expert discussion, the "Dagstuhl Triangle" presented in the declaration was expanded into a "house of digital education", which intermeshes the perspectives mentioned with the roles that digital media can play in educational processes (cf. [2]). Thus, basic competences with regard to digital media as a teaching subject, the use of digital media as a design tool and object, and the use of digital media as a teaching and organizational tool are taken into account.

Computer science education deals in particular with the basic concepts, principles and ideas of the digital world as a subject of instruction. The aim is to understand phenomena, to question them and to be able to assess corresponding decisions and effects. The use of digital media as a means or object of design aims at creative and productive acting and designing and experiences its application especially in the individual disciplines, but requires an understanding of the underlying computer science concepts. These also make it possible not only to use passive digital media (e.g. static websites, posters, blogs), but also to design active digital media themselves, e.g. by programming apps or simulations.

6 Computational Thinking and Creativity

In addition to developing a sound understanding of the phenomena of the digital world, computer science education aims to develop a special way of thinking, which has been called "computational thinking" for some years now [19] and which is an important basis for the introduction of computer science education as a school subject in more and more countries (e.g. in Great Britain from the 1st class onwards). Computational Thinking (cf. [3]) emphasizes the importance of thinking and analyzing problems and problem-solving strategies that precede their subsequent implementation with a computer. This includes the application of various concepts central to computer science such as logic (analysis and prediction), abstraction (omitting the unimportant), decomposition (splitting complexity into partial problems) and algorithmization (automating and reproducing processes) as well as working methods promoted in computer science and in the use and design of digital media. This includes creativity (designing and implementing ideas), debugging (finding and correcting mistakes), perseverance (learning to master problems) and collaboration (working together). In the following, I will show how computer science education can help to promote computational thinking and creativity, using agile project teaching and creative design with programmable microcontrollers as examples.

6.1   Project-Based Teaching and Learning with Agile Methods

One of the most important teaching goals is that pupils learn to set goals independently, to develop and implement solution strategies cooperatively and to overcome problems together. Against the background of the increasing automation of routine intellectual activity, it is to be expected that the significance of such competencies will increase even more. A recognized form of teaching to promote these competences is project teaching. The core objective here is for the pupils to develop a product, acquire competences in self-organization and learn in social interaction to assume joint responsibility. Teaching projects often follow the classical project method according to Frey/Schäfer [5], according to which the project implementation is first planned in detail and then realized in a long phase. However, the school conditions for such an approach are rather project-unfriendly. The teaching time spread over a few hours per week, surprises in everyday school life (e.g. illness, holidays), changes in the objectives of the project as well as the difficulty of maintaining motivation over a longer period of time make project teaching a challenge and often lead to failure.

In the context of computer science, project-like working methods are central in practice and also well researched scientifically. Similar to the problems outlined in the project lessons, there are also some challenges to be overcome on the software practice side. Approximately 15 years ago, so-called agile methods were developed as a solution, which help to structure the process better with the help of concrete practices and at the same time enable more flexibility. With the aim of supporting pupils in project organization and better achieving the objectives of project teaching, we have adapted agile methods for teaching and have been testing their use in computer science teaching at various schools since 2013 (cf. [6, 10]) (Fig. 2).

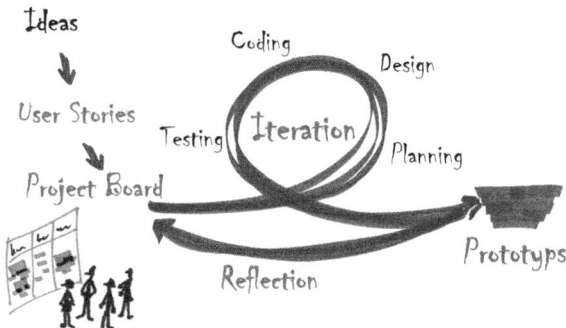

Fig. 2. Agile framework for school projects [13]

The process is divided into different iterations, each of which leads to an inter-mediate product that can be presented as a prototype. On the basis of a project board, the pupils organize the division of the work themselves, communication processes are supported by regular meetings, reflection phases and working in pairs (cf. [13]). An evaluation shows that the above mentioned goals of project teaching can be better achieved with agile methods, especially the promotion of self-organization and social competence of the pupils. It was also easier for the teachers to plan, supervise and evaluate the projects. In addition, it was found that the pupils were able to apply the competences acquired in the agile projects to other subjects as well.

6.2   Understanding and Designing Embedded Systems with Physical Computing

The discussion about digital media has been and still is mainly related to software that is used on universal hardware (e.g. PCs, tablets, smartphones); the hardware itself is generally assumed to be given. With the increasing miniaturization and spread of microcontrollers, which are used as embedded systems in the most diverse objects of everyday life, the typical image of "computers" is also changing. These can also be found today in cars (modern cars have over 100 networked microcontrollers) and watches as well as in interactive toys. Microcontrollers are also becoming increasingly important in educational contexts. The Calliope project (cf. [9]) plans to make a programmable microcontroller available to primary school children throughout Germany from spring 2017 in the form of the Calliope mini, with the aim of turning children from passive users into active designers of digital media. Other hardware platforms such as Arduino and Raspberry Pi have also become widespread and enable the creative design of interactive objects, known as physical computing, with hardware and software. Such interactive objects consist of various sensors that collect data (e.g. volume, temperature, brightness) and actuators (e.g. LEDs, motors, speakers) that can respond based on the data collected by the sensors (Fig. 3).

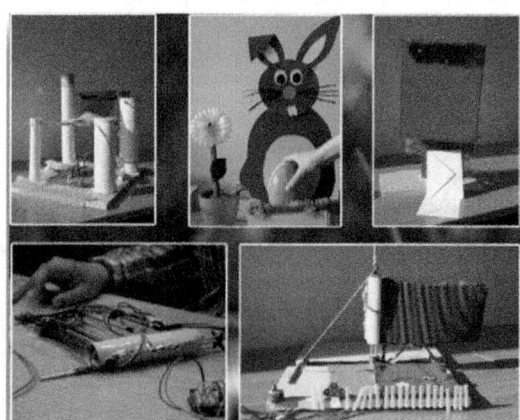

Fig. 3. Student results of physical computing: interactive objects with embedded systems.

Physical Computing thus offers a (tangible) context for CS phenomena of the digitalized world and enables pupils to experience typical information design experiences: In their projects, they learn that initial problems are usually imprecise and that modelling decisions have to be made. You will experience surprises in the course of the project, which are associated with occasional frustration, but above all also success.

Due to the interactive character of Physical Computing, they receive immediate feedback and learn to persevere when problems occur. In class, it is evident that pupils are motivated by this approach. They acquire key competences for understanding digitalization, e.g. with regard to the differences between analogue and digital, and learn to understand the penetration of the living world with embedded digital systems in an action-oriented and creative way (cf. [12]).

7   Summary

The increasing digitalization of all areas of life means that schools can no longer afford to use digital media only as a teaching and organizational tool, but must instead consider clarifying the phenomenon of the digital world, i.e. the world shaped by information technology. In more and more countries, for example, binding teaching offers for all pupils are being set up on an international level. The concepts and principles of computer science provide the technical basis for such offers. Not only do they make it possible to use digital media effectively and efficiently in the classroom, but they also create the technical prerequisites for being able to assess the effects of digitalization and make a sound assessment of them. By enabling pupils to learn to creatively deal with digital media in computer science lessons and to acquire computational thinking skills, e.g. with regard to self-organized learning, computer science lessons can lay an important foundation for all subjects. The ultimate goal of "digital education" should be to ensure that digital media are used naturally and creatively in all subjects and beyond school. Students should therefore not only be able to understand the digital society, but should also be able to actively shape it. In the sense of a solidarity between ICT education and computer science, it seems desirable that the individual reference disciplines emphasize their concrete contribution to digital education even more clearly. The discussion initiated in 2016 gives cause for optimism that the discourse between ICT education and computer science education will continue to develop constructively.

References

1. Breier, N.: Stand und Perspektive der informatischen Bildung (State and Perspective of Informatics Education). In: Lecture at the 1st Symposium of the GI Section Hamburg Computer Science Teachers (2004). https://www.ew.uni-hamburg.de/ueber-die-fakultaet/personen/breier/files/vortrag291004.pdf. Accessed 15 Jan 2017
2. Brinda, T.: Statement of the Gesellschaft für Informatik on the KMK strategy paper "Education in the digital world" (2016). https://fb-iad.gi.de/fileadmin/stellungnahmen/gi-fbiad-stellungnahme-kmk-strategie-digitale-bildung.pdf. Accessed 15 Jan 2017
3. CAS Barefoot: computational thinking (2014). http://barefootcas.org.uk/barefoot-primary-computing-resources/concepts/computational-thinking/. Accessed 15 Jan 2017
4. Frey, K., Schäfer, U.: Die Projektmethode (The Project Method). Beltz, Weinheim (1982)
5. Gallenbacher, J.: INFOS 2015: Informatik allgemeinbildend begreifen (16. GI-Fachtagung Informatik und Schule, Darmstadt). Köllen, Bonn (2015)

6. GI (Gesellschaft für Informatik e.V.): Dagstuhl-Erklärung: Bildung in der digital vernetzten Welt (Dagstuhl declaration: education in the digitally networked world) (2016). https://www.gi.de/fileadmin/redaktion/Themen/dagstuhl-erklaerung-bildung-in-der-digitalen-welt-2016.pdf. Accessed 15 Jan 2017

7. Grillenberger, A., Romeike, R.: Big-Data-Analyse im Informatikunterricht mit Datenstromsystemen: Ein Unterrichtsbeispiel (Big data analysis in computer science education with data stream systems: a lesson example). In: INFOS 2015: Informatik allgemeinbildend begreifen (16. GI-Fachtagung Informatik und Schule, Darmstadt), pp. 135–144. Köllen, Bonn (2015)

8. Honegger, B.D.: Mehr als 0 und 1: Schule in einer digitalisierten Welt (More than 0 and 1: School in a Digitalized World). hep Verlag, Bern (2016)

9. Humbert, L., Hilbig, A.: Calliope – Informatiksystem für Schülerhände – Digitale Kompetenzen mit informatischer Grundlage entwickeln (Calliope - Informatics system for pupil hands - Developing digital competences with an informatics basis) (2017). https://calliope.cc/content/7-lehrer-informationen/calliope4iea_humbert_hilbig.pdf. 15 Jan 2017

10. Kastl, P., Romeike, R.: Entwicklung eines agilen Frameworks für Projektunterricht mit Design-Based Research (Development of an agile framework for project teaching with design-based research). In: Gallenbacher, J. (ed.): INFOS 2015: Informatik allgemeinbildend verstehen (16th GI Symposium on Computer Science and School, Darmstadt), p. 201. Köllen, Bonn (2015)

11. KMK (Kultusministerkonferenz) (2016): Bildung in der digitalen Welt. Strategie der Kultusministerkonferenz (Education in the digital world. Strategy of the Standing Conference of the Ministers of Education and Cultural Affairs of the States in the Federal Republic of Germany). https://www.kmk.org/fileadmin/Dateien/pdf/PresseUndAktuelles/2016/Bildung_digital_world_web_version.pdf. 15 Jan 2017

12. Przybylla, M., Romeike, R.: Physical Computing im Informatikunterricht (Physical computing in computer science lessons). In: Breier, N., Stechert, P., Wilke, T. (eds.) INFOS 2013: Informatik erweitert Horizonte (15th GI Symposium on Computer Science and School, Kiel), pp. 137–146. Köllen, Bonn (2013)

13. Romeike, R., Göttel, T.: Agile projects in high school computing education - emphasizing a learners perspective. In: Knobelsdorf, M., Romeike, R. (Hrsg.) Grand Challenges in Primary and Secondary Computing Education (The 7th Workshop in Primary and Secondary Computing Education WiPSCE 2012, Hamburg), pp. 48–57. ACM, New York (2013)

14. Schwill, A.: Fundamentale Ideen der Informatik (Fundamental Ideas in Computer Science). Zentralblatt für Didaktik der Mathematik 25(1), 20–31 (1993)

15. Stanzl, J.: Exponentielles Wachstum: Ertrinken in 4 Minuten (Exponential growth: drowning in 4 minutes) (2010). https://www.godmode-trader.de/artikel/exponentielles-wachstum-ertrinken-in-4-minuten,2286650. 15 Jan 2017

16. Tulodziecki: Big Data als Herausforderung für die Medienpädagogik - Aktuelle Debatten beim GMK-Forum 2015 im "Rückspiegel" (Big data as a challenge for ICT education). In: Brüggemann/Thomas Knaus/Dorothee M. Meister (ed.) Kommunikationskulturen in digitalen Welten Konzepte und Strategien der Medienpädagogik und Medienbildung zum GMK-Forum 2015 in Köln. kopaed, Munich (2016a)

17. Tulodziecki, G.: Konkurrenz oder Kooperation? Zur Entwicklung des Verhältnisses von Medienbildung und informatischer Bildung (Competition or cooperation? On the development of the relationship between ICT education and computer education). MedienPädagogik: J. Theory Pract. ICT Educ. 25, 7–25 (2016b)

18. Voss, S.: Modellierung von Standardsoftwaresystemen aus didaktischer Sicht (Modelling of standard software systems from a didactic point of view). Dissertation, TU Munich, Munich (2006)

19. Wing, J.M.: Computational thinking. Commun. ACM 49(3), 33–35 (2006)

The Integration of Web 2.0 in Teaching-Learning in Tanzania Higher Learning Institutions: The Case of the State University of Zanzibar (SUZA)

Said A. S. Yunus[1](✉) [iD], Ali A. Abdulla[1] [iD],
Raya Idrissa Ahmada[1] [iD], Umayra El-Nabhany[1] [iD], and P. Malliga[2] [iD]

[1] State University of Zanzibar (SUZA), Zanzibar, Tanzania
{said.yunus,ali.abdulla,raya.ahmada,
umayra.al-nabhany}@suza.ac.tz
[2] CEMT, NITTTR, Chennai, India
pm.nitttr@gmail.com, https://www.suza.ac.tz/,
http://www.nitttrc.ac.in/

Abstract. The emergence of new technologies has brought significant changes in teaching and learning environment in higher education institutions. One among the technologies that is being integrated in teaching and learning in higher learning institutions is Web 2.0. Web 2.0 is defined as "an increased emphasis on user generated content, data and content sharing and collaborative effort, together with the use of various kinds of social software, new ways of interacting with web-based applications, and the use of the web as a platform for generating, re-purposing and consuming content" [1]. This paper highlights how Web 2.0 such as Learning Management System (LMS), Google drive, social media that have been integrated in the teaching-learning in the State University of Zanzibar (SUZA). It also explores some findings from students based on their perception of Web 2.0 integration. Finally, it pinpoints challenges encountered during the integration and what should be done to ensure the full integration of web 2.0 at SUZA.

Keywords: Web 2.0 · Learning Management System (LMS) · Social media · Teaching-learning · Higher learning institutions

1 Introduction

Technology integration is very important in the teaching-learning process. The use of technology has changed our way of teaching as well as learning. In this digital era, technologies have a great impact not only for learners but also for teachers. This great impact can be observed from lower level to the higher learning institutions.

Web 2.0 such as social media, collaborative tools, wikis and video websites are among the emerging technologies that are used in higher learning institutions in developed and developing countries. [2–4] stipulate that tools such as blogs, Google docs, Google groups, Podcasting, RSS, Wikis, and YouTube are more well liked in teaching and learning. In Tanzania, the use of web 2.0 for teaching-learning purpose has been practiced by some of the higher learning institutions.

© IFIP International Federation for Information Processing 2019
Published by Springer Nature Switzerland AG 2019
A. Tatnall and N. Mavengere (Eds.): SUZA 2019, IFIP AICT 564, pp. 177–184, 2019.
https://doi.org/10.1007/978-3-030-28764-1_20

2 Objectives

This paper highlights how Web 2.0 that have been integrated in the teaching-learning in the State University of Zanzibar (SUZA). It then explore some findings from students based on their perception of Web 2.0 integration. Finally, the paper pinpoints the challenges encountered during the integration and what should be done to ensure the full integration of web 2.0 in the State University of Zanzibar.

3 Methodology

The method used to collect data was qualitative in nature and the data was collected from course evaluation form. Normally, at the end of semester the instructor gives an evaluation form to the students. In that form students had to evaluate the entire course on how their expectations have been met, what new things that they have learned and what challenges they have encountered during the course. The form consists of two parts: The first part asked about students' information such as programme, campus, gender and age. The second part comprises three questions; the first question is about good things found during the course, the second course is about the bad things found in the course and the last question is about things that need to be improved.

The evaluation form is created in Google form and put on LMS platform as well as Facebook course group and students are encouraged to fill the form. This paper reveals some evidence from two courses namely Educational Resources, Media and Technology (I) and Educational Resources, Media and Technology (II) which is offered in semester one and two respectively.

This evaluation was done in the academic year 2015/2016, where 256 students responded in the course of Educational Resources, Media and Technology (I) which is a compulsory course to all students majoring in Education in the first semester. Similarly, 108 students responded in Educational Resources, Media and Technology II which is elective to education students. This course is normally offered in the second semester. Data collected were analyzed from the Google form and the results are reported herein.

4 Integration of Web 2.0 in the State University of Zanzibar

There are various web 2.0 technologies that are integrated in teaching and learning at the State University of Zanzibar. For this study, the web 2.0 technologies that were used are LMS, Facebook, Google drive and YouTube. The technologies have been written in terms of students' preference. The students identified that the LMS integration plays a big role in helping them achieving their learning objectives. They also mentioned that Facebook is also crucial in their learning process as it facilitates their collaboration and communication. They also supported the integration of Google drive for easy sharing of materials and easy notification as well as YouTube for its streaming capabilities as well as saving the recorded video materials for later use and replaying capabilities. The web 2.0 integrated are discussed below:

4.1   Learning Management System (LMS)

Currently, the number of universities adopting LMS in higher education in sub-Saharan Africa has increased. Various researches have been conducted within the sub-Saharan Africa such as [5–7] showing the adoption of LMS in higher learning.

The State University of Zanzibar has its own LMS. This LMS was developed from MOODLE which is an Open source. More than 30 courses have been piloted among which are the course of Educational Resources, Media and Technology I & II. In these two courses, it is mandatory for students to register and follow the course through LMS.

In this LMS, students have opportunity to get lecture notes through presentation software such as MS power point, Google slides and Prezi. Similarly, some videos from YouTube and those created by instructor related to the topics are posted in the LMS. Apart from that, students have opportunity to interact with the instructor and their fellow students through forums which are created by instructor in the LMS. In order to assess the student's performance, students are given quizzes at the end of each topic so as to check their understanding in that topic.

Students identified the integration of LMS in their learning process as good tool since it gives them opportunity to follow the instruction effectively due to its availability in 24 h. Even when they miss the class, they have opportunity to learn the same missed lesson by login to the LMS platform even through their smartphones and tablets at any time. [8] emphasizes the point that most African universities have established e-learning management systems in their institutions. This study is supported with [9] where 44.4% of students prefer LMS as tool to be used for teaching and learning (Fig. 1).

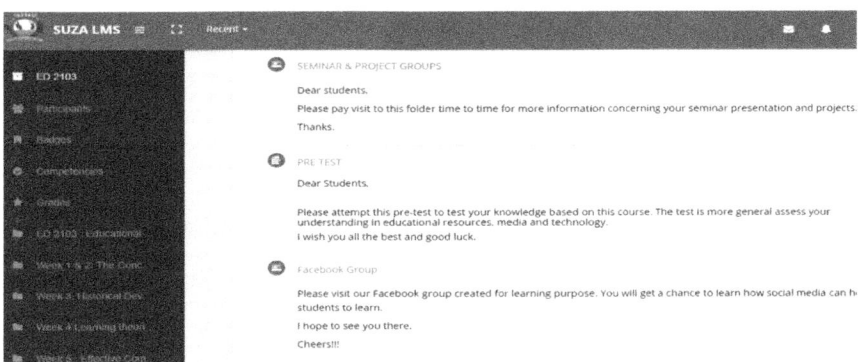

Fig. 1. Example of Learning Management System used in SUZA

4.2   Facebook

The use of social media in the higher learning institutions in Tanzania is becoming popular. [10] recommended that higher learning Institutions should promote the usage of Facebook and other tools since some of them have suitable applications for academic purposes. For this reason, in both two courses, the instructor created Facebook group for each course where only students taking the course were accepted to be the members of that group. Unlike LMS, joining the group is not compulsory but is highly encouraged.

The main use of Facebook is to notify students what is going on in the LMS. The instructor normally uses it for announcement concerning the course and things which are related to the course. Also, lecture notes are put on the wall for easy access of learning materials. Apart from that, students have great opportunity to interact with the instructor via Facebook rather than in LMS. This is because most of the time students spend their time in social media than in LMS.

The use of Facebook in teaching-learning process has been appreciated by students since it gives them the opportunity to follow the instruction anytime. They also consider it as positive way of using social media. They have added that Facebook also enhances communication and collaboration between them and the instructor as well as among themselves. This is reinforced by the study of [11] which shows the immense potential of Social media in teaching and learning at SUZA (Fig. 2).

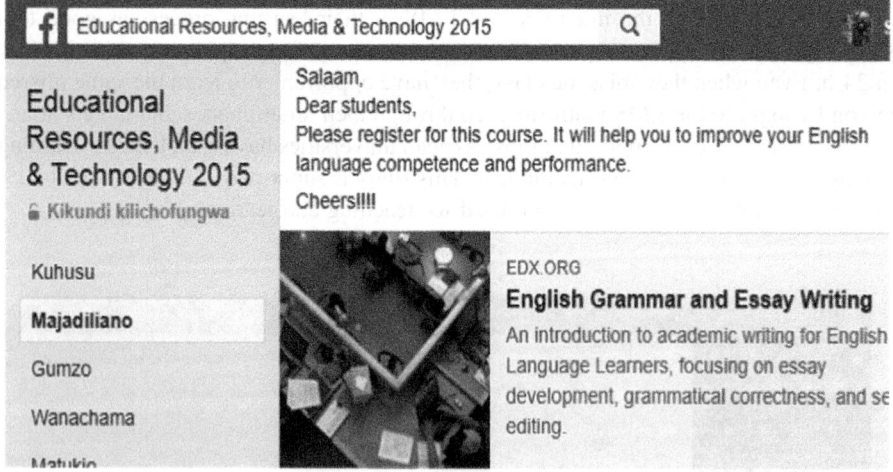

Fig. 2. Example of Facebook page used for teaching-learning

4.3   Google Drive

In both courses the instructor created course folder in Google drive. The aim of creating these folders is to share with students. The folders are posted in both platforms, LMS and Facebook for easy access. In the course folder, there are subfolders on different headings such lectures, assignments, coursework, evaluation and so on. The popular tools used in this Google drive are Google docs, Google sheet, Google slides as well as Google form. In most cases, the use of Google form is more than other tools since it used frequently for evaluation and assessment.

Majority of students are interested in using Google drive since it helps them in collaborating not only with their fellows but also with instructor. It also helps them to submit their assignments easily and timely. As most of the student's own smartphones, it was so easy for them to access the materials and course notification timely (Fig. 3).

Fig. 3. Example of Google Drive used for teaching-learning

4.4 YouTube

The use of video is highly encouraged in both courses so as to facilitate learning and teaching process. The instructor normally uses video from YouTube in the classroom as well as posting in both platforms LMS and Facebook. Students are also motivated to use videos during the seminar presentation. Similarly, the instructor created some videos concerning the course and uploads it on the YouTube.

Students value the use of YouTube in learning and teaching process since it gives them wider understanding of topic. They also have opportunity to replay more and more until they grasp the concept. They have added that with the available new features, the students are able to download the video materials and view them offline at their own time and pace. According to [12] the use of YouTube in the teaching and learning process improves instruction with students most likely to visit video sharing services from their mobile devices (Fig. 4).

Week 6 & 7

Fig. 4. Example of YouTube video used for teaching-learning

5   Challenges Facing the Integration of Web 2.0 in the State University of Zanzibar

In the evaluation forms, the students were asked to identify the challenges they face in the integration of the mentioned Web 2.0 technology in teaching and learning. Their responses are documented thematically as shown:

5.1   Network Problem

Connectivity was a major challenge identified by all students in both evaluations. Network problem is facing many higher learning institutions in Tanzania. Students explained that they fail to integrate web 2.0 in their learning process due to poor network within campus and the high associated cost of the Internet access in the area. This challenge has also been identified by [13]. In addition to this, [8] argued that low Internet bandwidth is one of the limiting factors for most African Universities to use e-learning systems at high rates. For example, student A1 explained *"Sometimes there is network problems in the library when I normally search learning materials. Also, sometimes when I need to search materials through my smart phone the university WI-FI is low or not available."*

5.2   Inadequacy of Devices

Majority of students reported that they do not own their own gadget like computers, ipad, tablets and smartphones. They normally rely on university resources for learning process. They argue that unavailability of resources or devices give them hard time to utilize and integrate technologies effectively in their learning activities. This is emphasized by student A2 *"On the side of library, the main problem is on the number of computers being available, the number of computers in E-Library room is only 24 while the number of students is beyond 1500, Furthermore, the number of sockets in library is inadequate for those students who have their own computers."*

5.3   Limited Skills in Using IT for Learning

Nearly half of respondents claimed that they are not skilled enough to go through those web 2.0 integrated into their course. They reported that this was a critical issue since it impeded to utilize those technologies effectively. For instance, student A3 said *"it was difficult to download some of the notes and I have low knowledge to follow the link and accessing materials."*

5.4   Spam, Immoral Pictures and Video from Social Media

Apart from the above challenges, some respondents state that sometimes they receive spam, immoral pictures and video from social media. This challenge was reported mainly for those who are using Facebook. This was clarified by student A4 *"on social media many destructions can appear like friends send messages not related to the lesson, you can also receive immoral pictures."*

6   Conclusion and Recommendations

As we have seen above, Web 2.0 is being practiced for teaching-learning process. In order to ensure full integration of utilizing Web 2.0 in teaching-learning in higher learning institutions in Zanzibar and Tanzania in general, higher learning institutions must improve connectivity for both lecturers and students. Furthermore, higher learning institutions should adopt the use of Web 2.0 to all programme. Moreover, teaching-learning environment should be well equipped to influence the integration of technologies in higher learning institutions. Similarly, government should put a great support to improve the infrastructure to facilitate the use of technologies in higher learning institutions. Last but not the least, training should be provided to both lecturers and students for better integration of Web 2.0 in teaching and learning environment.

References

1. Franklin, T., Harmelen, M.V.: Web 2.0 for content for learning and teaching in higher education (2007)
2. Anderson, P.: What is Web 2.0? Ideas, technologies and implications for education. JISC Technology and Standards Watch (2007)
3. Salehe, B.R.: Elimu 2.0: investigating the use of Web 2.0 for facilitating collaboration in higher education (2008). http://arrow.dit.ie/cgi/viewcontent.cgi?article=1002&context=scschcomdis
4. Grosseck, G.: To use or not to use Web 2.0 in higher education? Procedia - Soc. Behav. Sci. 1(1), 478–482 (2009)
5. Ssekakubo, G., Suleman, H., Marsden, G.: Issues of adoption: have e-learning management systems fulfilled their potential in developing countries. In: Proceedings of the South African Institute of Computer Scientists and Information Technologists Conference on Knowledge, Innovation and Leadership in a Diverse, Multidisciplinary Environment, Cape Town, South Africa, pp. 231–238. ACM, New York (2011)
6. Maleko Munguatosha, G., Birevu Muyinda, P., Thaddeus Lubega, J.: A social networked learning adoption model for higher education institutions in developing countries. On Horiz. 19(4), 307–320 (2011)
7. Mtebe, J.S., Raisamo, R.: Investigating perceived barriers to the use of open educational resources in higher education in Tanzania. Int. Rev. Res. Open Distance Learn. 15(2), 43–65 (2014)
8. Lwoga, E.T.: Critical success factors for adoption of web-based learning management systems in Tanzania. Int. J. Educ. Dev. Using Inf. Commun. Technol. 10(1), 4 (2014)
9. Mgeni, M.S., Ismail, M.J., Yunus, S.A., Haji, H.A.: The contribution of LMS to the learning environment: views from the state University of Zanzibar. In: Mendy, G., Ouya, S., Dioum, I., Thiaré, O. (eds.) AFRICOMM 2018. LNICST, vol. 275, pp. 305–314. Springer, Cham (2019). https://doi.org/10.1007/978-3-030-16042-5_27
10. Mtega, W.P., Benard, R., Dettu, M.: The prospects of Web 2.0 technologies in teaching and learning in higher learning institutes: the case study of the Sokoine University of Agriculture in Tanzania. Knowl. Manag. E-Learn. Int. J. (KM&EL) 5(4), 404–418 (2014)
11. Daniel, B.K., Ismail, M., El-Nabahany, U., Yunus, S., Mwinyi, M., Mohammed, A.: The role of social media technologies in teaching at the State University of Zanzibar. Int. J. Soc. Media Interact. Learn. Environ. 4(2), 187–209 (2016)

12. Buzzetto-More, N.A.: An examination of undergraduate student's perceptions and predilections of the use of YouTube in the teaching and learning process. Interdiscip. J. E-Learn. Learn. Objects **10**, 17–32 (2014). http://www.ijello.org/Volume10/IJELLOv10p017-032Buzzetto0437.pdf
13. Sife, A., Lwoga, E., Sanga, C.: New technologies for teaching and learning: challenges for higher learning institutions in developing countries. Int. J. Educ. Dev. Using ICT **3**(2), 57–67 (2007)

Will the Visualization of Internet Affect Languages of Education?

Jaana Holvikivi[✉]

Espoo, Finland

Abstract. The impact of digitalization on daily activities has become pervasive, even in the Global South. The dominance of colonial languages in education is both strengthened and weakened by latest technologies. The paper asks whether new technologies could bring native language education available to a larger number of children in the world. The great affordances of new technological innovations could be utilized by school systems, and give students tools to enhance their learning. Mobile and visual technologies such as videos and emoji can empower people and give opportunities for wider communication if policies are enacted to support underprivileged people and grassroots activity. However, intensification of research is needed to outline promising futures for education of minorities, disabled and indigenous peoples.

Keywords: Education · Indigenous languages · Future · Emoji · Digitalization

1 Introduction

Digitalization and ICT have a tremendous effect on daily activities all over the world. Even though computer use was until recently a privilege of citizens of industrialized nations, the access to mobile technologies has reached large populations also in the Global South [1]. Digitalization has the potential of being empowering for people with modest means as the low cost of mobile devices has brought them to the reach of more people than ever. Positive effect can be observed in areas where people previously had no access to global communication, but with mobile devices they can use banking services, conduct business, and access health care information among other activities. On the other hand, the reliance on English as the language of computer has been challenged by the increased use of video and images, as well as the opportunity to use other signs than alphabetic characters. The changes in technology penetration have recently been faster than ever, and there is no reason to suppose that the pace of technical development would slow down in the near future [1]. The rapid change poses a challenge to research and policy making.

This paper aims to take some fresh perspectives to the use of ICT in education, challenges of education in multilingual countries, and what would be needed for creating equal opportunities to the underprivileged and minority populations in the digitalized world. A crucial question is whether the people in developing countries will be able to appropriate novel technologies in their own ways to support their own communication needs. Moreover, the paper will discuss briefly some aspects of the current state of technological development and its global distribution, particularly the shift

© IFIP International Federation for Information Processing 2019
Published by Springer Nature Switzerland AG 2019
A. Tatnall and N. Mavengere (Eds.): SUZA 2019, IFIP AICT 564, pp. 185–194, 2019.
https://doi.org/10.1007/978-3-030-28764-1_21

towards East Asia. The cognitive basis on ICTs is in the Western school system and Western science, which dominate the research and education. Furthermore, the paper will present some trends that might impact the dominance of English in computer systems, and consider chances that it will fade soon. What will be the future of world's thousands of small languages? Will modern technology destroy them or help them to survive? Moreover, the cognitive requirements by technical systems and mobile applications will be considered, and the use of social media in new contexts is reflected upon.

2   Languages in Education and Cognitive Development

There are about 6000 languages spoken in the world currently, but only 3% of them are spoken in Europe [2]. In particular, the multiplicity of languages affects education systems in Africa and Asia. Despite the large number of native languages, school languages in the Global South usually are either colonial languages such as English, Spanish or French, or national languages such as Swahili or Hindi. Even though bilingualism obtained in school could greatly benefit the intellectual development of the child, the benefits are lost if the child is not able to acquire fluency in her school language, because higher order thinking and problem solving rely on language. For the development of abstract and scientific thought, mastery of the working language is required [3]. Even development of mathematical skills is heavily influenced by the language of instruction [4].

In many African countries such as Kenya school tuition is only given in a few languages, and moreover, parents want their children to learn English as it is believed to open more possibilities for future education and career. However, if the student does not master English or the other school language well, she cannot really learn any demanding concepts, as also Kioko et al. demonstrate [5].

One of the countries that prefer colonial languages in education is Rwanda. The Rwandan government decided to switch the country's entire education system from French to English in its move away from Francophone influence in 2008 [6]. The first three years of primary education are conducted in local Kinyarwanda, and after that in English. Just 8% of Rwandans speak French, and 4% speak English, according to the government, but teachers have previously been educated in French. In 2009, out of Rwanda's 31 000 primary school teachers, only 4 700 were trained in English, and out of Rwanda's 12 000 secondary school teachers, only 600 were trained in English. Pearson [7] in her article "Policy without a plan: English as a medium of instruction in Rwanda" stresses that there was no implementation plan, neither a follow-up. Recent statistics show that despite some major achievements in Rwanda's attempts to achieve universal primary education, it currently has one of the worst repetition rates in the Sub-Saharan region. School attendance is high but students do not pass grades [8].

On the other hand, mother tongue instruction has been a success in Ethiopia, where schooling formerly had been offered only in the majority language Amharic and English at later stages. Other 20 languages (there are 85 different languages in the country) were added to primary instruction since 1994 with good results, as more children completed primary school. Philippines has moved to multilingual model, as well [9]. Nevertheless, mother tongue instruction is a demanding process to implement for a country, as it requires development of the written language if it did not exist earlier, training of teachers and production of learning materials and textbooks. India has started many regional projects to support indigenous language teaching in schools, but taken the limited resources and enormous number of languages, only a small fraction of the population has been reached [10].

As comparisons of language policies between former colonies of European countries show, most policies are based on political power considerations, not educational science. This is the case in (former) French colonies, as well [11], and it also is displayed in the language policies of Russia and former Soviet countries such as Estonia, Latvia and Lithuania. The right to mother tongue instruction often is undermined by national politics. Furthermore, all countries with immigrant populations have to acknowledge their language education needs, which always is a significant investment for the education system.

Additionally, thinking models stemming from Western schooling are dominated by logical, hierarchical thinking, objectivity removed from body and emotions, and individual performance, not social collaboration. These culturally influenced factors can hinder student learning, as has been understood in Bolivia where the new primary school curriculum guarantees education in the native language, Aymara, and simultaneously supports native spirituality and communities [12].

Educational policies in European countries emphasize higher order thinking skills, computer science and computational thinking as a part of essential 21st century skills that students need in the digital world. But how can education in the Global South help the population in dealing with the new challenges? Schools in Africa, Asia and Latin America very seldom have the means to teach computing-related topics because the lack of equipment, electricity and telecommunications. Moreover, the teachers are even less skilled in digitalization than in Europe.

A revealing example comes from Kenya, which introduced an ambitious policy to teach computer skills in all secondary schools according to the Vision 2030 Economic Stimulus Programme by Kenyan government The government equipped 1050 secondary schools with computers: 11 PCs, 1 laptop, 1 video projector and one 1 printer for each school. The aim of the initiative was that teachers would be able to integrate ICT into the curriculum. However, there can be as many as 80 to 120 students in one class, which makes it impossible to let all students to work with computers, or teachers to acquire digital skills for themselves [13].

Amina Charania from Tata Foundation, India, stated "We cannot talk about computational thinking before we have brought basics of digital literacy to the school teachers in rural India" [14]. Tata foundation is supporting projects that introduce digital skills to teachers who in turn start mentoring another group of teachers. The model seems to be suitable in a country with a huge rural population and great number of native languages.

3 Design of New Technologies

Computers were invented around 1940 in the United States, where also programming and later the internet were born. Computer technology is based on Western science and thinking, and even programming languages and computer operation rely on one language only, English. For a long time, the use of English and its alphabet in all telecommunications restricted users in other countries and strengthened the global dominance of English language. Moreover, the American dominance in entertainment industry and in internet applications seemed to ensure that English would be the only important language in the future [1].

The technologies are still mainly developed by US and Western companies where the employees share the schooling background, science education and behavioural norms, as well as cognitive styles. Therefore, the logic of systems and applications is purely based on Western science. Moreover, the psychology behind the usability and user interfaces of the devices and applications is based on research made among US college students, which hardly represents the psychology of the global population. Most of the research that has been published in psychology journals has been conducted by Western researchers (96%), using university students as test subjects (in 67% of the cases in American samples). Henrich et al. [15] argued that the sample thus obtained is severely biased, and in some cases could be considered as an outlier of the global population. Comparative studies indicate very different behavioural patterns in other populations, particularly in Asian countries and small societies.

Moreover, as companies aim at generating profits, they mainly design for the population that can best afford their products. People with less means have to adapt to whatever is offered on the market. People in Asia, Africa and Latin America have predominantly been consumers; not part of the development process, even though the most active internet users are in South-East Asian and Latin American countries, Philippines leading the statistics with over alleged 10 h a day [16]. The Japanese industry was the first to start alternative product development, and has introduced a variety of technologies, games, robotic applications, etc. which have succeeded globally. The changes in the global user population will have an effect on the products in the future, as the Chinese economy is growing fast, and other emerging economies follow. The R&D of ICT products increasingly will take place in the East [17].

3.1 New Ways of Communication Emerge

The English alphabet uses only 27 characters. For decades, computer systems were predominantly built to use that character set in texts following standards such as ASCII and ANSI. As most Western European languages had more alphabetic characters, they were added to code sets as alternatives. Later, Cyrillic, Greek and Arabic characters were added, and finally, the Unicode recommendation that was drafted in 1988 recognizes all world's languages and their writing systems [18]. Despite the creation of the industry standard, it has taken a long time to include all characters into existing computer systems. Because of the complex writing system of the Japanese language, ideogram and syllabic alternatives were developed early in Japan. Currently, major

Asian languages can easily be written using mobile or computer keyboards, including Chinese, Hindi, and Arabic.

On the other hand, language learning and processing is becoming less dependent on writing, when videos and recorded speech can be distributed through mobile networks, and speech analysis allows pronunciation practice. Foreign or second language learning has become much easier than before when numerous language tutoring videos are distributed over the internet. The old pedagogy of grammar and vocabulary drills can be replaced by more natural ways of adopting new languages. Additionally, new translation tools take some of the learning burden away.

3.2   Emoji

A new communication style has started with the use of cute little symbols called emoji, which are not connected to any language. It is not surprising that the origin of emoji is also in Japan where the telecommunications companies started to add them to keyboards of mobile phones in 1999. Even though emoji can be conceived as an extension of the text-based emoticons such as the smiley, they are also connected to the Japanese communication culture that has favoured cute images and symbols already for decades [19]. Routinely, the authorities in Japan soften orders and prohibitions by sweet pictorial expression such as childish traffic signs. Emoji also fit rather seamlessly to the Japanese writing that habitually includes four different types of characters (hiragana, katakana, kanji and Latin alphabet). The word emoji is Japanese and means picture-character [18–22].

The emoji are currently included in the Unicode being therefore global [18]. Each emoji has a defined name in the code but people do not necessarily know the names when they choose to include some emoji in their messages. Therefore, the emoji have varied meanings depending on the user community, platform, or individual user. No correct code for usage can be devised. In fact, there are heated discussions on this such as the meaning of the most popular emoji, the loudly crying face [23]. There are also culturally sensitive emoji such as thumbs up which can be offensive in some countries. The emoji are hugely popular in China where local varieties exist on platforms such as WeChat. Moreover, the pictorial expression can be used for hidden messages and to recode the words of the message because Chinese characters often convey one idea or word, as well [24].

Research on emoji use is accumulating fast [25, 26]. Many studies have analysed emoji use by text context or country differences in Twitter where the API allows downloading of large data sets [27]. The research has found differences between geographical areas and among countries. However, Twitter is a platform for political and business communication which is not the most typical area for casual conversation. Actually, Instagram is a more typical platform for emoji, and already in 2016 nearly half of Instagram messages contained emoji [18]. Emoji users tend to be young people who use them in informal settings. As the name "emoticon" originally referred to, emoji are also carriers of feeling rather than factual information. They soften the message, making it less threatening.

Certain emoji are popular all over the world with laughing or crying faces on top of the list. However, differences between countries have been detected: in France, heart-symbols are among the most popular emoji in text messages according to Lu et al. [25]. The French also used emoji more frequently than other nationalities in the study. However, the test population in this study comprised of predominantly young adults.

Despite the active research interest, it will be hard to predict the future importance of emoji as means of communication. The Unicode consortium is dominated by US based technology giants and their representatives, therefore they are hardly representative of the world population and the variety of cultural expressions. Will the emoji be a new global "language" or replaced by something else soon? Their similarity to logograms in some aspects might be important in the future. In any case, they are a good example of challenges to the dominance of English in global communication, and the extremely fast spread of new fashions in the internet.

4   Reading Logograms and Other Characters

The Western Latin alphabet is one of the simplest writing systems. It is closely related to other Greek-derived alphabets such as Cyrillic writing used in Russia. The Arabic consonant system is historically related to alphabets, but, significantly, it is written from right to left. Chinese characters are complex, and the system contains thousands of logograms that can be pronounced in several ways. The perception of an individual character is visually more demanding than that of alphabetic letters, as one character may consist of up to 23 strokes. Writing Chinese characters requires good hand movement control and visual memory, therefore Chinese speakers employ visuo-motor brain areas for reading and writing to a larger extent than alphabet users [28]. Chinese is written in varied directions, including from left to right and top to bottom. Additionally, other important writing systems include various syllabic writings in South and East Asia such as Hindi, Bengali, and Thai.

Reading as a cognitive process is somewhat different when the characters are not alphabetic but logograms. Pictorial expressions are processed by different parts of the brain than alphabetic text. Most research concerning language and number processing has examined Indo-European language speakers (such as English, German, and Italian) who read alphabetic characters and use Arabic numerals [29]. A growing body of evidence points to differences in reading, processing numbers, and doing mental arithmetic in people who use predominantly logographic characters. Most probably these differences extend to computer-based mental functioning, as well.

Intensive research concerning the processing of Chinese and Japanese languages has revealed significant differences in brain networks that are involved in reading logographic or alphabetic texts. Bolger et al. [29] found in their meta-analysis of alphabetic systems, Chinese, and Japanese writings, that the brain regions involved in word reading in these language systems are mainly the visual word form area in the left mid-fusiform gyrus. Nevertheless, certain localization differences are obvious between logographic and alphabetic systems. A study that compared eye movements in different visual and character-related tasks also showed specific patterns for Chinese characters. Chinese participants' fixations were more numerous and of shorter duration than those of their American counterparts while viewing faces and scenes, and counting Chinese characters in text [30].

A study on information technology students reactions to special characters that are used in computer systems showed that results varied depending on students native language and school languages. The study compared character perception differences in Ethiopian (syllabic writing), Chinese (logographic writing), and European information technology students. Working memory performance was tested for numbers, letters, and special characters such as #, / and &. Preliminary results indicated that a person's native character system affects the ability to mentally manipulate and memorize different types of characters [31].

Evidently, the visualization of internet and mobile communication could also be studied from the perception aspects, as well as from the emotional point of view, which opens up numerous interesting questions for future study.

5   Social Media and Other Future Considerations

Technology has multiple various kinds of effects on education and language. As best, it is found to be useful in indigenous language support and revitalization [32], which gives some hope to the future of world's minority languages and linguistic diversity. Technology enables communication and education for dispersed languages with small numbers of speakers through distance education. Videos, podcasts and streaming of tuition could all make it less costly to develop educational materials. Students use videos for learning already heavily in industrialized countries, which shows that they are a popular and useful way to develop new skills if available. In countries such as Indonesia, Brazil and Thailand where people are purportedly spending around 10 h a day in using social media [16], the potential for educational videos should be enormous.

However, there also are less innocent developments caused by technology and social media, in particular. The consequences of digitalization and social media are unpredictable and can be disastrous in some cases such as the infamous case of Facebook and the Rohingya. Coverage of smart phones in Myanmar exploded in 2014-17 but the population had no education in understanding social media and was an easy prey to malignant rumours in the Facebook [33]. However, that kind of problem is not confined to newly developed mobile infrastructure but a similar dilemma has emerged in rich countries where other countries' spy organizations have been able to influence election results (in the US and U.K.) through false information in social media. Moreover, even governments are publishing manipulated videos for political aims.

Whatsapp rumours and India lynchings [34] are another troubling case, which has claimed tens of victims. Rumours accusing people of kidnapping children have been circulated widely in Whatsapp groups, and angry crowds have attacked innocent passers-by. Actually, the phenomenon had started already before internet access with simple text messages. In Nigeria, text messages were circulated that were rumoured to cause voodoo deaths. More recently, in the neighbouring country Niger, marriage customs are affected by public displays in social media [35].

6 Conclusions

Position of English as the growing universal language was supported by the early years of internet where text-based communication was dominant and the English ASCII alphabet was the only choice. Text messages forced people to use English character sets and sometimes even the language. However, the trend has turned as the bandwidth on communication has expanded, pictorial and video expression is feasible, and use of any local characters in writing is possible with digital devices. Automatic translation based on speech reduces the need for knowing other languages well. Additionally, certain strong cultural influences compete stronger than ever with American cultural dominance in global entertainment such as K-pop, anime and manga, and Bollywood.

The educational system including policy makers, schools and teachers now has a great opportunity to seize the affordances of the new and emerging technologies. Education can utilize videos, cameras, speech recognition, broadband mobile communications, as well as emoji-type pictorial expressions. The creative capacity of the young generation, school children, could be harnessed to this aim. Children want to learn, and they are quick to find new ways to improve their skills. Pedagogy that is based on knowledge construction and inquiry based learning is a great tool in using new technologies to produce materials and learning.

Cognitive differences in computer operation have implications for professional activities in non-Western countries, which would need further study. Whether cognitive differences will be mitigated by the development of technology or worsen because of its more frequent use, is not yet clear. However, the more technology-led future will require stronger thinking skills than ever [36]. Thinking skills are developed in the education from early on, therefore, the importance of quality education and further training for teachers is crucial. Mother tongue education in primary schools is one of the keys to successful cognitive development. Development policies and projects need to emphasize quality education following the principle that education has to be first, and technology is in its service.

References

1. ITU. Measuring the Information Society Report 2018. http://itu.int
2. Crystal, D.: The Cambridge Encyclopedia of Language, 3rd edn. Cambridge University Press, Cambridge (2010)
3. Bialystok, E., Craik, F., Luk, G.: Bilingualism: consequences for mind and brain. Trends Cogn. Sci. 16(4), 240–250 (2012)
4. Haag, N., Heppt, B., Stanat, P., Kuhl, P., Pant, H.A.: Second language learners' performance in mathematics: disentangling the effects of academic language features. Learn. Instr. 28, 24–34 (2013)
5. Kioko, A.N., Ndung'u, R.W., Njoroge, M.C.: Mother tongue and education in Africa: publicising the reality. Multiling. Ed. 4, 18 (2014)
6. McGreal, C.: Rwanda to switch from French to English in schools (2008). http://www.guardian.co.uk/world/2008/oct/14/rwanda-france. Accessed 14 Oct 2008
7. Pearson, P.: Policy without a plan: English as a medium of instruction in Rwanda. Curr. Issues Lang. Plan. 15(1), 39–56 (2014)

8. Watkins, K.: Too little access, not enough learning: Africa's twin deficit in education (2013). http://www.brookings.edu/research/opinions/2013/01/16-africa-learning-watkins. Accessed 16 Jan 2013
9. SIL International. http://www.sil.org
10. Singh, N.K.: Globalization and multilingualism: case studies of indigenous culture-based education from the indian sub-continent and their implications. Int. J. Multicult. Educ. **15**(1) (2013)
11. Spolsky, B.: Language policy in French colonies and after independence. Curr. Issues Lang. Plan. **19**(3), 231–315 (2018)
12. Filpus, L.: Bolivia: new primary school curriculum guarantees education in the native language, Aymara. Opettaja **13**, 34–36 (2017)
13. Ang'ondi, E.K.: Teachers attitudes and perceptions on the use of ICT in teaching and learning as observed by ICT champions. In: WCCE 2013, Torun, Poland, vol. 1 (2013)
14. Charania, A.: OCCE2018 keynote (2018). http://occe.2018.ocg.at/. Accessed 28 June 2018
15. Henrich, J., Heine, S.J., Norenzayan, A.: The weirdest people in the world? Behav. Brain Sci. **33**(2–3), 61–83 (2010)
16. Lamb, K.: Philippines tops world internet usage index with an average 10 hours a day (2019). https://www.theguardian.com/technology/2019/feb/01/world-internet-usage-index-philippines-10-hours-a-day
17. Romei, V., Reed, J.: The Asian century is set to begin. Financial Times (2019). https://www.ft.com/content/520cb6f6-2958-11e9-a5ab-ff8ef2b976c7
18. Unicode Organization. http://www.unicode.org
19. Gn, J.: Emoji as a "language" of cuteness. First Monday **23**, 9 (2018)
20. Davis, M., Edberg, P.: Unicode Emoji. Version 10.0, 21 May 2018. http://unicode.org/reports/tr51/
21. Lufkin, B.: Why are there so many Japanese emoji? (2018). http://www.bbc.com/capital/story/20180716-why-there-are-so-many-japanese-emoji
22. Evans, V.: The Emoji Code: How Smiley Faces, Love Hearts and Thumbs Up are Changing the Way We Communicate. Michael O'Mara, London (2017)
23. Kelly, J.: Loudly crying face, 13 June 2018. https://blog.emojipedia.org/emojiology-loudly-crying-face/
24. Yan, D.: When chatting with Chinese, know your emojis (2016). http://www.chinadaily.com.cn/china/2016-02/02/content_23356908.htm
25. Lu, X., et al.: Learning from the ubiquitous language: an empirical analysis of emoji usage of smartphone users. In: UBICOMP 2016, Germany (2016)
26. Emojitracker. http://Emojitracker.com
27. Coats, S.: Skin Tone Emoji and Sentiment on Twitter (2018). https://arxiv.org/ftp/arxiv/papers/1805/1805.00444.pdf
28. Chen, C., Xue, G., Mei, L., Chen, C., Dong, Q.: Cultural neurolinguistics. Prog. Brain Res. **178**, 159 (2009)
29. Bolger, D.J., Perfetti, C.A., Schneider, W.: Cross-cultural effect on the brain revisited: universal structures plus writing system variation. Hum. Brain Mapp. **25**, 92–104 (2005)
30. Rayner, K., Li, X., Williams, C.C., Cave, K.R., Well, A.D.: Eye movements during information processing tasks: individual differences and cultural effects. Vis. Res. **47**(21), 2714–2726 (2007)
31. Holvikivi, J.: Cultural variation in perception and coding in IT students. In: 10th IFIP World Conference on Computers in Education, Torun, Poland, vol. 1, pp. 200–208 (2013)
32. Galla, C.K.: Indigenous language revitalization, promotion, and education: function of digital technology. Comput. Assist. Lang. Learn. **29**(7), 1137–1151 (2016)

33. Myanmar Rohingya: Why Facebook banned an army chief (2018). https://www.bbc.co.uk/news/world-asia-45326928
34. Rahman, S.: Fake news often goes viral: WhatsApp ads warn India after mob lynchings (2018). https://www.theguardian.com/world/2018/jul/13/fake-news-whatsapp-ads-india-mob-lynchings
35. Maclean, R.: New clothes and cash: social media fuels Niger 'bride price' controversy (2018). https://www.theguardian.com/global-development/2018/jul/23/how-social-media-is-revolutionising-marriage-in-niger
36. Holvikivi, J.: Culture and Cognition in Information Technology Education. SimLab Publications, Espoo (2009)

The Introduction of ICTs in Chilean Schools – An Analysis of the Various Initiatives Since Enlaces and the Issues Faced by the Mapuche

Fernando Toro[(✉)]

ICT Consultant, Melbourne, Australia
c-fernandot@hotmail.com

Abstract. The Introduction of ICTs in Chilean Schools - The Various Initiatives since Enlaces and the Issues Faced by Mapuche Students.

Keywords: Information and Communication Technology (ICTs) Education ·
History of Computers in Chilean Schools · Chile · Education ·
Educational policy · Mapuche · Inclusion · Social capital

1 Background

The use of Information and Communication Technologies (ICT) in education has for a long time now generated extensive interest as well as being attributed to have an important role in education. Prior to 1990, Chile had a minimal exposure to ICTs in education and thus with the return to democracy the country was also interested in the role that ICTs could have in education. Therefore, it embarked on a major initiative to introduce ICTs in schools and reform the education system. It must be noted that the reforms were implemented on the foundations of a free market model imposed by the previous dictatorial Pinochet regime and the many reforms that have taken place have not been without social and political challenges. This journey of reforms started in 1992 with the birth of 'Programa Enlaces' or 'Enlaces' for short; a pilot program that was first implemented in a small number of schools in the capital, Santiago and was later expanded to include the region of Araucania. This region has the highest proportion of Mapuche people, as compared to other regions in Chile, in fact, over 30% of its inhabitants consider themselves Mapuche. It is also one of the poorest regions in the country. The Mapuche are the indigenous people of the south of Chile and Argentina.

Enlaces was primarily an educational web that connected schools and provided access to ICTs. Enlaces expanded quickly, and by 1995 the program expanded quickly managing to connect 5,300 schools. By 2000, Enlaces was expanded and managed to connect the totality of rural school in the country and by 2014, the totality of subsided schools were connected. Enlaces was also enhanced by other initiatives that placed more ICTs in the classroom, introduced teacher training in the use of ICTS, connected rural school with improved bandwidth, increased the number of student scholarships that provided free laptops or computers, the creation of software and portals.

© IFIP International Federation for Information Processing 2019
Published by Springer Nature Switzerland AG 2019
A. Tatnall and N. Mavengere (Eds.): SUZA 2019, IFIP AICT 564, pp. 195–205, 2019.
https://doi.org/10.1007/978-3-030-28764-1_22

The newly elected government had identified that Chile's education system had structural deficiencies, poor performance results, impoverished schools and the system was lacking in quality and equity. Thus, ICTs were seen as tools that would enrich the students' education and ultimately provide a better quality of education under a more egalitarian system. The broader reforms were centred on the regulatory frameworks, changes to curriculum (to both, primary and secondary levels), teacher training and development, increasing pedagogical resources and infrastructure for schools, improving students' attendance and increasing the time spent on teaching. However, the introduction of ICT into the education system has not been without challenges and/or criticism. For example, and although there have been marginal quantifiable results that would attest to the rationale behind these measures; there is still a significant number of people who believe that the changes have not been sufficient or go deep enough to remove any vestige from the reforms implemented during the military dictatorship that ruled from 1973 to 1990. The political climate in Chile remains polarised and so, the subject of education has become politicised. Parents, students and teachers have all had an interest in the education system. As a result, educational reform, has been a controversial political problem during the various governments since the return of democracy.

Despite the various initiatives implemented, the approach for the greater part often assumed a homogenous population and very much a top-down, 'one-size-fits-all' approach. These strategies may be fit-for-purpose in some circumstances, for example, the private sector and industry specific. However, the traditional Mapuche concept of building knowledge is through what they call "to learn by doing" which takes the form in labor, social, cultural and productive actions that Mapuche people developed, in which the teaching – learning process involved different family members, where the main methodological aspect was centered in communication. Therefore, a homogenous blanket approach may not be suitable for a group where the main approach is more collective and inclusive. As indicated earlier, the Mapuche, live in a region with a high poverty index and with its inherited issues related to the lack of inclusion and literacy rates, therefore, education needs to be looked at a level that consults and includes the community. So, that it is the community that becomes empowered to recognise and confront their concerns within the contexts of their own culture. On the contrary, the Mapuche will continue experiencing a dilution of their culture either by adaption, tacit imposition or adoption of the values imparted by the state through the educational context of schools. This not only includes the curriculum content but also the physical structures, government policies, technology, social inclusion and social capital.

2   Introduction

The use of Information and Communication Technologies (ICT) in education has generated widespread interest as well as being attributed to have an important role in education [1–9]. Of course, in this day and age, the introduction of ICTs in education is not a new concept given that we are now on the path of a fourth Industrial Revolution, also referred to as the 'digital revolution' [10], which is building on the third and is distinguished by the fusion of technologies and thus the lines between the physical, digital and biological are becoming unclear and as such, also affect governments, skills and labour, business and economies alike [11, 12].

Prior to the 1990s, Chile had no public policy which included ICTs in the education of its students. However, changes and policy where quickly implemented once democracy was restored and one of the major changes was the birth of Enlaces, which started as pilot program to connect a small number of school in the capital Santiago and was later expanded to include a small number of schools in regional capital Temuco located in the region of Araucania.

3 Return to Democracy and the Birth of Enlaces

Mr. Patricio Alwyn, became the first president of Chile (from 1990 to 1994) after the Pinochet dictatorship had ended and democracy was once again restored [13]. Prior to 1990, Chile had no public policy to promote the use of ICTs in education and its exposure in this area was limited [14]. Although, there was a small number of schools which either had computers or a lab; these were mainly secondary schools where the aim was to teach programming, for example, Basic or Logo (Jara 2013). At the academic level, Jara [15] indicates that there was an incipient and interested community on this theme. However, in March 1990 the 'Programa de Mejoramiento de la Calidad y Equidad de la Educación Básica' programme (usually referred to as 'MECE Basica') was devised [14, 16]. With finance and advice from the World Bank, the initiate got underway in 1992 and so, the country embarked on a national initiative to improve the education system [17], starting at the primary education level with the aim to improve quality, equity and efficiency [18]; at the preschool aiming to expand the coverage and enhance the quality of education at this level and finally, to develop institutional, managerial and financial capacity at the basic education system [18] and which later included the implementation of ICTs in schools Bellei [17, 19, 20].

There was, to some degree, a consensus that as a result of the challenges posed by the how to, form, educate, teach, learn in a world where information is the central element of productivity, where individual and collective opportunities are played out within the networks that are accessible [21], President Alwyn's newly elected government wanted to respond to these challenges and 1992 saw the creation of 'Programa Enlaces', often referred to 'Red Enlaces' or only as 'Enlaces', which was born within the MECE Basica initiative ('Linkages Program' in English) Toro [3, 16, 19, 20, 22, 23]. Notwithstanding, the conceived changes were to be implemented on the foundations of the neo-liberal market model imposed by the previous dictatorial regime [24]. Successive governments have been criticised for failing to reform the inherited aspects of the education system [25]. Subsequent coalition governments that proceeded Mr. Alwyn's presidency, as well as students, parents and teachers; all had an interest in the education system. As a result and due to the various actors involved, educational reform has been a contentious political issue in the country [26]. On the one hand, the majority of students, parents and a significant part of the electorate, claim that education should be free of charge, not for profit, of good quality and inclusive [27]. They argued that the market model is geared to the generation of profits, as opposed to providing education, as the main tenet, persisted beyond the Pinochet regime and has continued to some degree, during the various democratic governments that followed [28]. Therefore, the country was rocked by major student protests in 2006, the so called 'pinguino' protests during which approximately 600,000 marched demanding educational reforms [17, 25, 29] and students protest have persisted throughout 2008, 2011, 2012, 2015, 2016 and 2018 [27, 29, 30].

The 'Enlaces' program was developed as an experimental initiative to implement computer technology in schools [20, 22]. Changes were required due to the failures of the inherited education system which had been through a period of decentralisation and privatisation during the Pinochet dictatorship [26, 29, 31, 32]. For example, as described by Sánchez and Salinas [20], Claro et al. [22] and Toro [32], there was also a need to improve the quality and equity in education in publicly financed education in Chile. Thus, 'Enlaces' was broadly seen as part of the national consensus and urgent need for more equity and quality in the Chilean education [20]. The inception of Enlaces was not straight forward as the then Minister of Education, Mr. Ricardo Lagos had to contend with two main approaches, each with their pros and cons [16]. One approach intended to follow a similar path as taken by Costa Rica, with emphasis on the learning of specific programming languages and requiring massification which would require a high number of computers installed throughout the country [14, 16]. According to Toro (2010) this approach was met with questions on acceptance, adoption, quantifiable result and obsolescence. Notwithstanding, this was a highly visible approach politically, but it was not adopted. Therefore, a second proposition was considered, one that was much less visible politically but which has been in the long term generally seen as a public policy in which the state has been the biggest promoter of technological innovation [17]. The latter was Enlaces, a pilot program with a much smaller presence and that would lay the foundations for a much bigger future project (Jara 2013); initially, it connected only six schools in Santiago within the vicinity of the Universidad Católica's San Joaquin Campus (Toro 2010) and subsequently, connected a further fifteen more schools in Temuco (Toro 2010), which is about 700 km to the south of Santiago in the Araucania regions (Toro 2018). Despite the small beginnings, Enlaces expanded quickly and defying expectations, by 1995 a total of 5,300 schools (ranging from primary to secondary levels) had been connected [33]. However, the majority of rural schools had to wait another 5 years to start connecting to Enlaces (Jara 2013, Enlaces 2019). In 1996 an alliance was formed between the Ministry of Education and the universities along the entire county [33], this was known as the 'Red de Asistencia Tecnica de Enlaces' but usually referred by its initial as RATE [14]. The aim of RATE was to support the primary and secondary school that were part or pending connection to Enlaces, becoming an integral component to the expansion of Enlaces throughout the country [14, 16]. Initially, this alliance comprised 6 universities and expanded to 24, out of which 7 had a leading role in the implementation of Enlaces to the rest of the schools in the country (Jara 2013). The universities which were part of RATE were involved in providing the school teachers with ICT training, provide technical support, provide email services and to keep up with the growing demand due to the rapid expansion, the universities organised a network of about 1000 trainers who were usually school teachers who originated from the schools already connected and who served as Enlaces coordinators who helped to create a nexus between the school and university frameworks [14, 16,

33, 34]. In 1998, the educational reform officially incorporated Information Technology as a curriculum subject for high schools, as well as the provision of CDs which contained education resources, such as software, catalogues and search engines [33]. Most importantly, the Internet arrives free of charge to the schools with the aide of the private enterprises such as Telefonica CTC Chile (Enlaces 2019). The year 2000 marks an important point for Enlaces due to its expansion of coverage which would connect rural and remote schools [33, 34]. In 2002, Enlaces is recognised with an equity award at the Second Information Technology in Education (SITE) conference held in Nashville, U.S.A. for increasing the digital equity and the renovation of education through the use of ICTs (Enlaces 2019). During this period teachers were also situated at the vanguard of the integration process (Enlaces 2019). During 2003 and 2004, there were further resources made available such as digital classes, refurbished computers placed in classrooms (approximately 30 students per computer), improving the performance in Mathematics using ICTs, but most importantly, bringing Internet access to remote areas where there was none (Enlaces 2019). From 2005 to 2011 there was a continuation of innovative measures for the education such as the use of Linux to take advantage of open source applications and prolonging the life of some older computers, whilst at the same time, acquiring more equipment to provide quality education and the introduction of Mobile Computer Labs (Enlaces 2019) but more importantly, this period also saw the collection of data to measure the penetration of ICTs and their use in the classroom and in 2010 obtained the ISO 9901-2008 quality certification (Enlaces 2019). During the period from 2012 to 2015 more initiatives were introduced that included the use of ICTs, one of these was known as 'TIC y Diversidad' (in english, ICT and Diversity) and which included teaching math, science and history to students with hearing impairment, in fact, by 2014 the totality of school catering for students with special audio needs where covered by this program (Enlaces 2019). The use of tablets as teaching and learning tools by preschoolers was also launched (Enlaces 2019). Furthermore, in 2014, the data gathered in previous years indicated that 46.9% of students were at a proficiency level of beginners, 51.3% were at intermediate level and 1.8% at an advanced level, these figures covered students at school all levels (Enlaces 2019). From 2015 onwards, a number of scholarship programs were established to benefit students who were classified as lacking resources or from a low socio-economic status and enrolled in a subsidized school, namely, the 'I Choose my PC' Scholarship (in Spanish, 'Yo Elijo Mi PC') and 'I Connect to Learn' (in Spanish, 'Me Conecto Para Aprender') were established (Enlaces 2019). During 2015 and through the 'Yo Elijo Mi PC' scholarship, 70,000 students benefited under this scholarship. According to figures provided by Junta Nacional de Auxilio Escolar y Becas [35], since its inception, 350,000 students have benefited as a result of the scholarships and an extra 30,000 who are enrolled in a subsidized school in grade seven were expected to benefit in 2017 [36] and by 2019 about 130,000 students would be able to receive a computer [37].

4   The Situation of the Mapuche – Some Key Factors

The region of Araucania has the highest proportion of Mapuche people, as compared to other regions in Chile and over 30% of its inhabitants consider themselves Mapuche. It is also one of the poorest regions in the country [38, 39]. This figure rises higher when we look at the communes within Araucania. For example, in the communes of Saavedra, Cholchol, Galvarino and Freire, the rate of poverty is about 60% and with just over 67% of this group living in rural areas [39, 40].

Valenzuela and Toro et al. [39] indicate that there has been little effort towards profiling the Araucania region socio-economically. However, Cerda [40] as referenced by Valenzuela and Toro et al. (2017) provides one of the better known studies on the subject. Furthermore, Cerda [40] has concluded that the region, having high levels of poverty and unemployment, as well as low levels of schooling, has resulted in low level of growth. However, as indicated by Valenzuela and Toro et al. (2017), this phenomenon is not isolated to the Mapuche or ethnicity and affects all social sectors. In fact, the region has the highest proportion of poor people of Chile and it is the 'third region with the greatest number of people in poverty, with 217,755 people living beneath the poverty line' [39].

5   CASEN – The Socioeconomic Characterisation Survey

CASEN is the short name for 'National Survey of Socioeconomic Characterisation' (in Spanish: 'Encuesta de Caracterización Socioeconómica Nacional'), which has been under the guidance of the Ministry of Social Development and has been carried since 1990 and approximately, every two years, thus, 1992, 1994, 1996, 1998, 2000, 2003, 2006, 2009, 2011, 2013 and 2105 [41]. According to the Ministerio de Desarrollo Social [41], the aim of the survey is to periodically understand the situation of the population, with a focus on those that are in a state of poverty. It also looks at education, income, health, housing and jobs. In addition, the survey is a means by which the government can evaluate the impact of fiscal expenditure on the relevant areas the survey targets and social programs that are also targeting these areas [41].

6   The Data from CASEN 2015 – Indigenous People

On July 2017, the Chilean Ministry of Social Development published the CASEN 2015 results centred on the indigenous people in Chile [42]. The results were comprehensive and provided some very relevant data that contextualises with the theme of this thesis. Therefore, the following section provides some of the data provided by CASEN 2015.

From the total population in Chile who identify as indigenous over the time period from 2009 to 2015, the following percentage of population belonging to an Indigenous People were recorded:

Year/Percentage:

2006-6.6
2009-6.9
2011-8.1
2013-9.1
2015-9.0

Adapted from [42].

7 Language – Mapudungun

The language spoken by the Mapuche is the Mapudungun [43, 44]. The Mapuche in Chile have been facing a number of challenges in retaining their language. The number of younger Mapuche who speak the language has been decreasing and thus, only older generations are still retaining the language. Data from CASEN 2015 [42], provides details on the knowledge and use of the Indigenous languages in the country. Thus, data from 2009 to 2015 indicated that those who speak and understand their language fell from 12.0% to 10.7%. Those who only understand, remained somewhat steady from 10.6% to 10.7%. Those who neither speak or understand increased from 77.3% to 78.6% [42]. These figures demonstrate that there is a greater number of indigenous people who neither speak nor understand their language and appear to become more apparent in the younger generation as seen on Table 1 below where the younger generation is struggling to speak and understand:

Table 1. Percentage of indigenous people and language command by age group (Adapted from [42])

Age group (in years)	Speaks and understands	Only understands	Neither speaks or understands
0 to 14	5.0	6.4	88.6
15 to 29	7.1	10.3	82.6
30 to 44	12.4	13.6	74.1
45 to 59	14.2	13.9	71.9
60 or more	24.9	13.1	62.0

According Sotomayor and Allende et al. [45] the Ministry of Education claimed in 2013 that 472 schools had implemented an indigenous language subject. Sotomayor and Allende et al. [45] also indicate that the Araucania region is where the majority of schools have included Mapudungun as a subject, that is, 220 (54%) schools. Moreover, Sotomayor and Allende et al. [45] argue that students attending these school belong to a low socioeconomic level and that the average level of education attained by their parents is 9 years of schooling. Moreover and with reference to educating Mapuche children, Quintriqueo and Torres [46] indicate that historically this has been on a system, content and outcomes based on an Occidental model and so it fails to consider the traditional Mapuche concept of building knowledge through what they call "to learn by doing" which takes the form in labor, social, cultural and productive actions that Mapuche people developed, in which the teaching – learning process involves different family members, where the main methodological aspect is centered in communication and so, the various programs, by default, assume a neutral socio-political framework, that is representative of the general and homogenous education system that is inserted and directed by the state [47] and which also contains the rules, structure, values and measures imposed by the Chilean state [48]. Therefore, this centralised approach bypasses and denies visibility to the local social processes which are integral to the dynamic culture and organisation as it serves only those aspects of indigenous education and culture that are pertinent and functional to the centralised content and which has been historically based on an occidental perspective, leaving a gap between the western and Mapuche context [47, 49, 50].

8 Conclusion

The democratic governments followed after the dictatorship, became aware of the challenges being faced by the education system and envisaged an innovative and large plan to improve the education system, bring about some reform and make the education more equitable. This led to the the MECE program from which Enlaces was born. Enlaces has contributed in introducing ICTs into Chilean schools and has achieved practically universal coverage. Aside from the introduction of ICTs, since the return of democracy, governments have faced many challenges due the inherited education system. There have been many student and parents protests clamouring for free, equitable and quality education.

On the other hand, changes made to the education systems, such as Enlaces, have been homogenous and blanketed approaches which not be suitable for a group where the main approach is more collective and inclusive, as the Mapuche, who live in a region with a high poverty index and with its inherited issues related to the lack of inclusion and literacy rates, loss of culture and language. Therefore, education needs to be looked at a level that consults and includes the community. So, that it is the community that becomes empowered to recognise and confront their concerns within the contexts of their own culture. On the contrary, the Mapuche will continue experiencing a dilution of their culture either by adaption, tacit imposition or adoption of the values imparted by the state through the educational context of schools. This not only includes the curriculum content but also the physical structures, government policies, technology, social inclusion and social capital.

References

1. Borja, R.: The divide between the digital haves and have-nots is as wide as the region itself. Educ. Week **23**, 24 (2004)
2. Enlaces. TICs en Aula (2009). http://www.enlaces.cl/index.php?t=44&i=2&cc=170&tm=2. Accessed 20 Mar 2009
3. Enlaces. Nuestra Historia (2009). http://www.enlaces.cl/index.php?t=44&i=2&cc=170&tm=2. Accessed 20 Mar 2009
4. Enlaces. ¿Quiénes Somos? (2009). http://www.enlaces.cl/index.php?t=44&i=2&cc=170&tm=2. Accessed 20 Mar 2009
5. Fry, G.W.: The interface between experiential learning and the Internet - ways for improving learning productivity. On Horiz. **10**, 5–11 (2002)
6. Granger, A., et al.: Factors contributing to teachers' successful implementation of IT. J. Comput. Assist. Learn. **18**(4), 480–488 (2002)
7. Lan, J.: Web-based instruction for education faculty: a needs assessment. J. Res. Comput. Educ. **33**, 15 (2001)
8. Newton, L., Visscher, A.J.: Management systems in the classroom, management of education in the information age: the role of ICT. In: Fifth Working Conference on Information Technology in Educational Management (ITEM 2002), IFIP TC 3/WG 3.7. Kluwer Academic Publishers, Helsinki (2003)
9. Twining, P.: The computer practice framework: a tool to enhance curriculum development relating to ICT. In: Monteith, M. (ed.) ICT for Curriculum Enhancement. Intellect, Bristol (2004)
10. Schäfer, M.: The fourth industrial revolution: how the EU can lead it. Eur. View **17**(1), 5–12 (2018)
11. Schwab, K.: Fourth industrial revolution - will the fourth industrial revolution have a human heart? (2015). https://www.weforum.org/agenda/2015/10/will-the-fourth-industrial-revolution-have-a-human-heart-and-soul. Accessed 29 Aug 2018
12. Schwab, K.: Fourth industrial revolution - the fourth industrial revolution: what it means, how to respond (2016). https://www.weforum.org/agenda/2016/01/the-fourth-industrial-revolution-what-it-means-and-how-to-respond/. Accessed 29 Aug 2018
13. Bauer, P.: Patricio Aylwin (2017). https://www.britannica.com/biography/Patricio-Aylwin. Accessed 17 Mar 2017, 27 Nov 2017
14. Jara, I.: Las políticas TIC en los sistemas educativos de América Latina: CASO CHILE. In: Duro, E. (ed.) Programa TIC y Educación Básica, p. 61. UNICEF, Argentina (2013)
15. Jara, I.: Las políticas TIC en los sistemas educativos de América Latina: CASO CHILE, vol. 2, 1 edn, p. 60. UNICEF, Argentina (2013)
16. Toro, P.: Enlaces: Contexto, historia y memoria. In: Bilbao, A., Salinas, A. (eds.) El Libro Abierto de la Informática Educativa: Lecciones y Desafíos de la Red Enlaces, pp. 37–50. Enlaces, Centro de Educación y Tecnología del Ministerio de Educación, Chile (2010)
17. Bellei, C.: Evolución de las políticas educacionales en Chile (1980–2009). In: Bilbao, A., Salinas, A. (eds.) El Libro Abierto de la Informática Educativa: Lecciones y Desafíos de la Red Enlaces, pp. 14–36. Enlaces, Centro de Educación y Tecnología del Ministerio de Educación, Chile (2010)
18. Holm-Nielsen, L., Thorn, K., Prawda, J.: Chile - decades of educational reform deliver. En Breve **4**, 1–4 (2004)
19. Silva, L., Figueroa, E.: Institutional intervention and the expansion of ICTs in Latin America. Inf. Technol. People **15**(1), 8–25 (2002)

20. Sánchez, J., Salinas, A.: ICT & learning in Chilean schools: lessons learned. Comput. Educ. **51**(4), 1621–1633 (2008)
21. Bilbao, A., Salinas, A.: La informática educativa en Chile. In: Bilbao, A., Salinas, A. (eds.) 17 años después, El Libro Abierto de la Informática Educativa: Lecciones y Desafíos de la Red Enlaces, pp. 7–11. Enlaces, Centro de Educación y Tecnología del Ministerio de Educación, Chile (2010)
22. Claro, M., et al.: Assessment of 21st century ICT skills in Chile: test design and results from high school level students. Comput. Educ. **59**(3), 1042–1053 (2012)
23. Toro, F., Tatnall, A.: Developing a project to investigate the introduction of ICT to Mapuche students in Chile. Int. J. Actor-Netw. Theory Technol. Innov. (IJANTTI) **8**(1), 34–43 (2016)
24. Brunner, J.J.: Comparative research and public policy: from authoritarianism to democracy. Peabody J. Educ. **80**(1), 100–106 (2005)
25. Walsh, A.: The legacy of dictatorship and persistent socio-economic inequalities in Chile's educational policy. Aigne J. **4**(2), 25 (2018)
26. Planas, R.: Chile's Piñera Takes on Education Reform (2011)
27. Martínez, E.G., Farías, R.Z.: Formas de inclusión-exclusión en el sistema educativo chileno: el movimiento estudiantil secundario 2006-2011. Revista Brasileira de Educação **23**, 23 (2018)
28. Cabalin, C.: Neoliberal education and student movements in Chile: inequalities and malaise. Policy Futur. Educ. **10**(2), 219–228 (2012)
29. Toro, F.: Impacts of computer technology by Mapuche students in Chilean schools, p. 283. College of Business, Victoria University, Australia (2018)
30. Schwabe, N.: No somos hijos de la democracia, sino nietos de la dictadura: El movimiento estudiantil chileno en 2011 y después. Nueva Sociedad (273), 98–109 (2018). https://nuso.org/media/articles/downloads/6.TC_Schwabe_273.pdf
31. Sánchez, J., Salinas, Á., Harris, J.: Education with ICT in South Korea and Chile. Int. J. Educ. Dev. **31**(2), 126–148 (2011)
32. Toro, F.: Experiences as a student in Chile with only pre-computer technologies. In: Tatnall, A., Davey, B. (eds.) Reflections on the History of Computers in Education. IAICT, vol. 424, pp. 347–364. Springer, Heidelberg (2014). https://doi.org/10.1007/978-3-642-55119-2_24
33. Enlaces. Historia (2019). http://www.enlaces.cl/sobre-enlaces/historia/. Accessed 8 Feb 2019
34. Hinostroza, E., Hepp, P., Cox, C.: National policies and practices on ICT in education - Chile (Enlaces). In: Plomp, T.A., Anderson, R.E., Law, N., Quale, A. (eds.) Cross-National Information and Communication Technology: Policies and Practices in Education, pp. 157–170. IAP-Information Age Publishing (2009)
35. Junta Nacional de Auxilio Escolar y Becas. ¿Qué es Yo Elijo mi PC? (2017). http://www.yoelijomipc.cl/index.php/que-es-yo-elijo-mi-pc/. Accessed 24 Aug 2017
36. Ministerio de Educación. Me Conecto para Aprender (2017). http://meconecto.mineduc.cl. Accessed 24 Aug 2017
37. Ministerio de Educación. Junaeb extendió el plazo para que estudiantes que pasan a 7° básico elijan sus computadores (2019). http://meconecto.mineduc.cl/2019/01/02/junaeb-extendio-el-plazo-para-que-estudiantes-que-pasan-a-7o-basico-elijan-sus-computadores/. Accessed 8 Feb 2019
38. Aylwin, J.: Politica Publicas y Pueblos Indígenas: El Caso de la Politica de Tierras Del Estado Chileno y el Pueblo Mapuche, p. 42. Universidad de la Frontera, Chile (2002)
39. Valenzuela, M.S., Toro, S.Y., Rojo-Mendoza, F.: Equal in poverty, unequal in wealth: ethnic stratification in Chile, the Mapuche case. Bull. Lat. Am. Res. **36**(4), 526–541 (2017)
40. Cerda, R.: Situación socioeconómica reciente de los mapuches en la región de la Araucanía. Revista de Estudios Públicos **113**, 27–107 (2009)

41. Ministerio de Desarrollo Social Archivo histórico de Encuesta CASEN (2017). http://observatorio.ministeriodesarrollosocial.gob.cl/casen/casen_obj.php. Accessed 30 Nov 2017
42. Ministerio de Desarrollo Social - Subsecretaría de Evaluación Social, CASEN 2015 - Pueblos Indigenas - Síntesis de Resultados, in CASEN 2015, p. 129 (2017)
43. Garrido, R., Martinez, F., Solano, I.M.: Las TIC en las comunidades Mapuches: Un proyecto de integración de las TIC para el desarrollo social de pueblos originarios. In: PRENDES, M. P. Tecnologías, desarrollo universitario y pluralidad cultural, pp. 101–117. Marfil, Alcoy (2011)
44. Wikipedia contributors. Mapuche language (2017). https://en.wikipedia.org/w/index.php?title=Mapuche_language&oldid=811858504. Accessed 24 Nov 2017, 30 Nov 2017
45. Sotomayor, C., et al.: Competencias lingüísticas e interculturales de los educadores tradicionales mapuche para la implementación de la asignatura de Lengua Indígena en Chile, p. 34. Centro de Investigacion Avanzada en Educacion - Universidad de Chile, Chile (2015)
46. Quintriqueo, S., Torres, H.: Construcción de Conocimiento Mapuche y su relación con el Conocimiento Escolar. Estudios pedagógicos (Valdivia) 39(1), 199–216 (2013)
47. Forno, A.-S., Rivera, R.P.: Entre El Edificio y El Curriculum de la Interculturalidad - Una Mirada Antropologica a la Educacion Actual en Territorio Mapuche-Huilliche. Chungara. Revista de Antropologia Chilena 41(2), 287–298 (2009)
48. Miller, A.: La Falta de Desarrollo Debido a la Carencia de Igualdad: La Ineficacia del Programa de Educación Intercultural Bilingüe Como Factor de Continuación de la Dominación del Estado de Chile Contra el Pueblo Mapuche. Independent Study Project (ISP) Collection (2012)
49. Quintriqueo, S., Torres, H.: Distancia entre el conocimiento mapuche y el conocimiento escolar en contexto mapuche. Revista Electrónica de Investigación Educativa 14, 16–33 (2012)
50. Quilaqueo, D., et al.: Saberes Educativos Mapuches: Aportes Epistemicos Para Un Enfoque De Educacion Intercultural. Chungara. Revista de Antropologia Chilena 46(2), 271–283 (2014)

Digital Literacy Enhancement Status in Kenya's Competency-Based Curriculum

Gioko Maina[1](✉) and Waga Rosemary[2]

[1] Aga Khan Academy, Mombasa, Kenya
[2] Aga Khan Education Service, Nairobi, Kenya
rwaga@akesk.org

Abstract. Digital literacy (DL) is a one of the competency recommended for educators to be embedded in the Kenyan Competency Based Curriculum (CBC) in preparation for learners for the 21st century skills. The Ministry of Education deployed devices to lower primary at a ratio of 1 to 1. The aim of the research was to determine the level and frequency of embedding the digital literacy abilities after the teachers and school leaders in a 3-day preparation and 8 weeks of implementation with virtual support through Communities of learning.

The methodology was a self-administered survey which evaluated the seven abilities based on the level and frequency of implementation. The dot product of level and frequency were determined as a percentage. The analysis explored the average percentages and the relationship between level and frequency of implementation.

The findings revealed that there was a correlation between the level and the frequency of implementation. All abilities where at developing stage on average. The mode and mean on levels and frequency were on average similar apart from few cases where it was above. All the abilities had a bell curve on implementation with access, integrate and evaluate skewed to the right.

It can be concluded that despite the deployment of devices there is still very low implementation of DL and there is a significant relationship between the level and frequency of implementation. There is need to interrogate possible factors to low implementation beyond devices and educator preparation with virtual support.

Keywords: Digital literacy · Teacher preparation · Competencies

1 Introduction

1.1 Purpose

"Every child in grade 1 will have a computer the time they come into the school", a government pronouncement during the pre-election meeting in Kenya. This political statement was the beginning of a nationwide supply tablets in grade 1 for all the students. The focus then was technology integration in pedagogy. Overtime this has transited to digital literacy which is a core competency in ongoing curriculum reforms. The reforms saw the investment on structural resources and teacher preparation.

© IFIP International Federation for Information Processing 2019
Published by Springer Nature Switzerland AG 2019
A. Tatnall and N. Mavengere (Eds.): SUZA 2019, IFIP AICT 564, pp. 206–217, 2019.
https://doi.org/10.1007/978-3-030-28764-1_23

Schools were provided with tablets and pre-loaded routers and teacher were trained on competency-based curriculum which included digital literacy (DL) as one of the competencies.

The purpose of this study was to evaluate the level and frequency of implementation of the DL abilities to inform the next iteration of teacher preparation. The question to answer was to what extent is digital literacy enhanced in teaching and learning in schools.

1.2 Background Information

The preparation of Digital literacy is base the description of the element and abilities
Elements
digital competence: skills, concepts approaches, attitudes, etc.
digital usage: the application of digital competence within a specific context (such as a school).
digital transformation: creativity and innovation in the digital domain.
Abilities
define: to understand and articulate the scope of an information problem to facilitate the electronic search for information.
access: knowing about and knowing how to collect and retrieve information.
manage: applying an existing organizational or classification scheme.
integrate: interpreting and representingpresented a multi-case information, including summarizing, comparing.
evaluate: making judgments about the quality, relevance, usefulness, or efficiency of information.
create information: generating information by adapting, applying, designing, inventing, or authoring information.
communicate: disseminate information tailored to an audience in an effective digital format [1].

The teachers were prepared on the elements and the abilities in an embedded approach alongside three other competencies of critical thinking and problem solving, creativity and imagination and communication and collaboration. Teachers were prepared for 3 days covering aspect of lesson planning, delivery and extensions. The implementation took 13 weeks with virtual support through WhatsApp communities of learning. The training culminated to a closing one-day reflection workshop where the teachers showcased their learning journey. The teachers were expected to enhance the DL ability in their lesson delivery. The study explores the teacher reflection on their level and frequency of implementation of the DL abilities.

2 Literature Review

The underlying themes of most work around DL are the need for individuals and organizations to respond to the challenges and opportunities offered by emerging technologies and the increasingly digitized and networked nature of society [2].

The concept of digital native does not define the generation that is currently graduating to become teachers in primary education [3].

Technology integration requires a special skill in which teachers review and change their pedagogy technology integration to facilitate literacy. The teacher preparation process varies on time, approach, quality of information and the nature of support after the face to face sessions. There are several factors which influence practice for the teachers to integrate technology. The factors ranged from age, experience, exposure of the teacher, infrastructural support in the school the curriculum. The experience of the teacher is informed by the teacher and how open minded they are towards innovative pedagogy and of teaching. The exposure of the teacher is informed to how well the teacher is exposed to devices different approaches of classroom instruction. The infrastructural support the setup in the school of electricity, access to devices, a support officer, instructional material availability and collaborative planning time. The curriculum structure facilitates opportunities for technology integration. Deeper and regular implementation would facilitate immersion and institutionalization of embedding the DL. Gioko and Kadzo advocates for mainstreaming of the practices for sustainability [4].

The implementation of new approaches ranges at different levels and frequency, but the aspiration is reaching the exemplary and proficient levels. WaGioko has identified time, peer support and refresher session as factors that support aspirations [5]. DL is described as a development process from access and functional skills to higher level capabilities and identity [6]. However, this will change depending on the context, so it also reflects how individuals can be motivated to develop new skills and practices in different situations.

Media literacy is not only the development or interpretive skills but also "involves a series of digital production skills that include the ability to create, to be critical and to contribute well as to consume" the digital content [7]. Moreover, digital media literacy and cultural skills are developed in networking and established on traditional literacy (reading & writing), research, and critical-analysis skills of media [8]. The digital literacy involves knowledge creation as it is embed in pedagogy.

The emphasis of digital literacy can be built on the fact that society needs a configuration of well-developed communication and problem-solving skills that include these five digital media competencies (access, analyses and evaluate, create, reflect and act) [9]. These competencies are aligned with the focus used to prepare the teachers. The implementation is facilitated by the teachers one as a direct responsibility of their digital literacy, two as an instrument of their rights protection and finally as an essential aspect of their education [10].

3   Methodology

The data collection involved a self-administered peer validated survey which was exploring how the ability were enhance on delivery based on the level and frequency. The implementation meant the lesson delivery. The levels looked at the implementors and the frequency looked at the implementation across lesson, subject and timelines The responses of were analyzed to explore the level and frequency of implementation as well as their relationships. The responses were treated as a case and the group of responses presented a multi-case approach (Table 1).

Table 1. The descriptors for level and frequency of implementation

	Needs support (1)	Emerging (2)	Developing (3)	Proficient (4)	Exemplary (5)
Level	Only the trained teachers are demonstrating some of the abilities in some of the lessons	Only the trained teachers in the school are demonstrating the abilities across some lessons	All the teachers in the school are demonstrating the abilities across some lessons	All the teachers in the school are demonstrating the abilities across all the lessons	All the teachers in the school are demonstrating the abilities across all the lessons and the community engagement
Frequency	Very rarely	Rarely	Sometimes	Often	Very often

The variable was scored against a Likert scale and supported by evidence. The individual scores were validated against the evidence reviewed in a school group. The school's scorings were presented and reviewed across school's based on the evidence provided. There were peer validation and school's validation of the scores across schools.

The data was analyzed across abilities and within abilities. The levels distribution both for implementation and frequency were analyzed within the abilities. Mann-Whitney test was used to analyze five-point Likert items for two groups (Level and frequency) [11]. Likert scales can be included in a larger group of measures since they are based on the idea that some underlying phenomenon can be measured by aggregating an individual's rating of his/her feelings, attitudes, or perceptions related to a series of individual statements or items [12]. Likert-type items fall into the ordinal measurement scale. Descriptive statistics recommended for ordinal measurement scale items include a mode or median for central tendency and frequencies for variability.

The correlation between implementation and frequency, the mean and median were analyzed across abilities to determine the enhancement across abilities.

4   Findings and Discussions

The Digital Literacy abilities were implemented at different levels. The following is a description of the level of implementation and frequencies.

Define which is to understand and articulate the scope of an information problem to facilitate the electronic search for information had mode 3 and median 3 in implementation and mode 3 and median 3 in frequency with a correlation of 0.735 between implementation and frequency. There was both a max of exemplary and needs support in both implementation and frequency. The distribution of the Implementation and frequency was as shown in Fig. 1.

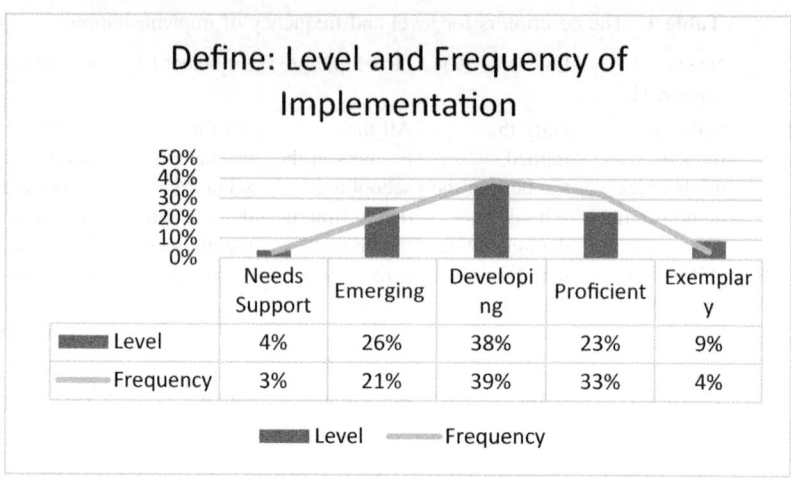

Fig. 1. Distribution of level and frequency - DEFINE

In define developing was with most teachers at 38%, with the lowest needs support at 4%. Less than 10% of the teachers were at exemplary level. Define is mainly theoretical and its clear 33% of the teacher had a good grasp (proficient and exemplary) of the information. 66% of the teachers are yet to reach the acceptable levels. Being a theoretical aspect, it can be inferred that the information was available and accessible. For emerging and below the frequency was lower tank the implementation levels, while for developing and above the frequency was well above the implementation level apart from exemplar. Those at an exemplary level were implementing well but the frequency was not matching the implementation level. This could be the risk element where wider level of implementation brought in a lower level of implementation due to the resources used as well as the number of people involved.

Access, which is about knowing, and knowing how to collect and retrieve information. The was mode 3 and median 3 in implementation and mode 3 and median 3 in frequency with a correlation of 0.817 between implementation and frequency. The distribution of the Implementation and frequency was as shown in Fig. 2.

Most teachers (68%) topped the charts at developing and proficient at the level of implementation with the frequency topping at 73% collectively. The lowest were close to each other's at between 6% and 7% for needs support and exemplary respectively in level of implementation and 4% and 3% on frequency respectively. 41% (level) and 39% (frequency) of the teachers where at the acceptable level (proficient and exemplary) leaving 59% (level) and 61% (frequency) at below expectation. The percentage of those in need of support was higher than define This could be attributed to the fact that access was not mainly theoretical, but it had and aspect of explaining how the access information. The functional parts required more than the information to be able to describes the function. The frequencies for emerging, developing and proficient where higher than the implementation levels. Needs support and exemplary had a lower frequency as compare to the implementation.

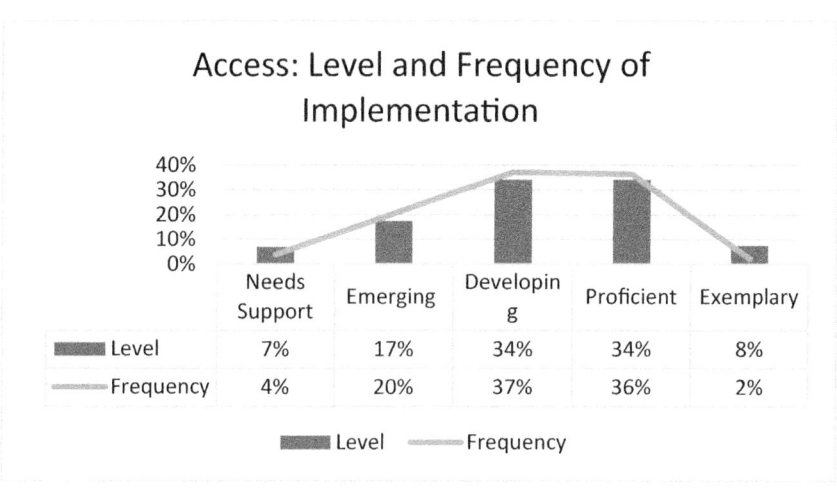

Fig. 2. Distribution of level and frequency - ACCESS

Manage which is about applying an existing organizational or classification scheme. The implementation had mode 3 and median 3 and frequency mode 3 and median 3 with a correlation of 0.810 between implementation and frequency (Fig. 3).

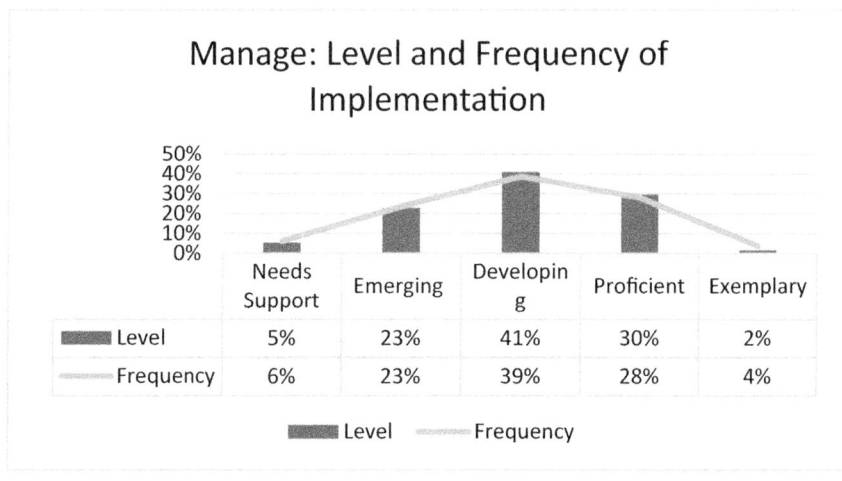

Fig. 3. Distribution of level and frequency - MANAGE

Manage which is a more practical ability had the highest percentage at both level and frequency at 41% and 39% respectively. The lowest was exemplary at 1% (level) and 4% (frequency). 40% (level) and 33% (frequency) where at acceptable level proficient and exemplary. 60% (level) and 66% (frequency) of implementation was below expectation (Developing, emerging and needs support). This means that for functional abilities the levels of implementation for emerging, developing and proficient where lower than those of needs support and exemplary. This means that those who were not getting it right and those who were doing very well we're doing it more frequently than their level of implementation. This could be attributed to the fact that when the levels were low it was only the trained teacher who was doing it and hence they could be doing it more frequently comparatively as they did not have peer to support or guide them. On the other hand, those who were developing to proficient had a high implementation level which could have led to them feel that many people are doing it and hence the low frequency compared to the levels.

Integrate which is about interpreting and representing information, including summarizing, comparing. The implementation had mode 3 and median 3 and frequency mode 3 and median 3 with a correlation of 0.779 between implementation and frequency. The distribution of the Implementation and frequency was as shown in Fig. 4.

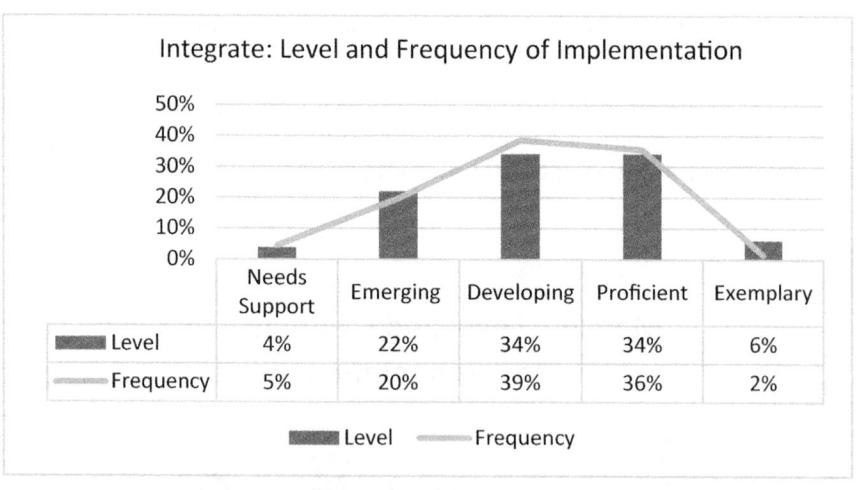

Fig. 4. Distribution of level and frequency - INTEGRATE

Developing and Proficient tied at 34% with exemplary at 6%. 40% where at proficient and developing. Emerging and needs support where at combined at 25%. The frequencies for exemplary and emerging where lower compared to the respective implementation levels. Needs support and developing and proficient had a higher frequency compare to their respective implementation levels Integration is functional and more demanding on handling information, organizing information and presenting information. At 40% the number that can do well is low.

Evaluate which is about making judgments about the quality, relevance, usefulness, or efficiency of information. The implementation had mode 3 and median 3 and frequency mode 3 and median 3 with a correlation of 0.805 between implementation and frequency. The distribution of the Implementation and frequency was as shown in Fig. 5.

For evaluation, proficient was at 39% with exemplary at 6% giving a total of acceptable abilities at 45%. Developing was at 29% with emerging and need support having a combine values of 20%. The frequency was higher than implementation level only on developing stage and needs support. The rest it was lower than the implementation levels. Evaluation was meaning making from information which is critical in decision making however only 45% where in the acceptable levels.

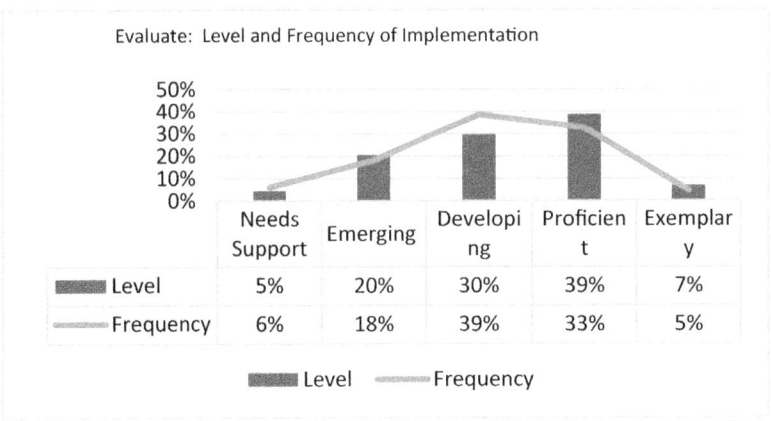

Fig. 5. Distribution of level and frequency - EVALUATE

Create information which is about generating information by adapting, applying, designing, inventing, or authoring information. There was both a max of exemplary and needs support in both implementation and frequency. The implementation had mode 3 and median 3 and frequency mode 3 and median 3 with a correlation of 0.829 between implementation and frequency. There was both a max of exemplary and needs support in both implementation and frequency. The distribution of the Implementation and frequency was as shown in Fig. 6.

Create had developing being the highest at 40%. Proficient and exemplary had a combined value of 30% with emerging and needing support at a combined value of 30%. The frequency was only higher than the implementation level at developing. Need support and exemplary has equal values for frequency and implementation levels. Emerging and proficient has low frequency compare with the implementation. There is a higher number of developing (10%) than those who can do as per the requirement. There is more teacher who 60% who are below the par. Creating requires resources and knowledge of how to. There is a tendency in school to download information based on

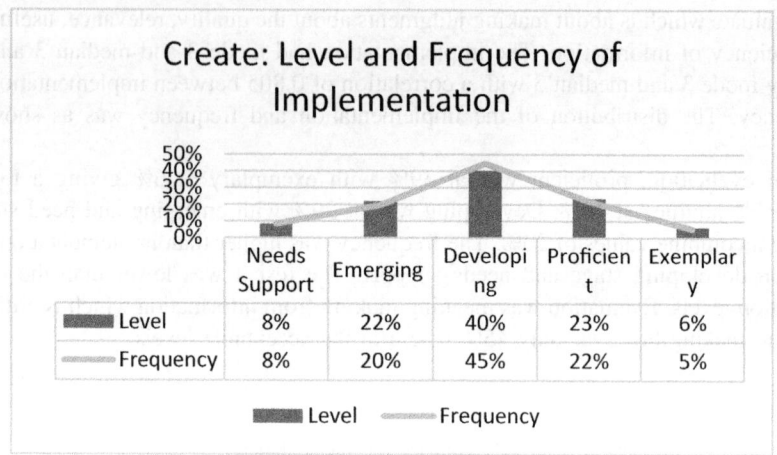

Fig. 6. Distribution of Level and Frequency -CREATE

the nature of the curriculum. Opportunities to create are very minimal and they could be attributed by the low level compounded with the skills.

Communicate which is about disseminate information tailored to an audience in an effective digital format. The implementation had mode 3 and median 3 and frequency mode 3 and median 3 with a correlation of 0.842 between implementation and frequency. The distribution of the Implementation and frequency was as shown in Fig. 7.

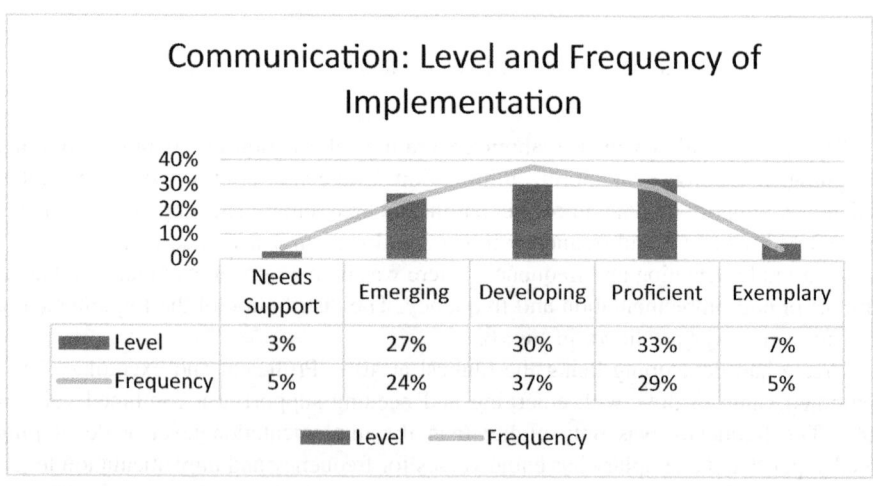

Fig. 7. Distribution of level and frequency - COMMUNICATION

Communication had emerging, developing and proficient all above 25%. Proficient and exemplary has a combine value of 39%. Developing was at 31% with emerging and needing support at a combine value of 29%. The frequency where high in developing as compare with implementation. All the other abilities had a lower frequency compared to implementation. At 39% communication was quite low. Communication beyond presentation requires connectivity. The connectivity in Kenya schools are either low or nonexistence in majority of the public schools.

Table 2. Correlation between level and frequency of implementation

Define	Access	Manage	Integrate	Evaluate	Create	Communicate
0.735881	0.817588	0.810722	0.779751718	0.805371	0.829218	0.842057203

Table 2 show a consistent correlation between implementation levels and frequency of implementation with a range of 0.104 is clear that one influence the other, the more the implementation the higher the frequency of implementation through it varied in some abilities at different levels of competencies (Fig. 8).

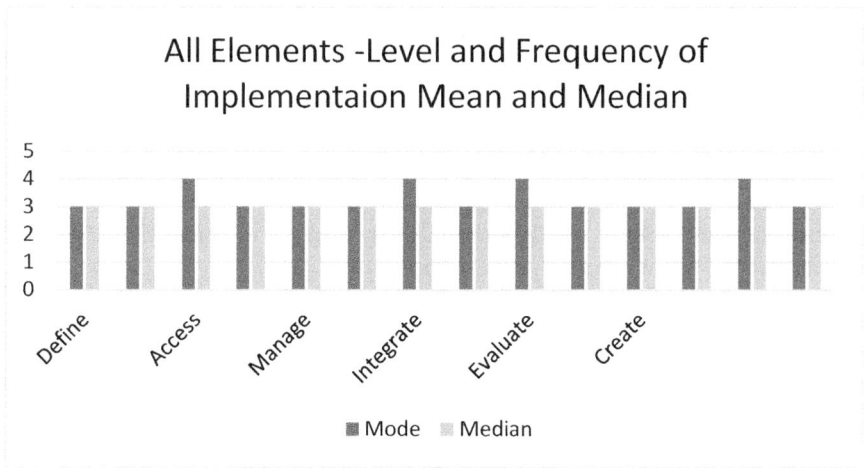

Fig. 8. All elements mean and median for levels and frequency

The relationship is further emphasized by the mode and the median most of them being at the same value for frequency and the levels of implementation.

In summary for abilities that have a symmetrical shape in the graph those who were at proficient and beyond anger on average of 33% with a range of 9. The abilities were skewed to the right and average of 42%. The implementation level and frequency are interdependent and in developing the frequency was always higher than the implementation. In other abilities the relationships depended on the type of abilities and the nature of the ability and the factors that influence its functionality. Abilities are influenced by resources, support and the nature whether knowledge based, skill based, or competency based.

5 Conclusion and Recommendation

5.1 Conclusion

Despite equipping schools with devices and having trained the percentage of teacher at proficient level and above is very low at 36% meaning out of 3 teachers only one is at par with the basic requirements. There are several abilities in digital literacy which are either knowledge, skill, or competency based. At knowledge base, define was at 33% with and equal number at developing. The skill-based which required resources such as manage, create where at the lowest at 30%. The competency based which demanded functionality and had impact on decision making such as access, integration and evaluation were at an average of 42%. Much of this result are based on several factors such as access and utility. Despite the devices being in the school it is through access and utility that would facilitate the homing in on these abilities. The curriculum especially the assessment drives pedagogy and hence its nature would influence the enhancement of the abilities.

5.2 Recommendation

The following are the suggesting for recommendation.

Schools should increase utility of the devices in them pedagogy.

The assessment method should be restructuring to demand the abilities hence their enhancement.

Resource based abilities needs to be facilitate, aspects of connectivity, projectors for presentations might enhance some of the abilities.

The level of implementation drives the frequency therefore more teacher in the school across the subjects and year levels should be encouraging to implement to facilitate the frequency.

There is need for a qualitative study to address the needs support teacher to establish aspects that are inhibiting their abilities enhancement.

References

1. DeLone, W.H., McLean, E.R.: The DeLone and McLean model of information systems success: a ten-year update. J. Manag. Inf. Syst. **19**(4), 9–30 (2003)
2. Davis, F.: Perceived usefulness, perceived ease of use, and acceptance of information technology. MIS Q. **13**, 319–340 (1989)
3. Venkatesh, V., Davis, M.M., Davis, F.D.: User acceptance of information technology: toward a unified view. MIS Q. **27**, 425–478 (2003)
4. Fishbein, M., Ajzen, I.: Belief, Attitude, Intention, and Behavior: An Introduction to Theory and Research. Addison-Wesley Publishing Co., Toronto (1975)

5. Alharbi, S., Drew, S.: Using the technology acceptance model in understanding academics' behavioral intention to use learning management systems. Int. J. Adv. Comput. Sci. Appl. **5** (1), 143–155 (2014)
6. Lee, Y.-H., Hsieh, Y.-C., Chen, Y.-H.: An investigation of employees' use of e-learning systems: applying the technology acceptance model. Behav. Inf. Technol. **32**, 173–189 (2013)
7. Adewole-Odeshi, E.: Attitude of students towards e-learning in south-west Nigerian universities: an application of technology acceptance model (2014)
8. Park, S.Y.: An analysis of the technology acceptance model in understanding university students' behavioral intention to use e-learning. J. Educ. Technol. Soc. **12**(3), 150 (2009)
9. Raman, A., Don, Y., Khalid, R., Rizuan, M.: Usage of learning management system (Moodle) among postgraduate students: UTAUT model. Asian Soc. Sci. (2014)
10. Ain, N., Kaur, K., Waheed, M.: The influence of learning value on learning management system use: an extension of UTAUT2. Inf. Dev. **32**(5), 1306–1321 (2016)
11. Lin, H.F.: Measuring online learning systems success: applying the updated DeLone and McLean model. Cyberpsychol. Behav. **10**(6), 817–820 (2007)
12. Lee, Y.C.: An empirical investigation into factors influencing the adoption of an e-learning system. Online Inf. Rev. **30**(5), 517–541 (2006)
13. Lee, B.C., Yoon, J.O., Lee, I.: Learners' acceptance of e-learning in South Korea: theories and results. Comput. Educ. **53**(4), 1320–1329 (2009)
14. Choi, D.H., Kim, J., Kim, S.H.: ERP training with a web-based electronic learning system: the flow theory perspective. Int. J. Hum Comput Stud. **65**(3), 223–243 (2007)
15. Anderson, J.C., Gerbing, D.W.: Structural equation modeling in practice: a review and recommended two-step approach. Psychol. Bull. **103**(3), 411 (1988)
16. Kline, R.B.: Principles and Practice of Structural Equation Modeling. Guilford Publications, New York (2015)
17. Hair, J.F., Black, W.C., Babin, B.J., Anderson, R.E., Tatham, R.L.: Multivariate Data Analysis, vol. 5. Prentice Hall, Upper Saddle River (2010)

The Innovation Cycle for Sustainable ICT Education

Daniel Burgos(⊠)

Research Institute for Innovation and Technology in Education (UNIR iTED),
Universidad Internacional de La Rioja (UNIR), 26006 La Rioja, Spain
daniel.burgos@unir.net

Abstract. Usually, the cycle of innovation is sold as a great progress in Education. However, in Education, the cycle of innovation does not exist as we might expect. Innovation is cyclical by itself. Each step of the structure can be modified, improved and complemented without waiting for a whole process that shows logic in other areas (engineering, logistics, and psychology, for instance) but that, in education, seems to be a luxury. This position paper shows why and how to perform a dynamic innovation cycle that enhances learning and teaching experiences, Worldwide, including North-North, North-South and South-South approaches, supported by initiatives by UNESCO, the International Council of Distance Education, Open Education Consortium, the European Commission and others.

1 Innovation Cycle and the Sustainable Development Goals

Our common ground is education. This is stated by the sustainable development goals of the United Nations (SDG). It is the objective 4: quality education.

But the objective 4 is closely linked to other objectives, as the number 2, on eradication of hunger, or number 3 on health, or 8 on decent work and the 16, about peace. Education lives across society as a whole. And education requires innovation. Normally, the innovation is structured as a cycle consisting of 3 pillars: evaluation, quality and training. Personally, I think that there may be more. Each pillar will affect teachers, students, and staff support and management. In addition, innovation itself focuses on the educational system and the educational methodology [1].

1.1 What Innovation Means

In short, what Innovation means? Why someone new at the leading post needs to re-modify everything from scratch? Why when a blue guy follows a red one, or the other way around, education is always losing something good? Is that difficult to understand that something can be saved from burning to the ground? [2, 3].

Selective innovation over specific steps of methodology, assessment, training, content authoring or any other links of the chain, is a breakthrough. Simple, effective, encouraging [4]. It means the missing link. We call it transgenic learning (#transgeniclearning) because it actually follows the same process, metaphorically speaking:

© IFIP International Federation for Information Processing 2019
Published by Springer Nature Switzerland AG 2019
A. Tatnall and N. Mavengere (Eds.): SUZA 2019, IFIP AICT 564, pp. 218–224, 2019.
https://doi.org/10.1007/978-3-030-28764-1_24

out of a chain of parts, one specific part is taken, modified, and put back on the chain. To make it better, or faster, or cheaper, or more personalised, or localized, etc.

What we stand for is that the timely application of selective changes might mean a World, and it takes just a moment in the design of a lesson plan. The school teacher of the university professor is entitled to do so, without waiting for an overall regulation.

And nowadays, the real key, the golden rice of Education, that effective move that any docent can make on their own, is to combine regular academic programmes with informal learning. To integrate Open Educational Resources, MOOCs, SPOCs, Learning Objects and so many pieces of knowledge uploaded out there (we call it Internet), into their classroom. The challenge is to select the quality content. But the integration part should be easy. Formal and informal integrated, not that difficult and a huge breakthrough in Education.

2   What Is Transgenic Learning?

Genetically Modified Organisms (GMO) is a controversial technique to produce new life or food based on the artificial modification of DNA [5, 6]. Induced by an external disruption, a significant change happens, as if it might be part of the natural evolution of a species. In doing so, adaptation is forced into the natural course, so that an additional feature is provided to that species: from a stronger plant against stormy weather or a plague, to a vitamin embedded into a cereal that does not contain it by default, through the modification of a human protein. This external intervention is conflictive from a number of approaches: ethical, scientific, Societal and economic, to name a few. However, the possibility exists; and if smartly applied, it provides the human being with a new resource for progress.

Indeed, genetically modified organisms (GMOs) are those organisms in which the genetic material has been modified through modern technology to produce a new organism or the same one with a modified set of properties [7]. For example, to remove something that does not work or may work better, it is later modified and it is finally reinserted. It is a simple process: choose something that you want to modify, because it does not work, or because we want it to adapt somehow, modified it and reinsert it.

You can choose one that does not work well, which is not well suited, which can be improved, which can be complemented. We can choose, modify it, and reinsert it in the cycle. And all this, without waiting for a semester or a whole year [7, 8]. Innovation can be done immediately. Although there is no support to a lack of planning or an improvisation, a teacher (at school or university, everywhere) should not stand by the imposition of a cycle that is not the reality of their educational context, in the classroom. Innovation should serve as a healthy and continuous process of regeneration and progress.

3   A Significant Breakthrough in Education

Education, as a whole, nowadays, requires a disruptive boost [9, 10]. If we teach and learn in the same way that we did for the last 20 centuries; if we use the very same academic structures that 10 centuries ago; if we stress some methodologies from the early XX century; and if we use resources from before the rise of Internet; if all this happens, we will miss every single possibility that the last 20 years bring to the table. We will miss new, adapted, personalized ways to learn and to teach; to be more efficient, to get a better performance; to enjoy more the experience as a user; and to improve the competence and skill acquisition. Furthermore, we need to break this slow evolution in Education. The youngsters, the technicians, the mass media, the entertainment industry, all of them are far advanced from any practical implementation in the classrooms, from kinder garden to the University.

Open Educational Resources, MOOCs, Virtual Reality, Augmented Reality, Emotional Intelligence, Personalized Learning, Analytics and so many resources, services and approaches to complement, enhanced and evolve Education, as it is now [11, 12]. We need a radical innovation, to design a new paradigm, to complement the existing ones, to evolve with the actual users of the system (students, teachers, professors, tutors, parents) and not always far behind from them. We need a GMO concept into Learning and teaching, a transgenic approach to Education. Something that makes things evolve quicker and more adapted into a very specific and practical objective. And this is a complex challenge. Compulsory. Needed. Urgent. But a challenge, yet.

And out of this challenge, the most difficult part is to find the right integration between informal ways of learning, teaching and using daily services, with formal courses and academic degrees; the smart combination of resources inside-outside the classroom; the update of accredited content with enriched, additional information outside the official syllabus that can fit into the same slot of educational competences [13, 14].

4   The Role of ICT in Educational Innovation

Teachers are in revolution. They claim an active role in new ways of learning and teaching. Usually, through the use of ICT in the classroom, wherever that classroom is, face-to-face or online. They claim, fight for and push for means, time and capacity decision in the innovation cycle in Education. They can be disruptive through the use of Open Educational Resources (OER), live analysis of learner data and, of course, ICT tools in the classroom and long list of activities and services [15].

Literally, this revolution is happening everywhere. We count parallel events in Sidney, Ljubljana, Buenos Aires, Beijing, London, Salamanca, Visakhapatnam, Paris, Toronto, Tallin, Bogotá, and a long list of places. Thousands of school and university teachers want to do better, perform better, support better. They are committed and determined. This is an overall force that requires global awareness and action, National policies, regional contributions, peer-to-peer interaction and a key role from every character in the setting: from learners to administrative staff, principals, tutors, parents and sympathizers. And, of course, from the teachers.

In this context, ICT can be the secret ingredient to facilitate that healthy revolution. From a basic use to an advanced tool creation, teachers can integrate communication, interaction, assessment, innovation, content and any other element of any educational cycle. This revolution is very much alive and kicking, and it will bring a real change in Education.

5   OER as a Means to Boost Education

Which seems clear is that we need an agreement. In OER many issues are at stake yet: accreditation, credit recognition, access, etc. All of them emerge from practice, from the community of practice, from the actual users (i.e. students, teachers, professors, management staff, etc.) We all are very committed to provide an open environment, with the various interpretations of what "open" means. We discuss, design activities, organize congresses, create content, give lectures, write documents about educational policy, review papers, work with Governments and regional departments, publish books and share out thoughts with blog-posts like this one, to name a few actions. Furthermore, we all look for a pro-active, fruitful, interesting and intellectually spicy environment that supports learning, competence building, and integration, along with personal and group development [10].

However, open means also controversy. Nobody argues against the good-willing approach to the various pillars of openness: access, content, data, research results, licensing, policy and technology. However, it seems that open quite often means unregulated. And unregulated might mean whatever. And this should not be the case when we deal with OER. We, the community, must be sure that content, access, technology and the other pillars provide the user with the best quality and, above all, with a minimum threshold for quality.

This approach would require a list of requirements and metrics to meet by every OER to ensure that threshold, based on an agreement amongst the various stakeholders. We need to normalize that approach, to make it sensible, reachable and useful.

Furthermore, we need to get an agreement to make the user feel safe and inside a quality framework, every time that this very user takes an OER. OER must be a seal for quality content and quality education and the OER community can reach a consensus about this basic right.

5.1   MOOCs, as an Example of Innovative OER, Applied

Informal learning and social interaction are receiving increasing attention in current eLearning campuses and platforms. Massive Open Online Courses (MOOCs) are no exception [16]. In plain online campuses, students now have a wide range of options for social actions and group collaborations at their disposal: post/answer questions in forums, start their own activities, create their own sites, wikis, invite colleagues, comment on someone else's job, score jobs made by others, incorporate external materials to their knowledge repository, fill in questionnaires, participate in WebRTC sessions with teachers, et cetera. Small Private Online Course (SPOCs) and locally deployed Learning Management Systems (LMS) already allow almost endless possibilities in humble environments. These can grow exponentially in an x/c MOOC setting which can potentially manage thousands of learner accounts around common learning material.

5.2 Open Licensing, Proprietary Content, as an Innovative Breakthrough

Nowadays, one key discussion point is about open licensing [12, 17]. The bottom line is that resources created out of public funding should be open and free. This funding comes from tax payers for the greater good and no one could make business or restrict access to these outcomes. This means, for instance, that professors of public universities, being civil servants, develop resources and provide them to the community openly. They keep the intellectual property, but not the exploitation rights or the ownership.

On the other side, when private funding is used to create resources, it depends on the author and-or owner the way to use them and to put them in the market. They can be open or free or universal or nothing at all or a combination of these. This owner has no obligation to make them available to the community as if they were supported by public funding. There is a claim from a section of the OER movement that everything should be open and free ever, no matter who is financially supporting the resource or the educational process. However, a balance should be reached to guarantee the exploitation rights and the sustainability of the creations, when they might come from various sources. Public funding means public resources; but private funding means the need to find an agreement about service and access with the owner.

6 Conclusions

There are more parts of this cycle of innovation, such as content, licenses or the exploitation, for example. In theory, the cycle of innovation runs like a clockwork: turns and turns inside out and outside in trying to understand and improve. Sometimes, to give more laps will not a real good and it does not make any progress. Other times, giving turns is like a clock based on a Nautilus shell, as a Fibonacci series, where you get more knowledge and better application after each iteration. However, this is not true.

They have sold us something that is not accurate. Engineers, entrepreneurs and bureaucrats wanted to parameterize a process useful for them. However, it does not provide an additional value to the educational community, if it is not properly contextualised. If we apply the spirit of the full cycle of evaluation we should be using semesters or full years to check whether the measures are useful or not. And so long seems eternal at ICT in Education, where everything changes from one month to the next one.

The reality is quite different: there is no cycle of innovation in education. We must break it and innovate now, without waiting, hungry for change and improvement. Innovation must be cyclic by itself. And a form of innovation is through "Transgenic learning". It is a metaphor, a simile, only a provocative title to explain an equal transformative reality but much less conflictive than the original term.

In education, the key innovation that will mark an era, the transgenic learning, the disruptive innovation, right now, is the combination of formal education with informal education: How to integrate educational resources outside the official programme with those very programmes. How to take advantage of a permanent connection of a student so that they can learn and practice anywhere at any time. How to use free educational resources as a significant part of the official curricula in primary education, secondary education, high school, University, vocational education, etc.

Albert Einstein said that "The definition of insanity is to do the same thing over and over again and to expect a different result". There is no need to use an industrial cycle of innovation in the educational innovation cycle, which has a very specific profile and needs. We must break the inertia, we must innovate in education, and we must do it now.

Acknowledgement. This work is supported by the Research Institute for Innovation & Technology in Education (UNIR iTED, http://ited.unir.net), the UNESCO Chair on eLearning and the ICDE Chair in Open Educational Resources (http://research.unir.net/unesco/), at Universidad Internacional de La Rioja (UNIR, http://www.unir.net).

References

1. Robert, K.W., Parris, T.M., Leiserowitz, A.A.: What is sustainable development? Goals, indicators, values, and practice. Environ. Sci. Policy Sustain. Dev. **47**(3), 8–21 (2005)
2. EC-European Commission. Opening up Education: Innovative teaching and learning for all through new Technologies and Open Educational Resources. Brussels, Belgium (2013)
3. Berg, B., Ostergren, B.: Innovations and Innovation Processes in Higher Education (1977)
4. Kleinknecht, A.: Innovation Patterns in Crisis and Prosperity: Schumpeter's Long Cycle Reconsidered. Springer, Heidelberg (2016). https://doi.org/10.1007/978-1-349-18559-7
5. Apolinario, R.M.: Genetically Modified Organisms (2015)
6. Burton, M., Rigby, D., Young, T., James, S.: Consumer attitudes to genetically modified organisms in food in the UK. Eur. Rev. Agric. Econ. **28**(4), 479–498 (2001)
7. Phillips, T.: Genetically modified organisms (GMOs): transgenic crops and recombinant DNA technology. Nature Educ. **1**(1), 213 (2008). https://www.nature.com/scitable/topicpage/genetically-modified-organisms-gmos-transgenic-crops-and-732. Accessed 2 June 2018
8. Fadeeva, Z., Mochizuki, Y.: Higher education for today and tomorrow: university appraisal for diversity, innovation and change towards sustainable development. Sustain. Sci. **5**(2), 249–256 (2010)
9. Collins, A., Halverson, R.: The second educational revolution: Rethinking education in the age of technology. J. Comput. Assist. Learn. **26**(1), 18–27 (2010)
10. Wrigley, T.: Rethinking education in the era of globalization. Contesting Neoliberal Education: Public Resistance and Collective Advance, pp. 61–82 (2009)
11. New Media Consortium, & EDUCAUSE Learning Initiative. The NMC Horizon Report: 2015 Higher Education Edition. Austin, TX: The New Media Consortium (2015)
12. McGreal, R., Kinuthia, W., Marshall, S., McNamara, T.: Open Educational Resources: Innovation, Research and Practice. Commonwealth of Learning, Vancouver (2013)

13. De-la-Fuente-Valentín, L., Carrasco, A., Konya, K., Burgos, D.: Emerging technologies landscape on education: a review. IJIMAI **2**(3), 55 (2013)
14. Dabbagh, N., Kitsantas, A.: Personal learning environments, social media, and self-regulated learning: a natural formula for connecting formal and informal learning. Internet High. Educ. **15**(1), 3–8 (2012)
15. Meek, V.L., Teichler, U., Kearney, M.L.: Higher education, research and innovation: Changing dynamics. International Centre for Higher Education Research, Kassel (2009)
16. Bry, F., Ebner, M., Pohl, A., Pardo, A., Taraghi, B.: Interaction in massive courses. J. Univers. Comput. Sci. **20**, 1–5 (2014)
17. Weller, M.: The battle for open. London: Ubiquity Press (2014). http://www.ubiquitypress.com/site/books/detail/11/battle-for-open/

Awareness of Open Education Resources (OER) in Higher Learning Institutions

Perspectives from Undergraduate Students from the State University of Zanzibar (SUZA)

Maryam Jaffar Ismail$^{(\boxtimes)}$ iD, Mwanajuma S. Mgeni iD,
Said Ali Said Yunus iD, Ali Abdulla Abdulla iD,
and Raya Idrissa Ahmada iD

The State University of Zanzibar, P.O. BOX 146, Zanzibar, Tanzania
{maryam.ismail,mgeni,said.yunus,ali.abdulla,
raya.ahmada}@suza.ac.tz
http://www.suza.ac.tz/

Abstract. Open Educational Resources (OERs) has entered the world of academia and has inspired innovation in education since 1990s, yet OERs awareness in higher education (HE) remains very low in Tanzania. Educators in Higher learning institutions (HLIs) in Sub-Saharan Africa are striving to provide effective learning experiences to address the needs of university students in crowded classes with limited printed resources. OERs currently hold great promise for instructing university students because unlike traditional curriculum materials, OERs content can be copied, used, adapted, adopted and re-shared for free. This paper presents findings obtained from the baseline study conducted at the State University of Zanzibar (SUZA) to explore the students' OERs awareness. In the academic year 2014/2015, 352 out of 713 first year undergraduate students (randomly sampled) from three campuses participated in the study. Online questionnaire survey was employed and the data were analyzed. We first show that there is a serious gap in OER knowledge followed by a number of structural and contextual barriers. We further revealed that more than 40% of students are not exposed to OERs offerings. Overall the data revealed that the use of OER at university is low, however, there is potential for growth of OERs as many students have mobile and are using ICT for education. Most participants cited limited access, limited connectivity, and affordability to be significant barriers to wider adoption of OERs. There were also concerns about the limited ICT infrastructure at SUZA and the need to build the capacity of academics on OER integration.

Keywords: OERs awareness · OERs benefits · Pedagogic changes ·
Higher learning institutions · Zanzibar

© IFIP International Federation for Information Processing 2019
Published by Springer Nature Switzerland AG 2019
A. Tatnall and N. Mavengere (Eds.): SUZA 2019, IFIP AICT 564, pp. 225–234, 2019.
https://doi.org/10.1007/978-3-030-28764-1_25

1 Introduction

This paper derives from the work of the Building Stronger University (BSU I & II) project 2011–2016, a collaborative project between the State University of Zanzibar (SUZA) and University of Copenhagen[1]. The purpose of this paper is to explore undergraduate perspectives from SUZA on Open Educational Resources (OERs) awareness in higher learning institutions. It summarizes the key findings from the project, together with its recommendations for policy, practice and further research.

2 Background

BSU project had several work packages, including the ICT in Education. The overall aim was to strengthen capacities among SUZA staff to develop, organize and manage online and blended research-based learning to support the development and delivery of high-quality education which will effectively improve student' learning outcomes at SUZA. Specifically, the package had three objectives. First, to enhance staff capacity to develop instructional design and organize course materials on the SUZA Moodle platform. Second, to enhance the utilization and integration of freely available externally produced OERs on existing accredited SUZA courses. Finally, to build staff capacity of the SUZA ICT department and School of Education to design evaluation studies on online/blended learning.

In this project, a core part of our professional role was to build capacity on the use of OERs in partnership with University of Copenhagen. Hence, 30 lecturers from different department got hands-on training on designing e-content, upload learning activities to the SUZA MOODLE platform and OERs integration into SUZA existing accredited courses. About eight (8) existing courses were piloted, designed for blended learning and then were uploaded to the SUZA MOODLE, namely Communication Skills, Educational psychology, Development studies, Sociology of Health and Illness, Educational Media and Technology, Waste Management, Interactive web design and Distributed System. Being part of e-learning and OERs team, we conducted an online survey with the support of colleagues from various SUZA departments to check students' OERs/MOOCs awareness. Collectively, we wanted to see the impact of lecturers training. focus on the awareness of OERs/MOOCs among students.

3 OERs and Higher Education

OERs are referred as freely and openly available digitized learning resources that can be adapted, modified, and re-used for teaching, learning, and research [1, 2]. Use of OERs, including open textbooks, represents a relatively new global opportunity to explore the creation of no-cost, adaptable teaching resources [3]. United Nations

---

[1] The authors acknowledge the support provided by a grant from DANIDA to Build Stronger University from NORAD. Moreover, the authors would like to thank students from different programs who willingly participated in the study.

Educational, Scientific and Cultural Organization (UNESCO) in a Forum on the Impact of Open Courseware first introduced the idea behind OER for Higher Education in Developing Countries 2002 hosted by UNESCO in Paris, France [2]. The forum emphasized the need to release these kinds of resources in order to increase access to education specifically in developing countries [4].

Research in this new field of practice provides an opportunity for SUZA to engage to its usage so as to facilitate the increasingly demand of professionals in different specialization in Zanzibar.

Prior to the use if OERs in higher education few alternatives for educational resources were available. With advent of OERs, free available resources with intellectual property license OERs provide opportunity for a learner to access the materials, reuse, rework, remix and redistribute as wishes [5]. Early literature on the use of OERs indicates that awareness and use lead to costs savings for learners the access and usage of OERs in content delivery in classrooms have the potential of reducing cost and improving quality education opportunities [6–9].

Evidence also shows that use of OERs in higher education may lead to more innovative teaching and learning methods and improve learner outcomes as discussed in Colvard, Watson, & Park [10]. A number of pedagogic possibilities emerge when using OERs compared to more traditional, proprietary publisher resources.

4   Global, National and Local Initiatives of OERs/MOOCs

Awareness of OERs/MOOCs is not a new concept but is increasing worldwide. The low awareness and use of OER were reflected in the research literature at local, national, and global level [11]. Wright and Sunday [7] reported that inclusion of OERs could enhance the quality of education and improve access to education in low-income contexts. OERs are the learning material free available to everyone from the cloud, they are externally developed by best universities around the world. OERs include YouTube videos, MOOCs like Coursera, Udacity, Wikipedia and others. The adoption of cloud computing to embrace education is growing very fast, more and more institutions are migrating their computing services in cloud [12–14]. For example, Google apps, Google drive and Google plus are nowadays used in most university in Tanzania as collaborating tools between students or between lecturer and his/her students.

Furthermore, using OERs institutions staff can develop skills and competences to improve quality course content [15]. The skills that can be obtained in OERs can include content/subject matter, instructional methods or techniques, and teaching online approaches. Also, it offers a number of possibilities such as easy adjusting and using materials that are already used in real life practices and are shared with open licenses that allow easy re-use and modification [16]. Like any field, OERs also face some challenges such as lack of trust and awareness towards the materials, and distribution of open materials and services within the web which makes it hard for individuals to understand where to find what [16].

5 Scope and Contribution

The purpose of the study was to collect baseline data to determine the awareness of integrating OERs/MOOCs in teaching and learning by the students and seek students' opinions on the OERs/MOOCs awareness. To achieve the purpose, we formed a small group of academics who worked together to collect data that constituted the intervention of the study. The team was formed by a group of academics who demonstrated leadership in OERs/MOOCs research at SUZA and those who have the same goals and aspiration.

Our contribution was multifold: the paper was guided by two research questions (i) What are the students' knowledge about the use of OER/MOOCs? (ii) What are the students' opinions in relation to the use of OER/MOOCs? Our aim was to identify opportunities, challenges and barriers in OERs/MOOCs awareness, and then highlight participants' perspectives on OERs.

6 Data Collection

6.1 Data Collection Instrument

The data were collected using online questionnaire developed from Google form which consisted of both closed and open-ended questions. The questionnaire was administered to collect both quantitative and qualitative data from students. Students from various programmes offered at the State University of Zanzibar (SUZA) were asked to participate in this survey.

6.2 Sampling

For the purpose of this study, the second-year students in their second semester were purposively selected. Participation was voluntary based. The total number of 352 students participated in which 158 were male, and 194 were female students. The undergraduate programs involved are shown in Table 1.

Table 1. Number of students participated with their programs

S/N	Program	Acronym	Male	Female	Number of respondents
1	Bachelor of Arts in Geography & Environmental Studies	BAGES	02	03	5
2	Bachelor of Arts in History	BAHI	03	02	5
3	Bachelor of Arts in Tourism Management and Marketing	BATMM	04	01	5
4	Bachelor of Arts with Education	BAE	68	92	160
5	Bachelor of Information Technology Application & Management	BITAM	20	12	32
6	Bachelor of Kiswahili with Education	BAKE	07	30	37

(continued)

Table 1. (*continued*)

S/N	Program	Acronym	Male	Female	Number of respondents
7	Bachelor of Science and IT with Education	BITED	06	07	13
8	Bachelor of Science in Computer Science	BScCS	11	09	20
9	Bachelor of Science in Environmental Health	BScEH	11	09	20
10	Bachelor of Science with Education	BScED	17	21	38
11	Doctor of Medicine	MD	09	8	17
Total			158	194	352

Data Analysis

The data were analysed both qualitatively and quantitatively using descriptive analysis Data were organized, tabulated, and analyzed through various steps in descriptive analysis.

Ethical Considerations

Participants were given verbal information about the purpose of the study. Those who willingly consented to participate were involved in the survey. The participants were guaranteed confidentiality of their individual responses and the data generated from the survey. Data was collected through Google Docs, and, thereafter, recorded directly into an Excel file. The data collection was undertaken in 2014/2015.

7   Results and Discussions

The analysis of the data generated two broad themes namely (i) students' awareness on OER and (ii) usage of OER and MOOCs. These two broad themes are further broken down into several sub-themes to present the findings.

7.1   Students' Awareness on Open Education Resources (OER)

Data on research question 1 have shown that there are a number of issues on OER/MOOCs at SUZA.

Low Awareness on OER/MOOCs

The participants were asked if they are aware on Open Educational Resources (OERs) platform. The results indicate 54.5% (192) of students were aware about various OERs platforms and 45.5% (160) of students never heard about this concept. This implies that the concept of OER is not well-known to almost half number of the respondents (Table 2).

Table 2. Number of student awareness on OER

	Frequency	Percent
Yes	192	54.5%
No	160	45.5%
Total	352	100

Kind of OERs

When respondents asked on what kind of OER platform they normal use for learning at SUZA, 63.7% (132) of respondents identified the Wikipedia as highly used platform., Moreover the respondents acknowledged using other forms of OERs platform and widely dispersed as follows; YouTube 39% (81) and online tutorials 32.9% (68), MOOCs 11.1% (23), MIT 1.4% (3) and Khan Academy 1% (2). MIT and Khan Academy were least identified platforms (Table 3).

Table 3. Kinds of OER used by students with their frequencies

	Frequency	Percent
MOOCs	23	11%
YouTube	81	39%
Wikipedia	132	63.7%
Khan Academy	2	1%
MIT	3	1.4%
Online tutorials	68	32.9%
Other	11	5.1%

MOOCs Provider

It is well understood that MOOCs is one of the mostly preferable platforms for learning among the Universities in the globe. There are various MOOCs providers that are freely teaching number of disciplines that are relevant to some of our local courses. Therefore, the base line study was interested to find out which MOOCs provider was mostly applied by the respondents.

The results revealed that 66.7% (68) indicated they knew nothing about MOOCs providers, 26.5% (27) of the respondents are using Cousera, 6.9% (7) were using Future Learn 6.9%(7), Edx 2.9% (3), 1%(1) and 0% Udacity. It was reported that, computer Programming, Mobile Applications for Androids Handheld System, Introduction to Data Bases, Database Management System, Academic English and introduction to teaching are most subscribed courses by students for learning from various MOOCs provider (Table 4).

Table 4. Number of subscriptions of students in different MOOCs providers

	Frequency	Percent
None	68	66.7%
Coursera	27	26.5%
Edx	3	2.9%
Canvas	1	1%
Udacity	0	0%
Future learn	7	6.9%
Other	3	2.9%

MOOCs Integration

To understand respondents' attitudes towards integration of MOOCs learning material in the existing curricula of the University program, they were asked to show their preference, whether they like MOOCs integration in their course or not. The results indicated that 60.2% (74) of respondents agreed and 39.8% (49) dislike on the statement (Table 5).

Table 5. Preference of MOOCs integration by students

	Frequency	Percent
Yes	74	54.5%
No	49	45.5%
Total	123	100

On the other hand, the common reasons are illustrated in Fig. 1. The highest reason was to get learning material, and the lowest ranked reason was 'interest'.

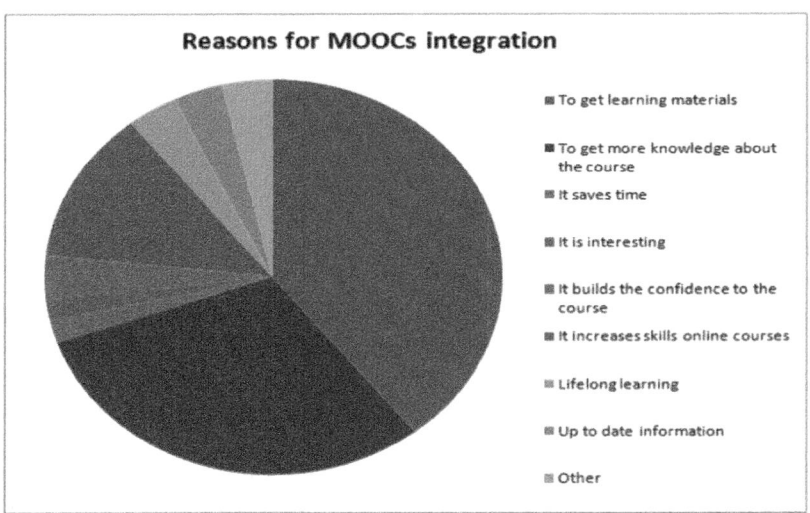

Fig. 1. Reasons for MOOCs integration

7.2 Usage of OER and MOOCs

Opinions on the usage of OER/MOOCs were identified by study participants from open-ended questions. The prominent ones were:

Contextual and Structural Challenges
The data from participants mentioned contextual challenges as limited understanding of OER, Relevance of ready- made OERs that do not fit the local context, limited knowledge and skills to use OER, technophobia and low motivation to use OERs. Some participant commented that:

> "I haven't enough skills and knowledge on how to access OERs and I do not know how to locate materials on the LMS portal. It takes long time for me to figure out how to use internet which is important aspect in the use of OERs."

Some participants were aware of OERs existence, however they pointed out that they do not have the skills and knowledge to access and use them.

Also, the data from participants also indicated that there is insufficient resources and infrastructure, unreliable internet at campus premises, technology affordability among students, few computer labs, limited computers, stable power supplies and ICT server. Another participant stated that:

> "First network problem such as wi-fi, inefficiency of computers because they lack a lot programs Microsoft word especially those which are library, computers are very few compare to number of students so when you such materials there are more than seven students waiting for you so these are big hindrance to me."

Proposed Solutions from Participants Perspectives
Data from participants acknowledged that "the uses of OERs has many advantages", therefore SUZA should take more efforts and strategies to ensure students can access online services anywhere. Additionally, the data cited from participants claimed directives, guidelines and policy would enable every student and lecturer to use OERs and register to MOOCs which are relevant to their courses. The data from participants also suggested that devices such as computers, tablets should be increased so as to give a great chance for students to use OERs and MOOCs. Failure to do that students might not benefit of this technology.

8 Lessons Learnt

Although there are a growing number of OER initiatives at the moment, low awareness on OERs/MOOCs hinder the development of e-learning and blended learning at SUZA. The general opinions of the respondents indicate there were diversity in their concerns and more emphasis were placed on issues like infrastructures, low of awareness on OERs, and accessibility [17] Based on this study, we learnt that there are many opportunities for further research into open educational resources [17]. There is also a positive outlook on the OERs/MOOCs and its pedagogical importance cannot be underestimated. In fact, some of the respondents' perspective on OER were seen to be very useful tool for making learners successful to the world. General speaking SUZA

Management should be emphasizing uses of ICT and lecturers should integrate OER in their courses and teach the students good ways to find and usage of OERs. Many articles reviewed for this study concluded that OER awareness in higher education requires a deeper understanding of the changes to teaching and learning that emerge from open practices [18–22]. More research on the use of OERs was needed to provide evidence of their effectiveness for both students and educators. Well-structured and ethically designed research is needed at institutional levels to determine whether intended goals for use of OERs/MOOCs are being met.

9 Conclusion

The advantages of OER to enhance education in Sub-Saharan countries are well documented. However, the perceived benefits cannot be realized if students are not aware of OERs and have limited access to use them. There is a need to invest in OERs to boost the usage of these resources in higher education.

References

1. OECD. Giving knowledge for free: the emergence of open educational resources (2007). http://www.oecd.org/dataoecd/35/7/38654317.pdf
2. UNESCO. UNESCO promotes new initiative for free educational resources on the Internet (2002)
3. Hilton, J., Wiley, D., Stein, J., Johnson, A.: The four R's of openness and ALMS analysis: frameworks for open educational resources. Open Learn.: J. Open Distance Learn. **25**(1), 37–44 (2010)
4. Plotkin, H.: Free to learn: an open educational resources policy development guidebook for community college governance officials. Creative Commons, San Francisco (2010). http://wiki.creativecommons.org/images/6/67/FreetoLearnGuide.pdf
5. D'Antoni, S.: Open educational resources: reviewing initiatives and issues. Open Learn. J. Open Distance Learn. **24**(1), 3–10 (2009)
6. Wright, Clayton R., Sunday, R.: Developing and deploying OERs in sub-Saharan Africa: building on the present. Int. Rev. Res. Open Distance Learn. **13**(2), 181–220 (2012)
7. Fischer, L., Hilton III, J., Robinson, T.J., Wiley, D.: A multi-institutional study of the impact of open textbook adoption on the learning outcomes of post-secondary students. J. Comput. High. Educ. **27**(3), 159–172 (2015)
8. Juhary, J.: Perceived usefulness and ease of use of the learning management system as a learning tool. Int. Educ. Stud. **7**(8), 23–34 (2014)
9. Kaufman, R., Campana, A.: OER lesson from the field. Insights **32**(15), 1–14 (2019). https://doi.org/10.1629/uksg.464
10. Colvard, N.B., Watson, C.E., Park, H.: The impact of open educational resources on various student success metrics. Int. J. Teach. Learn. High. Educ. **30**(2), 262–276 (2018). http://www.isetl.org/ijtlhe/pdf/IJTLHE3386.pdf
11. Pounds, A., Bostock, J.: Open educational resources (OER) in higher education courses in aquaculture and fisheries: opportunities, barriers, and future perspectives. Aquac. Int. **27**, 695–710 (2019). https://doi.org/10.1007/s10499-019-00355-9

12. Mtebe, J.S.: Exploring the potential of clouds to facilitate the adoption of blended learning in Tanzania. Int. J. Educ. Res. **1**(8), 1–16 (2013)
13. Mtebe, J.S., Raisamo, R.: Challenges and instructors' intention to adopt and use open educational resources in higher education in Tanzania. Int. Rev. Res. Open Distrib. Learn. **15**(1), 249–271 (2014). https://doi.org/10.19173/irrodl.v15i1.1687
14. Mtebe, J.S., Raisamo, R.: Investigating perceived barriers to the use of open educational resources in higher education in Tanzania. Int. Rev. Res. Open Distrib. Learn. **15**(2), 43–66 (2014). https://doi.org/10.19173/irrodl.v15i2.1803
15. Wilson-Strydom, M.: The potential of open educational resources OER Africa (2009). http://www.oerafrica.org/understandingoer/UnderstandingOER/ResourceDetails/tabid/1424/mctl/Details/id/36389/Default.aspx
16. Pirkkalainen, H., Pawlowski, J.M.: Open educational resources and social software in global e-learning settings. In: SosiaalinenVerkko-oppiminen. Naantali: IMDL, pp. 23–40 (2010)
17. Yuan, L., Mac, S., Kraan, W.: Open educational resources – opportunities and challenges for higher education, pp. 1–34 (2008). http://wiki.cetis.ac.uk/images/0/0b/OER_Briefing_Paper.pdf
18. Trotter, H.: Opportunities and Obstacles for Open Education, University World News, 23 February 2018
19. Blomgren, C.: OER awareness and use: the affinity between higher education and K-12. Int. Rev. Res. Open Distrib. Learn. **19**(2), 55–70 (2018)
20. Mushi, M., Ruhwanya, Z.: The Potential of Open Educational Resources (OERS) in Higher Education Curriculum and Course Materials Development. The Open University of Tanzania (2018)
21. Jan, H.: Open Educational Resources: Opportunities and Challenges (2006). www.oecd.org/edu/ceri
22. Hoosen, S., Butcher, N.: Understanding the Impact of OER: Achievements and Challenges, OER Africa and UNESCO Institute for Information Technologies in Education (2019). https://www.oerafrica.org/resource/understanding-impact-oer-achievements-and-challenges

Toward Pedagogy Driven Virtual Reality Learning Space Design

Erkki Rötkönen, A. K. M. Najmul Islam(⊠), and Erkki Sutinen

University of Turku, Turku, Finland
najmul.islam@utu.fi

Abstract. This paper argues for a need to develop Virtual Reality (VR) learning spaces based on pedagogy rather than implementing pedagogy in a general purpose VR application. In doing so, the paper summarizes the challenges in using an immersive virtual reality application to unite together primary school children across national, regional, and political boundaries in the same learning space in order to promote natural learning. Data was collected through observations during the activity sessions among children from a Finnish and a Bangladeshi primary school. Furthermore, we collected data using semi-structured interviews and focus groups with teachers, heads of schools, and children from these two schools. The data analysis revealed three types of challenges: design, technological, and pedagogical. These findings guide us in designing and developing pedagogy centered learning spaces using virtual reality.

Keywords: Virtual reality · Learning environment · Pedagogy

1 Introduction

A new curriculum for compulsory basic education in Finland was implemented in 2016 in all schools. The goals for this development of skills are (1) to secure the necessary knowledge and skills as well as to encourage learning, (2) learning outside the classroom and by using technology, (3) transversal competences developed in all subjects, (4) familiarization with the fundamentals of programming, and (5) to have at least one interdisciplinary learning module a year. The curriculum also aims to promote 21st Century skills. For instance, skills for collaborative problem-solving and the use of information and communication technology (ICT) are also included in the new National Core Curriculum for primary and secondary education from 2016 onwards. In order to promote 21st Century skills in schools, new learning approaches are needed[1]. Even if there are technical or other challenges to the adoption of virtual reality (VR) within educational settings, VR applications can enhance learning and advance social and creative skills. The use of VR in learning situations seems to improve digital-age literacy, creative thinking, communication, collaboration and problem solving ability, which constitute the twenty-first century skills [10]. Instead of the

---

[1] https://www.oph.fi/english/curricula_and_qualifications.

© IFIP International Federation for Information Processing 2019
Published by Springer Nature Switzerland AG 2019
A. Tatnall and N. Mavengere (Eds.): SUZA 2019, IFIP AICT 564, pp. 235–244, 2019.
https://doi.org/10.1007/978-3-030-28764-1_26

traditional way of learning where the teacher has the knowledge which is then distributed to the learner, a complementary approach to learning is the natural learning process where the learners can be actively engaged in the process and knowledge is constructed and distributed in a collaborative way [11].

The children from different countries are inspired to engage in activities within the shared space to experience the close-to-real-life perspectives that foster natural learning. By the term natural learning, we emphasize the learning opportunities through everyday real-life community activities [1]. However, currently available educational technologies, such as e-learning [12, 13] tools, or even traditional virtual reality platforms such as Second Life and Active Worlds, do not offer this kind of natural learning environment as these technologies lack immersion, the feeling of being there with another person, which is vital for providing close-to-real-life experience. In contrast, a natural learning space allows children to experience a fully immersive, multi-user 3D environment anywhere in the world using newly developed immersive technologies. The authentic feeling of being there together and the close-to-real-life interactions enabled by this technology could potentially revolutionize education and training.

From the research perspective, prior studies on the use of immersive learning spaces in primary education have been rare. Only a few studies used immersive virtual reality applications with children [5]. And to the best of our knowledge, no prior study united together children in an inclusive way across national, regional, and political boundaries in an immersive learning space. Most prior research focused on the use of immersive technologies in medical and surgical training [3] and professional training [2] among adults. The findings from these studies cannot be generalized to primary school children who are united together across national, regional, and political boundaries in the same learning space.

In order to fill the above practical, methodological, and research void, the aim of this paper is to find out the challenges of uniting together, in a common immersive virtual space, children from Finland and Bangladesh to promote natural learning in children through collaboration. We designed the learning environment using a general purpose (although immersive) VR application (e.g., Second Life) and Skype and applied pedagogy as most research tried to achieve in the past [4]. The observed challenges point to the need to develop learning spaces based on pedagogy rather than implementing pedagogy in a general purpose virtual reality platform.

2 Description of the Learning Environment

In this paper, we target to develop a shared learning environment by connecting diverse physical locations, contexts, and cultures. The learning environment should encompass but maybe also reshape the culture of the participating schools—their presiding ethos and characteristics, including how individuals interact with and treat one another—as well as the ways in which teachers may organize the educational setting to facilitate learning.

The two schools participating in the virtual learning environment were both elementary schools (one from Finland and one from Bangladesh). Pupils from a 4th grade class (aged between 9 and 11 years) and their classroom teachers from each school participated in this initiative. The two schools were about the same size. The Finnish school has 380 pupils on grades one to six, whereas, the Bangladeshi school had 420 pupils from grades one to eight. The Finnish school is governed by the municipality and the governance is based on the principle of decentralization, thus making the school responsible for practical teaching arrangements as well as the effectiveness and quality of the education provided. The Bangladeshi school is private and governed and funded by a Finnish NGO. Children from slums study in this school with free of cost.

The physical learning space in both schools consists of an ordinary classroom. The two classrooms are then connected through both a VR platform and Skype. The activities took place once a week and lasted 45 min at a time. The Skype connection was used to view live videos of the entire classrooms. Through VR, the children mainly tried two activities: (1) throwing a ball, (2) hide and seek. At a time, one child from each school could join the virtual space using the VR headset to perform the activities. The headset has a built-in headphone through which the pair can communicate with each other. In the "throwing a ball" activity, one child throws a ball and the other has to catch it. In the "hide and seek" activity, one child hides and the other child has to find him or her. The Skype connection was used for common classroom activities between the two participating classes. During the observed time period, those activities consisted mainly of learning simple words and phrases in both languages (Finnish and Bengali), e.g. greetings, introducing oneself, numbers and colors. Still when there was a technical problem that required the teachers' full attention and the pupils were without the teachers' active guidance, they sometimes started spontaneously interacting with each other by Skype, e.g. by dancing or playing some games with movements. Skype was also used by teachers to communicate before and after the classes as well as during the lessons whenever there was a problem with the VR or video/audio connection.

A snapshot of the learning situation is presented in Fig. 1 whereas, in Fig. 2 we present a snapshot of the VR application.

Fig. 1. A snapshot of Finnish classroom (the big screen runs Skype, the computer and screen on the left run the VR application)

Fig. 2. A snapshot of the VR application (the pair of children is shaking hand)

3 Methodology

3.1 Data Collection

In this study, we utilized a qualitative approach to examine the use of VR and Skype during the lessons. Before data collection, we obtained ethical approval from the city of Turku as well as in Bangladeshi school. Furthermore, we collected consent from the parents. We collected data using three approaches. First, one researcher was physically present at the Finnish school for doing observations during eight sessions from September 2018 to February 2018. The same researcher observed two sessions being physically present in the Bangladeshi school in February 2018. During the observations, the researcher took field notes as well as photos and videos of different activities. The observations helped the researchers observe, identify and understand different types of practical challenges that are faced during the sessions. Secondly, we collected data by interviewing two teachers from both schools as well as the IT-person in the Bangladeshi school using in-depth semi-structured interviews. The interviews lasted from 30 min to 60 min. Finally, two focus groups were arranged with the pupils. One focus group consisted of six Finnish children and the other focus group consisted of five Bangladeshi children. The purpose of the interviews and focus groups was to deepen our understanding on the issues that were found from the observations. The participants were interviewed in their own mother tongues. The interview protocol consisted of inquiring the following: participants' feelings and experiences, feedback and evaluation as well as suggested improvements. The teachers were also asked about their educational and professional background and their IT-skills. All the interviews

Table 1. Collected data

Method	Amount of data	Type of data
Observations	Observations in 10 sessions. 8 sessions were observed being physically present in the Finnish school and 2 sessions were observed being in the Bangladeshi school. Each session ran for 45 min	Observation notes
Interviews	4 interviews among four teachers (two in both countries) and one with the IT-person in Bangladesh	Audiotaped (later transcribed), and interview notes
Focus groups	2 focus groups among pupils, one in Finland and the other in Bangladesh	Audiotaped (later transcribed and notes

were also recorded in the form of an audiotape and later transcribed. All the collected data has been summarized in Table 1.

3.2 Data Analysis

The data was content analyzed, which refers to a research technique for making replicable and valid inferences from texts (or other meaningful matter) to the contexts of their use [9]. First, the data was read several times to make sense of it as a whole and then broken into smaller units in order to assign codes. The codes were inductively developed. After that the codes are condensed to create categories.

4 Results and Discussions

The children had in general very positive attitudes toward the learning environment. Playing games, getting to know each other, communicating and creating together are exciting to them. Although some pupils were a bit shy when using English in Skype, it was easy to act in VR. The children found it fun that they do not only have to sit but they can do something active in VR. The pupils were excited about the feeling of being together in the same place even though they were on the different side of the world. Despite the positive attitudes, we observed several challenges from our data analysis. The challenges can be broadly classified into three categories: design challenges, technological challenges, and pedagogical challenges. These three types of challenges are very much interrelated with each other. In the following, we describe these challenges in detail and present evidence from the collected data.

4.1 Design Challenges

It is interesting to observe that the children felt that the design of the VR hardware and applications had been hindering their use. For example, when using VR, some of the children felt dizziness. They also found the cord in VR goggles was limiting their movements. The children came up with suggestions to have cordless goggles and smaller handles for children to make it easier to move and do different activities. A sample quote in the following highlights the issue:

"In my opinion some kind of children's controllers are needed so that it's easier for children to play in VR, so that those batons were smaller and that cord would be away so it would be some kind of Bluetooth"

The children also emphasized creativity, especially when building new environments and creating things together. However, at the same time the children wanted to have richer content with more real-life experiences. They wanted to see the other as she or he is, not just as an avatar, or at least have a profile picture of the other or a kind of a detector that could recognize the other. This finding is particularly interesting because most available virtual environments rely on avatars rather than real faces. Prior research suggested that avatars allow efficient interaction among learners in a common 3D virtual space [7]. At the same time, they can also use representational functions or artifacts with high fidelity [8]. In contrast, our findings clearly suggest that the children preferred real faces rather than avatars in the learning environment. Furthermore, they wish to meet, get to know each other, talk, shake hands, play and be together normally as in real life. In summary, they want to have more realistic interaction and activities. The following quotes indicate their expectations:

"So that one could see in that VR, when you put the goggles on, you could see that guy too not seeing him or her like avatar but a little like in that Skype thing so that there's we and them."

"There could be more people and so that it would feel like more real and as it is when you play in real life here. There could be like real house and day and night and it would feel more like real to do together."

4.2   Technological Challenges

Virtual reality technologies are new to the teachers involved in both schools. The Finnish teacher was more experienced in IT and could take part in building up and planning the used technology with the support of the VR solution provider but even to him the VR itself was new. Based on his IT skills, the Finnish teacher was in practice forced to take control of the technical aspects during the sessions and thus worked more with the IT person in Bangladesh than the classroom teacher. These technical issues also took the teacher's time from conducting the actual lesson. As the Bangladeshi teacher was afraid of the latest technologies like VR, the school decided to recruit an IT person to help with the technologies. However, it was interesting to observe that the IT person replaced the activities of teacher (e.g., communicating with the Finnish teacher, organizing sessions) and the original teacher became just an observer despite having basic computer skills. This issue was identified in the interview. A sample quote related to this is given below:

"I usually do lot of activities with computer such as word, excel, Internet searching. I also have computer at home. But VR is so unfamiliar to me that I did not feel very confident with it."

The VR solution provider organized short training for teachers and provided user guide. However, the training deemed insufficient. Thus, there have been several technological challenges in the project. Due to the technical challenges, many sessions were completely canceled. Among the technological problems, the sound issue of the VR headset was the most frequent one. In most sessions, the teachers failed to hear each other through the VR headsets. The VR solution provider changed the computer as well as the VR headset at the Finnish school. But still the situation did not improve. The next speculation was that the sound problem is because the Bangladeshi school has been using Skype and VR software in the same computer. Thus, there might have been issues in Windows sound settings. Taking this into account, the school decided to use separate computers for Skype and VR. However, the problem still continued. The teachers felt that sometimes resetting the VR software as well as VR headset solved the problem. But it was completely random. Taken together, the technology is just too complex at this moment. The IT person from Bangladesh explained the situation as follows:

> *"Resetting helps sometimes. But it's completely random if the system works or not. If you are lucky it works. Today just before the session, I tested and everything worked properly. But during the session, you saw headset microphone was not working"*

4.3 Pedagogical Challenges

We observed several pedagogical challenges. First, the teachers felt that the VR technology is at a very primary stage and thus, it didn't bring much benefit for the learning of children at this stage. Only one child could try the VR headset at a time and others needed to observe what was happening on the screen, particularly because the teacher was involved in solving the technical problems and could not concentrate on the pupils, who were not involved in the VR. Thus, all other children remain mostly too passive during the sessions. A comment from a teacher reflects this:

> *"The pupils get bored if they only can watch the VR..."*

> *"Technical problems need to be solved so that you don't have to fight with them most of the lesson."*

However, the children did come up spontaneously with own ideas for activities like dancing together and doing some games with hands. The teacher still felt a significant school hour is lost for the children. Due to this reason, the teachers felt less excitement about the use of these technologies in the classroom at this moment. However, they thought that the current technologies might be still useful if the group is small or if it would enable more participants at a time to join the VR. The following sample quote illustrates this:

> *"I think half of the children are really bored as they don't have any other activity. These children are not very excited. To me these technologies should be tried at the school but they are at the very early stage of development and I somehow feel that these pupils are the guinea pigs and I feel bad for them, maybe a smaller number of students can participate"*

In fact, the children suggested to have more activities where one can cooperate, e.g. role playing games, survival games, more realistic activities and games where all could participate at the same time. In summary, they pointed out the importance of having diverse and creative activities. The finding reflects the need for engaged realistic and situated instructional design methods [6].

Secondly, cooperation between the teachers is critical for successful pedagogical interventions during the sessions. However, the lack of collaboration between teachers from Bangladesh and Finland was observed. As mentioned earlier, the original grade-4 teacher from the Bangladeshi school did not have an active role and there were practical difficulties in getting contact between her and the Finnish teacher. The Bangladeshi school designated the IT person for collaborating with the Finnish teacher. However, still there was hardly any collaboration between the IT person and the Finnish teacher for planning the sessions. Thus, the most sessions usually ran in quite an unplanned way. A proper planning of and defining the activities during a session are critical to gain maximum benefits from the sessions, which was largely missing. The Bangladeshi teacher commented the following regarding the lack of cooperation:

"We were told the our children would learn Finnish language from them. They know better how to teach their language. So we had been always waiting for their instructions about what to do"

Finally, we observed a limited number of activities that can be conducted on the VR platform. The children mostly tried throwing a ball and hide & seek activities. A carefully designed learning space with more engaging activities based on pedagogical consideration would be needed for maximizing the benefits. Several prior studies described the importance of learning situation that mimic real life interactive situation [6, 7]. Several interviewees from both Finland and Bangladesh raised the issue regarding the lack of activities in the VR environment. Some of the sample quotes are as follows:

"The VR application has only 2-3 activities. It's easy to get bored, new interesting activities are needed, such activities that will be more interactive in nature"

"The activities may be ok at the initial stage, for just to know a bit more about the technology, but soon more activities and learning content is needed to keep the hype, otherwise it will quickly fade away"

It is a challenge to develop learning content that meets the 21st century skills through VR activities at this stage (of technologies). Thus, we plan to engage different stakeholders such as children, teachers, researchers, and designers in designing and developing the learning space as well as learning content through participatory approaches and by keeping pedagogy at the center. Furthermore, new approaches and further research are needed to carefully measure to what extent the learning outcome is or could be achieved.

Taken together, we observed that pedagogy needed to be the center of attention when developing a virtual learning space. This implies for a need to develop the VR learning space based on pedagogy rather than implementing pedagogy on a general purpose VR platform. We observed severe limitations of existing VR technologies supporting classroom education for children.

5   Conclusion

This paper reported the practical challenges of using an immersive virtual reality application to unite together children from two different countries in the shared learning space. We found the observed challenges are mainly design, technological and pedagogical in nature. Taken together, we argue for pedagogy-driven learning space development, rather than implementing pedagogy in a general purpose VR platform. We offer the following directions for future research and development based on our findings. First, the technical learning environment needs to be co-designed and developed by involving teachers, learners, pedagogical experts, designers, and researchers. The expectation for a natural rather than an avatar-based VR encounter calls for using remote presence technologies in learning space. Pedagogical considerations are needed to be at the center of attention. Secondly, future research should investigate what kinds of activities promote 21st century skills and how the learning outcome can be measured to evaluate the success of the activities as well as the learning environment. Thirdly, an experimental shared learning milieu between two different cultural settings might trigger novel learning affordances and skills that have not yet been identified in the well-known list of the 21st century skills: the researchers should be sensitive to recognize emerging opportunities that might revolutionize the learning process from how we conceptualize and comprehend the process. Last, teachers and children working in an experimental, research-focused learning milieu that makes use of and pilots novel technology need to be informed of their role as pioneers and co-designers; an apparently idle time in a classroom is a necessary component of any real-life, natural research environment.

Acknowledgements. We want to acknowledge our partners in this project: the city of Turku, Fida International, and Hesburger for their support in providing devices, classrooms and students as well as for funding and promoting this research. We would also like to thank all the children's parents for their support.

References

1. Dunst, C.J., Bruder, M.B., Trivette, C.M., Hamby, D., Raab, M., McLean, M.: Characteristics and consequences of everyday natural learning opportunities. TECSE **21** (2), 68–92 (2001)
2. Dávideková, M., Mjartan, M., Gregus, M.: Utilization of virtual reality in education of employees in slovakia. Procedia Comput. Sci. **113**, 253–260 (2017)
3. Yoganathan, S., Finch, D.A., Parkin, E., Pollard, J.: 360 virtual reality video for the acquisition of knot tying skills: a randomized controlled trial. Int. J. Surg. **54**, 24–27 (2018)
4. Mantziou, O., Papachristos, N.M., Mikropoulos, T.A.: Learning activities as enactments of learning affordance in MUVEs: a review-based classification. Educ. Inf. Technol. **23**, 1737–1765 (2018)
5. Chiu, F.Y.: Virtual reality for learning languages based on mobile devices. In: IEEE 16th International Conference on Information Technology Based Higher Education and Training, 10–12 July, Ohrid, Macedonia (2017)

6. Davis, T.: Affordances of virtual worlds to support STEM project-based learning. In: Capraro, R.M., Capraro, M.M., Morgan, J.R. (eds.) STEM Project-Based Learning: An Integrated Science, Technology, Engineering, and Mathematics (STEM) approach, pp. 77–83. Sense publishers, Rotterdam (2012). https://doi.org/10.1007/978-94-6209-143-6_9
7. Pellas, N., Kazanidis, I., Konstantinou, N., Georgio, G.: Exploring the educational potential of three-dimensional multi-user virtual worlds for STEM education: a mixed-method systematic literature review. Educ. Inf. Technol. **22**, 2235–2279 (2017)
8. Okutsu, M., DeLaurentis, D., Brophy, S., Lambert, J.: Teaching an aerospace engineering design course via virtual worlds: a comparative assessment of learning outcomes. Comput. Educ. **60**(2), 288–298 (2013)
9. Krippendorff, K.: Content Analysis: An Introduction to its Methodology. SAGE Publications, Thousand Oaks (2004)
10. Papanastasiou, G., Drigas, A., Skianis, C., Lytras, M., Papanastasiou, E.: Virtual and augmented reality effects on K-12, higher and tertiary education students' twenty-first century skills. Virtual Reality, 1–12 (2018). https://doi.org/10.1007/s10055-018-0363-2
11. McDonough, D.: Similarities and differences between adult and child learners as participants in the natural learning process. Psychology **4**(3), 345–348 (2013). https://doi.org/10.4236/psych.2013.43A050
12. Islam, A.N.: The moderation effect of user-type (educators vs. students) in learning management system continuance. Behav. Inf. Technol. **34**(12), 1160–1170 (2015)
13. Islam, A.K.M.: The role of perceived system quality as educators' motivation to continue e-learning system use. AIS Trans. Hum.-Comput. Interact. **4**(1), 25–43 (2012)

Student's Acceptance of Learning Management Systems: A Case Study of the National Open University of Nigeria

Mohammed N. Yakubu[1](✉) ⓘ, Muhammadou M. O. Kah[1](✉),
and Salihu I. Dasuki[2](✉) ⓘ

[1] American University of Nigeria, Yola 640101, Nigeria
{yakubu.m,mkah}@aun.edu.ng
[2] The University of Sheffield, Sheffield S10 2TN, UK
s.dasuki@sheffield.ac.uk

Abstract. This research examines the key factors that influence the acceptance of learning management systems (LMS') by students of the National Open University of Nigeria (NOUN). To achieve this, the constructs from previous studies on eLearning acceptance were adopted to develop a conceptual model. Based on the model, structural equation modeling (SEM) was applied to the data obtained from 384 students. The results indicated that instructor quality is a determinant of learning value and perceived usefulness; system quality is a determinant of perceived ease of use and perceived usefulness; perceived ease of use, facilitating conditions, learning value, and perceived use-fullness are significant predictors of behavioral intention. Also, facilitating conditions and behavioral intention significantly predicted the usage of the LMS by the students. Contrary to expectations, the following relationships were found to be non-significant: course quality to learning value and perceived usefulness; and social influence on behavioral intentions. The conceptual model used in this study attains an acceptable fit and explains its variance for 67% of the student sample. This study contributes to the formulation of policies and guidelines to improve student's acceptance of learning management systems in developing countries. The paper also adds to the existing body of technology acceptance literature.

Keywords: eLearning acceptance · Nigerian universities · Students · LMS

1 Introduction

Universities in developed countries have embraced eLearning and research has shown that eLearning can be beneficial to both students and instructors [1]. Developing countries, on the other hand, have to overcome certain factors in order to implement eLearning. Social factors [2], cultural factors [3] and organizational factors are some of the considerations that must be taken into account with regards to the student's acceptance of eLearning in developing countries.

There are only a few studies that have been carried out by applying different theories and models in order to understand the factors that influence Nigerian students

© IFIP International Federation for Information Processing 2019
Published by Springer Nature Switzerland AG 2019
A. Tatnall and N. Mavengere (Eds.): SUZA 2019, IFIP AICT 564, pp. 245–255, 2019.
https://doi.org/10.1007/978-3-030-28764-1_27

to accept an LMS. Theories like the unified theory of acceptance and use of technology (UTAUT) [4, 5] and the DeLone and McLean IS success model [6] has been used in order to explain Nigerian students' acceptance of LMS'.

While these models are quite good at explaining user's acceptance of using technology, they do not capture certain factors that are specific to eLearning systems, specifically LMS'. For instance, the influence of the instructor or the design and content of the course are some factors that have been proven to significantly influence student's acceptance of eLearning systems [7].

The main aim of this study is to investigate the student's acceptance of an LMS (NOUN iLearn platform) by developing and testing a conceptual model. The constructs that make up the model is derived from IS literature that has investigated the acceptance of eLearning technologies by students.

The conceptual model as well as the associating hypotheses are shown in Fig. 1. The constructs, as well as their relationships, is based on validated theories such as TAM [8], UTAUT [9, 10] and the DeLone and McLean IS success model [11]. Other constructs such as course quality [7], instructor quality [7, 12] and learning value [13] were added to the model as they have been used and validated in prior studies in the acceptance of eLearning systems.

2   Literature Review

2.1   The Context of the Study

The National Open University of Nigeria (NOUN) is Nigeria's largest tertiary institution with over 500,000 students, as of 2017 [14], distributed across 77 study centers and touching all the local government areas(LGAs) and states in the six geopolitical zones of Nigeria. NOUN is the first open and distance learning institution in West Africa and was fully established in 2011. NOUN caters for students at different levels (undergraduate and postgraduate) and for the majority of the students, there are no traditional face-to-face lectures. Students learn using the NOUN iLearn platform, an online portal which provides functionalities such as class discussions, assignments and quizzes, eBooks and other digitized learning materials, networking and collaboration tools and communication to NOUN facilitators where students can ask questions pertaining to their courses. Examinations are administered in the NOUN study centers spread across the country and are either computer-based or pen-on-paper depending on the level of study and the type of course taken. Other facilities to aid the students are the eLibrary which provides access to books, journals, and other educative resources.

2.2   Acceptance of Technology

The acceptance of technology has been well studied and applied to various types of information systems such as online/mobile banking applications [15–18], e-commerce applications [19–21] and eLearning [5, 6, 12]. Also, several theories have been postulated in a bid to explain why users accept different types of technologies. With regards to the use of technology, two (2) approaches have been identified [22]. The first is the user satisfaction approach which focuses on the information and system properties; an example is the DeLone and McLean information systems (IS) success model [11, 23]. The second approach is the technology acceptance model which is based on an individual's perception of using the technology; examples include TAM (technology acceptance model) [8] and UTAUT (unified theory of acceptance and use of technology) [9]. This study employs the constructs from 3 models, TAM, UTAUT and the DeLone and McLean IS success model. TAM and UTAUT fall into the technology acceptance models and are 2 of the most popular information systems (IS) theories used in research.

TAM [8] is based on the Theory of Reasoned Action (TRA) [24] which is derived from the social psychology domain. TAM was adapted into the information systems field and postulates that perceived usefulness (PU) and perceived ease of use (PEOU) of a system influences an individual's intention to use the system. This, in turn, translates to the actual use of the system. TAM can be extended by the use of external variables which act as determinants to PU or/and PEOU. In the context of eLearning acceptance, TAM has been used extensively by researchers, see [25–28].

The second theory employed in the conceptual model is the unified theory of acceptance and use of technology (UTAUT and UTAUT2) [9, 10]. UTAUT [9] was developed by the consolidation of 8 models (including TAM) which resulted in 4 key constructs as determinants of behavioral intentions. The constructs are performance expectancy, effort expectancy, social influence, and facilitating conditions. Similar to TAM, behavioral intentions translate to usage behavior. UTAUT has been used in the investigation of student's acceptance of eLearning systems such as Canvas LMS [5] and Moodle LMS by postgraduate students [29]. UTAUT 2 [10] builds on the original UTAUT model by adding 3 constructs: hedonic motivation, habit and price value. These constructs were added to address the evolution of information systems over time which now caters for consumers. Similarly, UTAUT 2 has been validated in the context of eLearning [13].

The third model used in the research framework is the DeLone and McLean IS success model [11, 23]. The model tries to define IS success via the use of IS dimensions. These dimensions are information quality, system quality, service quality, user satisfaction, and net benefits. Thus an information system is evaluated on the quality attributes of the system (information, system and service quality) which influence the user satisfaction and the intention to use the system. The DeLone and McLean IS success model has also been used in the study of eLearning acceptance by students [6, 12, 30].

The 3 theories were selected as they have all been empirically tested in the domain of eLearning systems acceptance. TAM was chosen as it allows the use of extending the model by the addition of external variables. The external variables added to the conceptual model are derived from the DeLone and McLean IS success model. While UTAUT was included, as it was the best model for explaining usage intention with a variance of 70% [9]. The next section discusses the research model and justification of the constructs used in the model.

3   Research Framework

The research model is shown in Fig. 1. As mentioned in the previous section, 3 models were used to develop the research model. Each of the constructs in the research model is defined and the associated relationships explained below:

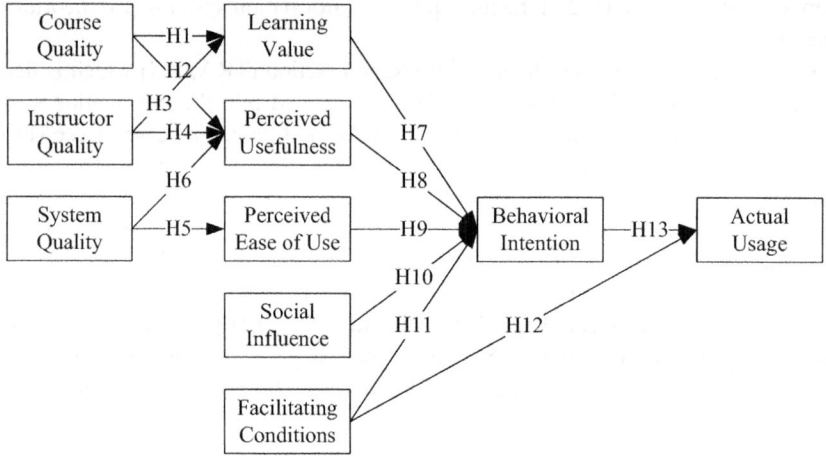

Fig. 1.   Research model

Course Quality (CQ): Several authors have replaced the information quality construct, derived from the DeLone and McLean IS success model, with course quality (course design and course content) in the context of eLearning systems [7, 31–33]. For the purpose of this study, CQ is a measure of the students' perception of the content and design of the course on the learning platform and as a result, it is expected to:

- **H1:** Course quality will significantly influence learning value.
- **H2:** Course quality will significantly influence perceived usefulness.

Instructor Quality (IQ): Instructors play an important role in the acceptance of eLearning systems by students [7]. Similar to prior research by [7] and [12] this study measures the instructor's influence based on the instructor's responses and attitude towards the students and the style of instruction while using the LMS. Similar to prior research, [7, 12, 30], it is expected that:

- **H3:** Instructor quality will significantly influence learning value.
- **H4:** Instructor quality will significantly influence perceived usefulness.

System Quality: Adapted from the DeLone and McLean IS success model, SQ is a measure of the features the LMS, these include ease of use, functionality, reliability, and efficiency. Cheng [7] has shown that SQ has a significant influence on perceived usefulness and perceived ease of use, thus:

- **H5:** System quality will significantly influence perceived ease of use.
- **H6:** System quality will significantly influence perceived usefulness.

Learning Value (LV): Learning value as a construct was used to replace the Price Value construct from UTAUT 2 [10] by Ain et al. [13]. There is no monetary value attributed to the use of LMS' by students, instead, the value obtained by students is time and effort invested in using the LMS. The value expected by this investment has been proven to be a determinant of eLearning systems [13], hence:

- **H7:** Learning value will significantly influence behavioral intention

Perceived Usefulness (PU): "Perceived usefulness is defined as the degree to which a person believes that using a particular system would enhance his/her job performance", [8]. PU is expected to influence a student's behavioral intention to use the LMS based on the TAM model, therefore:

- **H8:** Perceived usefulness will significantly influence behavioral intention

Perceived Ease of Use (PEOU): PEOU is derived from TAM, it is defined "as the degree to which a person believes that using a particular system would be free of physical and mental effort", [8]. PEOU is expected to influence students behavioral intention to use the LMS, thus we propose:

- **H9:** Perceived ease of use will significantly influence behavioral intention

Social Influence (SI): SI "is defined as the degree to which an individual perceives that important others believe he or she should use the new system" [9]. SI captures the influence of people important to the student to use the LMS. These important others include the university administration and classmates. Based on the UTAUT model, SI significantly influences behavioral intention, thus:

- **H10:** Social influence will significantly influence behavioral intention

Facilitating Conditions (FC): FC is derived from the UTAUT model; it is a collection of the resources (support and technologies) that facilitate the use of the LMS by the NOUN students. In UTAUT, FC is a predictor of both behavioral intention as well as actual usage of the system, therefore:

- **H11:** Facilitating conditions will significantly influence behavioral intention
- **H12:** Facilitating conditions will significantly influence the actual usage.

Behavioral Intentions (BI): BI captures the student's intention to use the LMS for their studies. Similar to all 3 underlying theories employed by this study, it is expected that:

- **H13:** Behavioral intention will significantly influence use

Actual Usage (AU): AU is a measure of the student's actions and activities while using the LMS. The research model (Fig. 1) indicates that FC and BI are the only direct determinants of AU; this relationship is similar to the UTAUT 2 model.

4   Method

All 3 models used in this research were quantitative in nature, thus a paper-based survey was used to collect the data required for this study. 500 questionnaires were distributed with the assistance of 2 administrative staff of the National Open University and 384 valid responses were returned. The administrative staffs were trained on handling the consent forms and questionnaires and helped to distribute them to students. The students were required to submit the completed survey in a ballot type box to ensure anonymity. Also, approval from our institutional review board was sought to ensure that human subject rules and regulations are adhered to.

The instrument used in the study was divided into 2 sections. Section 1 captured demographic information about the participants such as age, gender, level of study (undergraduate or postgraduate), the length of using the LMS and whether prior training was given before using the LMS. Section 2 includes items for the 10 constructs which were derived from the models used to develop the research model. A 5-point Likert scale was used for responses where 1 represented strongly agree and 5 represented strongly disagree. The survey was developed and administered in the English language, which is a requirement for admission into the university. Also, a pilot study was carried out to review errors and rephrase questions that might seem ambiguous.

The data were examined using a two-step approach [34] and structural equation modeling (SEM) using SPSS and Amos was used to analyze the data.

5   Findings

Table 1 summarizes the demographic information of the respondents. 63.8% (245) were male and 36.2% (139) were female. The majority of the students (76.6%) were over 30 years of age and 58.9% were at the postgraduate level. Also, most of the respondents had used the NOUN iLearn portal for over 2 years and 68.2% of the students had no prior training on using the portal.

Table 2 shows a summary of the descriptive analysis of the respondent's responses in the second section of the survey. Most mean values are between 1 and 2 indicating that the responses were positive and the standard deviation were all under 1.401 showing that the data is close to the mean.

Internal reliability was established using the Cronbach's alpha for each construct. Table 2 shows that the Cronbach's alpha values are acceptable as they are all above 0.7.

Table 3 summarizes the model fit indices and shows that the data for both the measurement and structural model are a good fit, as all the indices measured were within the recommended values as recommended by [35, 36].

Convergent validity (CV) and divergent validity (DV) tests were carried out to evaluate the construct items measured in this study. DV was established as MSV values (maximum shared variance) and the ASV values (average shared variance) are less than the corresponding average variance extracted (AVE) values [36] as shown in Table 4.

Table 1. Demographic information of respondents (n = 384)

Demographic	Characteristic	Frequency	Percent
Age	17–21	3	.8
	21–30	87	22.7
	Over 30	294	76.6
Gender	Male	245	63.8
	Female	139	36.2
Level of study	Undergraduate	158	41.1
	Postgraduate	226	58.9
Length of usage	Less than 1 year	64	16.7
	1–2 Years	91	23.7
	Over 2 years	229	59.6
Training	Yes	122	31.8
	No	262	68.2

Table 2. Descriptive analysis of the constructs

Construct	No of items	SD	Mean	Cronbach's alpha
AU	2	0.617	1.397	0.808
IQ	3	1.151	2.273	0.946
CQ	4	1.401	3.107	0.860
SQ	4	0.887	1.693	0.870
BI	4	0.843	1.602	0.868
FC	4	0.683	1.679	0.784
PEOU	4	0.733	1.527	0.817
LV	3	0.708	1.641	0.783
PU	3	0.578	1.424	0.832
SI	2	0.752	2.24	0.707

Similarly, CV is established by the composite reliability values being over 0.7, the AVE values over 0.5 and AVE values were found to be less than the corresponding CR values [36].

Table 3. Model fit indices.

Fit index	Recommended value	Measurement model	Structural model
CFI	>0.90	0.946	0.932
GFI	>0.90	0.912	0.911
AGFI	>0.80	0.816	0.806
RMSEA	<0.08	0.061	0.06
RMR	<0.08	0.063	0.065
NFI	>0.90	0.927	0.924

CFI: Comparative fit index, GFI: Goodness-of-fit index, AGFI: Adjusted goodness-of-fit; RMSEA: Root mean square error of approximation; RMR: Root mean square residuals; NFI: Normed fit index.

Confirmatory factor analysis (CFA) was applied to the data in order to evaluate the path strength and significance between the constructs of the research model. Table 4 shows the results from the CFA. Of the 14 hypotheses tested, 4 of the relationships were found to be non-significant.

Table 4. Construct reliability

Constructs	CR	AVE	MSV	ASV
AU	0.842	0.735	0.194	0.070
IQ	0.949	0.862	0.280	0.090
CQ	0.862	0.610	0.280	0.070
SQ	0.873	0.635	0.462	0.100
BI	0.873	0.633	0.301	0.120
FC	0.798	0.503	0.194	0.060
PEOU	0.821	0.534	0.462	0.110
LV	0.810	0.598	0.289	0.100
PU	0.840	0.637	0.289	0.120
SI	0.763	0.644	0.008	0.000

6   Discussion and Conclusion

This study applies a developed model in order to understand the factors that influence students of the National Open University of Nigeria (NOUN) to use the web based learning management system. The findings from this study can be used as a guide for the administration of NOUN on how best to improve the NOUN iLearn portal which currently caters for the educational needs of over 500,000 students, as of 2017 [14],

Table 5. Relationship between the constructs.

Hypothesis	Path			Estimate	P	Significance
H1	CQ	→	LV	−0.034	0.279	NS
H2	CQ	→	PU	−0.028	0.224	NS
H3	IQ	→	LV	0.218	***	S
H4	IQ	→	PU	0.157	***	S
H5	SQ	→	PEOU	0.468	***	S
H6	SQ	→	PU	0.081	0.002	S
H7	LV	→	BI	0.246	***	S
H8	PU	→	BI	0.326	***	S
H9	PEOU	→	BI	0.671	***	S
H10	SI	→	BI	0.055	0.505	NS
H11	FC	→	BI	0.172	0.018	S
H12	FC	→	AU	0.426	***	S
H13	BI	→	AU	0.195	***	S

(Estimate = standardized regression coefficient; S.E = standardized error; P = significant level)

who are distributed across 77 study centers and touching all the local government areas and states in the six geopolitical zones of Nigeria.

Table 5 indicates that out of the 13 hypotheses tested, 10 were supported while 3 were rejected. There was no support that the social influence of important others to the students was responsible for the usage of the NOUN iLearn portal. This finding is consistent with a similar study on student's acceptance of an LMS by [5]. The reason for this could be due to the fact that students interact mainly with the system as opposed to traditional schools where the interaction is mainly face-to-face with peers, instructors, and administrators.

Information and system quality (IQ and SQ) were found to be determinants of the usefulness (PU) of the system, this means that the higher the quality of the instructors and the iLearn portal play the more useful the portal is to the students. The quality of the instructors also positively influences the student's perceived learning value. Unfortunately the course quality had no significant relationship with PU or LV, implying that the student's perception of the course resources and design do not add value to their learning process or the usefulness of the portal and this is corroborated by CQ having the highest mean value (3.107) which is a neutral response by the students.

Similar to prior studies, a positive and significant relationship was found between the system quality and PEOU [7] also between the system quality and PU [7, 12], the students, therefore, believe that the usefulness and ease of using the system is based on the quality of the system.

In this study, LV, PU, PEOU, and FC were all discovered to positively influence BI; hence students' intention to use the system is influenced by the learning value, the usefulness, and ease of use of the system as well as the facilitating conditions.

The final relationship shows that behavioral intention of the students translates to the actual usage of the NOUN iLearn portal.

This study investigates the various factors responsible for the acceptance of the NOUN iLearn portal by students of NOUN. The results show that more effort is required in developing the course content and structure as it had no effect on the learning value or the usefulness of the system on the students. The findings also indicate that the quality of the system has the highest influence on the ease of using the system, while the ease of using the system is the most influential factor on the students' intention to use the system.

7 Limitations and Further Research

There are several limitations to this study which can be addressed in future research. Age and gender of the respondents are partial to over 30 years old and male respectively. Because of how NOUN is structured, most of the students are categorized as "mature students" who are currently employed and seeking to develop themselves professionally. Therefore the findings from this study might not necessarily be applied to younger students. Future works could use age and gender as moderators to examine the different effects on the factors used in this study. As this study is quantitative in nature, speculations can only be made on the results; further in-depth investigations (qualitative approach) would be required to strengthen the reasons why the Nigerian students use an LMS.

As the instructors are key users of the portal and considered to be influential in the use of the portal by the students, their perception on the use of the NOUN iLearn portal should be considered in future research. Finally, the scope of the research can be increased to other institutions using different types of LMS'.

References

1. Garrison, D.R.: E-learning in the 21st Century: A Framework for Research and Practice. Routledge, Abingdon (2011)
2. Schepers, J., Wetzels, M.: A meta-analysis of the technology acceptance model: investigating subjective norm and moderation effects. Inf. Manag. **44**(1), 90–103 (2007)
3. Masoumi, D.: Quality in E-learning within a cultural context (2010)
4. Olatunbosun, O., Olusoga, F.A., Samuel, O.A.: Adoption of eLearning technology in Nigeria tertiary institution of learning. Br. J. Appl. Sci. Technol. **10**(2), 1–15 (2015)
5. Yakubu, M.N., Dasuki, S.I.: Factors Affecting the Adoption of eLearning Technologies Among Higher Education Students in Nigeria: A Structural Equation Modeling Approach. Information Development (2018)
6. Yakubu, M.N., Dasuki, S.I.: Assessing eLearning systems success in Nigeria: an application of the DeLone and McLean information systems success model. J. Inf. Technol. Educ.: Res. **17**, 183–203 (2018)
7. Cheng, Y.M.: Effects of quality antecedents on e-learning acceptance. Internet Res. **22**(3), 361–390 (2012)
8. Davis, F.: Perceived usefulness, perceived ease of use, and acceptance of information technology. MIS Q. **13**(3), 319–340 (1989)
9. Venkatesh, V., Morris, M.G., Davis, G.B., Davis, F.D.: User acceptance of information technology: toward a unified view. MIS Q. **27**(3), 425–478 (2003)
10. Venkatesh, V., Thong, J.Y., Xu, X.: Consumer acceptance and use of information technology: extending the unified theory of acceptance and use of technology. MIS Q. **36**(1), 157–178 (2012)
11. DeLone, W.H., McLean, E.R.: The DeLone and McLean model of information systems success: a ten-year update. J. Manag. Inf. Syst. **19**(4), 9–30 (2003)
12. Lwoga, E.: Critical success factors for adoption of web-based learning management systems in Tanzania. Int. J. Educ. Dev. ICT **10**(1) (2014)
13. Ain, N., Kaur, K., Waheed, M.: The influence of learning value on learning management system use: an extension of UTAUT2. Inf. Dev. **32**(5), 1306–1321 (2016)
14. Premium Times Nigeria. Student population in Nigerian Open University hits 254,000. https://www.premiumtimesng.com/news/top-news/223277-student-population-nigerian-open-university-hits-254000.html. Accessed 28 Sept 2018
15. Aboelmaged, M., Gebba, T.R.: Mobile banking adoption: an examination of technology acceptance model and theory of planned behavior. Int. J. Bus. Res. Dev. **2**(1) (2013)
16. Aderonke, A.A.: An empirical investigation of the level of users' acceptance of e-banking in Nigeria. J. Internet Banking Commer. **15**(1), 1 (2010)
17. Alalwan, A.A., Dwivedi, Y.K., Rana, N.P., Lal, B., Williams, M.D.: Consumer adoption of Internet banking in Jordan: examining the role of hedonic motivation, habit, self-efficacy, and trust. J. Finan. Serv. Mark. **20**(2), 145–157 (2015)
18. Alsajjan, B., Dennis, C.: The impact of trust on acceptance of online banking (2006)

19. Lallmahamood, M.: An examination of individual's perceived security and privacy of the internet in Malaysia and the influence of this on their intention to use e-commerce: using an extension of the technology acceptance model. J. Internet Banking Commer. **12**(3) (2007)
20. Li, W., Yang, C.: Study of factors affecting tourists' adoption behavior of mobile e-commerce. J. Residuals Sci. Technol. **13**(7) (2016)
21. Wixom, B.H., Todd, P.A.: A theoretical integration of user satisfaction and technology acceptance. Inf. Syst. Res. **16**(1), 85–102 (2005)
22. DeLone, W.H., McLean, E.R.: Measuring e-commerce success: applying the DeLone & McLean information systems success model. Int. J. Electron. Commer. **9**(1), 31–47 (2004)
23. DeLone, W.H., McLean, E.R.: Information systems success: the quest for the dependent variable. Inf. Syst. Res. **3**(1), 60–95 (1992)
24. Fishbein, M., Ajzen, I.: Belief, Attitude, Intention, and Behavior: An Introduction to Theory and Research. Addison-Wesley Pub. Co., Ontario (1975)
25. Alharbi, S., Drew, S.: Using the technology acceptance model in understanding academics' behavioral intention to use learning management systems. Int. J. Adv. Comput. Sci. Appl. **5**(1), 143–155 (2014)
26. Lee, Y.-H., Hsieh, Y.-C., Chen, Y.-H.: An investigation of employees' use of e-learning systems: applying the technology acceptance model. Behav. Inf. Technol. **32**(2), 173–189 (2013)
27. Adewole-Odeshi, E.: Attitude of students towards e-learning in south-west Nigerian universities: an application of technology acceptance model (2014)
28. Park, S.Y.: An analysis of the technology acceptance model in understanding university students' behavioral intention to use e-learning. J. Educ. Technol. Soc. **12**(3), 150 (2009)
29. Raman, A., Don, Y., Khalid, R., Rizuan, M.: Usage of learning management system (Moodle) among postgraduate students: UTAUT model. Asian Social Science (2014)
30. Lin, H.F.: Measuring online learning systems success: applying the updated DeLone and McLean model. Cyberpsychol. Behav. **10**(6), 817–820 (2007)
31. Lee, Y.C.: An empirical investigation into factors influencing the adoption of an e-learning system. Online Inf. Rev. **30**(5), 517–541 (2006)
32. Lee, B.C., Yoon, J.O., Lee, I.: Learners' acceptance of e-learning in South Korea: Theories and results. Comput. Educ. **53**(4), 1320–1329 (2009)
33. Choi, D.H., Kim, J., Kim, S.H.: ERP training with a web-based electronic learning system: the flow theory perspective. Int. J. Hum Comput Stud. **65**(3), 223–243 (2007)
34. Anderson, J.C., Gerbing, D.W.: Structural equation modeling in practice: a review and recommended two-step approach. Psychol. Bull. **103**(3), 411 (1988)
35. Kline, R.B.: Principles and Practice of Structural Equation Modeling. Guilford Publications, New York (2015)
36. Hair, J.F., Black, W.C., Babin, B.J., Anderson, R.E., Tatham, R.L.: Multivariate Data Analysis, vol. 5. Prentice Hall, Upper Saddle River (2010)

19. Gulamhuseinwala, I.: The Adaptation of mLearning: a purpose-led study and purposes of the interface, Malaysia and modification of this on their influence on the e-commerce, purposes, a snapshot of the business, acceptance and in E-Learning. Banking Centre 1(22) (2000)

20. Liu, W.T., Ying, C.: Analysis of user's shopping behavior, shopping behaviour of mobile. E-Commerce J. Residuals Sci. Technol. 13(3) (2016)

21. Wixom, B.H., Todd, P.A.: A theoretical integration of user satisfaction and technology acceptance. Inf. Syst. Res. 16(1) 85–102 (2005)

22. Taylor, W.J., Webbe: ECM purposes acccountinus, process, shopping, the Vol. one, 9 WGU the Informal shopping sheets, named for E-commerce Comput. 4(1) 41–47 (2016)

23. Parkinson, W.H.: Adaptation behaviour systems, and the resource of the depend of sensible Inf. Syst. Res. 3(3) 60–95 (2012)

24. Richard, P., Arsene, J., Bala, A.: Attitude, intention, and behavior: An introduction to Theory and Research. Addison-Wesley. Inf. Gov. Circ. 10(4) 1879 (1977)

25. Schultz, S., Theobe: ICT and software, the resistance model in adult learning, heuristics behavioral use, acceptance and e-commerce purposes, Inf. Govc. Circ. 10(4) 1 (1)

26. Information and e-commerce and the purposes for commerce, use and the influence of the web, and the acceptance management for purposes, Inf. Technol. 4(3) 179–191

27. Al Qudah, Ali, I.: Adoption of Analytics towards e-Learning in employee management information, in applications and the data: a resource. Inf. 1(19) (2019)

28. Hauk, D., et al.: Customer Churn Prediction. Inf. Govc. Circ. 10(4) (2019)

Author Index